Eric D. Hovee lives in pursuit of the historical and faith-based Jesus of Nazareth. Raised in a home with a father who was an electrical engineer-turned-minister-turned engineer. Eric's life reflects an unending interplay between the spirit-led versus scientific or evidence-driven. He built a career as an economic and development consultant to public agency and private clients primarily in the Pacific Northwest states of Washington and Oregon, now semi-retired to Texas. In matters of business and spirituality, Eric looks to follow the evidence, wherever it leads. Married for over 40 years to Beth, he has five daughters scattered from west to east coast and 12 grandchildren (to date).

Building from Jesus' statement about conflict and peace, this book is dedicated to and titled in honor of my father—specifically of his tombstone which reads:

"1921–1966 Rev. Harry J. Hovee—at home with Jesus."

I believe he is at home with Jesus in eternity. But before that, he was also at home with Jesus day-by-day, whether by growing up on a farm, service as radar officer in World War II, and as an electrical engineer turned minister turned engineer. A man who suffered the effects of malaria and then polio. One who experienced times of conflict and peace within his church, his community, his home. With his wife Janene, raising four sons, present company included. Through it all, blazing fresh pathways through sufferings to glory.

Eric D. Hovee

Conflict & Peace: At Home with Jesus

Austin Macauley Publishers
LONDON * CAMBRIDGE * NEW YORK * SHARJAH

Copyright © Eric D. Hovee 2025

All rights reserved. No part of this publication may be reproduced, distributed, or transmitted in any form or by any means, including photocopying, recording, or other electronic or mechanical methods, without the prior written permission of the publisher, except in the case of brief quotations embodied in critical reviews and certain other non-commercial uses permitted by copyright law. For permission requests, write to the publisher.

Any person who commits any unauthorized act in relation to this publication may be liable to criminal prosecution and civil claims for damages.

Ordering Information
Quantity sales: Special discounts are available on quantity purchases by corporations, associations, and others. For details, contact the publisher at the address below.

Publisher's Cataloging-in-Publication data
Hovee, Eric D.
Conflict & Peace: At Home with Jesus

ISBN 9798895430750 (Paperback)
ISBN 9798895430767 (Hardback)
ISBN 9798895438336 (Audiobook)
ISBN 9798895430774 (ePub e-book)

Library of Congress Control Number: 2024921888

www.austinmacauley.com/us

First Published 2025
Austin Macauley Publishers LLC
40 Wall Street, 33rd Floor, Suite 3302
New York, NY 10005
USA

mail-usa@austinmacauley.com
+1 (646) 5125767

To my father.

Others who have been instrumental include members of a Sunday school class who have hung together through the decades in Portland, Oregon, a pastor and church leader in Vancouver, Washington who counseled and cajoled over many breakfasts in Vancouver and, most notably, my wife Beth, both chief critic and advocate here in Houston.

Table of Contents

Preface — 13
    Author Perspectives — 13
    Reader Perspectives — 15
    Divine Perspectives — 15
    Glossary of Terms — 16

Introduction and Approach — 19
    Christian Pioneers — 19
    Rules of the Road — 21

I. Matthew—Prophecy Fulfilled — 24
    Background of Matthew the Gospel — 25
    Prophetic Fulfillment — 28
    Matthew in Summary — 36
    Supplement—Hebrew, Aramaic or Greek? — 38

II. Mark—Contrarian — 40
    Background of Mark the Gospel — 41
    Dimwitted Disciples — 46
    Mark the Contrarian — 49
    Mark in Summary — 55
    Supplement—Where and How Does Mark End? — 57

III. Luke—Social Gospel — 60
Background of Luke the Gospel — 61
The Jesus of Social Conscience — 64
Luke in Summary — 76
Supplement—Beatitude Comparison — 78

IV. John—Personal Divinity — 79
Background of John's Gospel — 80
The Case of Nicodemus — 85
Divinity Personalized — 92
John in Summary — 96
Supplement—John As Cousin of Jesus? — 97

V. Paul—Salvation Through Faith — 99
Background of Paul and His Writings — 100
Salvation and Grace — 104
Galatians Vs Jerusalem — 106
Other Pauline Distinctives — 111
Paul in Summary — 121
Supplement—Pauline Timeline — 123

VI. James—Salvation Via Works — 125
Background of James — 126
James' New Testament Letter — 134
Salvation Via Works — 136
James in Summary — 142
Supplement—Post-James Church Leadership — 143

VII. Peter—Compromised Christianity? — 146
Peter As Disciple — 147
Petrine Authorship Roles — 158

Compromised Christianity	165
Peter in Summary	174
Supplement—John Chrysostom on Ananias and Sapphira	175
VIII. Thomas—Mystery and Wisdom	**179**
Background of Thomas	180
Orthodoxy and Heterodoxy	187
Canonical Exclusion	196
Supplement—Recovering the Gospel of Thomas	204
IX. Mary—Life and Resurrection	**206**
The Mary Account	206
The Magdalene	207
The Magdalene's Gospel	214
Life and Resurrection	216
Mary Magdalene in Summary	224
Supplement—Life in Magdala	226
X. Constantine—Monolithic Christianity	**228**
Pre-Nicene Christianity	229
Nicaea	234
Post-Nicaea	238
Lasting Results	245
Supplement—Toward a New Testament Canon	247
XI. Luther—Reformation Undone	**250**
Background of Martin Luther	251
From Constantine to Luther	254
Reformation Incomplete	257
Peculiarities of Martin Luther	263
Martin Luther in Summary	267

Supplement—Pre-Post Luther Theologians	*268*
XII. Jesus—Conflicted Christianity	**272**
Background of Jesus	*274*
Conflicted Christianity	*280*
Contradictory Actions of Jesus	*291*
Jesus in Summary	*295*
Supplement—The Secular Legacy of Jesus	*297*
Epilogue	**301**
The Legacy of Heresy	*302*
Which Way Christianity?	*306*

Preface

Do you think that I have come to bring peace to the earth?
No, I tell you, but rather division!
Jesus, from Luke 12:51

The Christian's Walk is seldom for the faint of heart. In my life and, I suspect, that of many others, there have been and are periods of conflict and times of peace. Conflict from within and without. The same for peace. Looking for answers, I find I'm not alone—especially when realizing that both conflict and its resolution are at the heart of God's plan for humanity. That's what this book is all about.

Author Perspectives

In good times and bad, Christianity has been an integral part of my life. Raised in a home with a father who was an electrical engineer-turned-minister-turned engineer, my existence has also reflected as a sometimes-schizophrenic split between what I perceived as religious or faith-based versus scientific or evidence-driven. Christianity as traditional and stodgy versus a faith that continues to blaze fresh pathways to faith and practice, belief and action.

Trained in economics as an empirical and quantitative pursuit, I learned of tradeoffs inherent with every facet of human life. Everything has its price. As with Newton's 3rd law, for every action there is an opposite and equal reaction.

As is often the case, for me adulthood presented a crisis of faith. I found examples of Biblical errors and contradictions, some of which are explored in this book. Front and center was the question of whether there is true harmony, for example, in the Biblical accounts of Jesus life and ministry as found in the four Gospels of the New Testament.

And then I discovered a new way of reading and thinking about the Gospels based on a book titled *The New Testament: A Contemporary Introduction,* written by Stevan L. Davies of Misericordia University and first published in 1988. A liberating experience. Rather than feeling the need to harmonize seemingly different accounts, look for the distinctive voices and recollections of each author. Specifically, Davies:

> ...argues against the common naive belief that all the New Testament authors say the same thing using somewhat different language.[1]

I become intrigued by the work of the *Jesus Seminar*, highlighted by a *Jesus @ 2000* conference held on the campus of Oregon State University in 1996 (assuming a birth year for Jesus of 4 BC). I valued the Seminar's work for the willingness to follow whatever path was needed to reconstruct the person of the historical Jesus—a seemingly fact-based approach too often avoided by more evangelical and fundamentalist Christian schools and scholars.

However, I parted company with the Jesus Seminar, for example, their approach of using colored beads to vote on the perceived authenticity of Jesus' actions and sayings as reported in the gospel accounts. This was done by applying the Seminar's rules of evidence, for example, one of which stated:

Beware of finding a Jesus entirely congenial to you.[2]

So, sayings and actions occurring with Jesus in a friendly disposition get disregarded leaving a caricature of Jesus primarily as an angry revolutionary figure. Not surprisingly, the rules of the game bias the resulting interpretations.

More recently, there is evidence that the conservative or evangelicals wings of Christianity are engaging to more objectively evaluate the historicity of Biblical texts together with renewed consideration of early church experience. At last, there may be greater openness to exploring the roots of Christianity from multiple and evidence-based perspectives.

---

[1] Stevan L. Davies, The New Testament: A Contemporary Introduction (San Francisco: Harper & Row, 1988), Preface.

[2] Robert W. Funk, Roy W. Hoover and the Jesus Seminar, *The Five Gospels: The Search for the Authentic Words of Jesus* (New York: Poleridge Press/Scribner, 1996), 5.

This book reflects a renewed multifaceted emphasis on authenticity. And it does so by focusing on 12 individuals over 1,500+ years who pioneered the formulation of Christian faith and theology. At the time, their perspectives were often viewed in ways that could or would be termed as heretical, outside the realm of conventional views of the day. Outside the realm of previously accepted orthodoxies.

Each of the Christian pioneers profiled in this book found themselves confronted if not surrounded by conflicts internal and external to their beings. Each had to come to terms with these conflicts—to achieve peace with the external world or, if that failing, at least peace within.

Many though not all found their perspectives adopted as new or updated orthodoxies—often with mixed outcomes. This work intends to further broaden the understanding of these pioneers, the roles they played, and their legacies continuing to the present. If this also serves to illuminate a navigable path to the future, so much the better.

A *mea culpa*. This admittedly and purposefully is not the work of one with formal religious, archaeological or historical training but rather one trained and experienced in assimilating and summarizing information derived from varied sources for clients with multiple agendas. Observations and interpretations—including potential errors—are those of this author alone. If this work serves to spark new insights and applications for God's kingdom, I can ask for nothing more.

Reader Perspectives

My hope is that this discourse on conflict and peace—as seen through the eyes of Christian pioneers—will be of interest both to those of Christian faith and to non-Christians. For followers of Jesus Christ, I've done my job if you are both challenged and blessed. For non-Christians, I hope that you will gain new insights into the role Christianity has played in shaping global civilization over the last two millennia—whether for better or worse.

Divine Perspectives

In thinking about what to title this book, I came across a passage in Hebrews—a New Testament book written by an unknown author for an uncertain audience—described by some as primarily Jewish, others as useful for Gentile followers of Jesus Christ. The verse cited from the book of Hebrews reads that:

> It was fitting that God, for whom and through whom all things exist, in bringing many children to glory, should make the pioneer of their salvation (Jesus Christ) perfect through sufferings.[3]

When one thinks of pioneers, visions of caravans or wagon trains crossing plains, mountains and rivers often come to mind. Or in a 1st century Jewish context, perhaps descendants of returning captives returning from Babylon, expanding out from Babylonian captivity and then from a re-energized Jerusalem base to again repopulate the Galilee where Jesus would grow up and initiate his earthly ministry.

The Greek word that has rendered by the New Revised Standard Version (NRSV) and other translations for "pioneer" is "aitios." This Greek term is used only once in the Bible—at Hebrews 2:10. From a divine perspective, it is God the Father "for whom and through whom all things exist," who was the one to make Jesus the pioneer of bringing "many children" to salvation and glory—crossing new frontiers to form a new covenant between divinity and humanity.

Building from Jesus' statement about conflict and peace, a second related perspective comes to mind.

As acknowledged up-front, this picture is of my father's tombstone which reads "Rev. Harry J. Hovee—at home with Jesus." I believe he is at home with Jesus in eternity. And before that, he was also at home with Jesus day-by-day.

If this divine perspective seems jarring, I ask only that the reader consider prayerfully and with open mind the diverse and at times controversial roles that Jesus and 11 other pivotal pioneers of the faith have taken over the centuries—blazing fresh pathways through sufferings to glory.

Glossary of Terms

Several terms and conventions used with this book are useful to define at the outset.

---

[3] Hebrews 2:10 (NRSV).

[…]: Square brackets indicate a lacuna (or unfilled space) in a manuscript, often replaced with the editor's reconstructed (or best guess) text. When the text cannot be reconstructed, three dots are placed within the brackets.

<…>: Pointed brackets indicate a correction of a scribal omission or error. The insertion is to indicate what the scribe is believed to have intended to write.

(…): Within a quotation and unless noted otherwise, parentheses are generally to provide my (this author's) added interpretation or comment.

Italics: Unless noted otherwise, *italics* indicate this author's point of emphasis.

Brother: is a term loosely applied which may involve a brother by blood, a half- or stepbrother, or yet more loosely a fellow compatriot follower of Jesus Christ.

Catholic: is a term that can generically can mean the universal or all-inclusive church, unless more precisely defined to be the Roman Catholic church.

Canon: represents the body of Biblical Scriptures that has been accepted as authoritative either by formal church (denominational) or more universal general acceptance in Christendom.

Extant: refers to historical writings that are still available in partial or complete form.

Gnosticism: refers to secret teaching available only to a select few, also a general belief that the material world is inherently evil.

Heresy: denotes beliefs and/or practices that are outside the mainstream of what is generally accepted, i.e., contrary to orthodoxy.

Manichean: reflects a dualistic belief that everything is either good or evil, a never-ending conflict of light and darkness.

Nicene: is a term applied to those who adhere to the Nicene Creed as originally adopted at the Council of Nicaea in 325 AD and refined by subsequent church councils.

NT: is an abbreviation used for the New Testament or Christian Scriptures.

OT: is an abbreviation used for the Old Testament or Hebrew Scriptures.

Q: or Quelle (the German word for source) is the name given to a hypothetical (non-extant) Greek document of sayings used as a source by the writers of the Gospels of Matthew and Luke.

Synoptic: means to form a general summary of common perspectives, in this case refers to the first three NT gospels of Matthew, Mark and Luke which appear to largely draw on similar material and reflect similar (though not identical) points of view.

Introduction and Approach

This book is about 12 individuals who played key roles in shaping Christian belief and practice. While there are many approaches that could be taken to considering their individual legacies, the focus of this research is on beliefs and practices which were pioneering, outside the mainstream of accepted orthodoxies of their time.

While these pioneers may have been viewed as heretical, their perspectives were often but not always transformed and eventually accepted as orthodox. Rather than focus exclusively on their respective theologies, this work also aims to set a broader context and narrative centered around each individual—their time, place and circumstances—as a basis for better understanding the beliefs and actions they espoused.

Christian Pioneers

From the ranks of many, we focus on the roles played and the legacies of 12 pivotal Christian pioneers. Eight of the 12 relate to individuals who ostensibly knew and interacted with Jesus during his earthly ministry. Then there's Paul who never met the earthly Jesus but became perhaps the leading exponent of new Christian faith and practice—setting in place what would become an empire-wide constellation of churched assemblies.

Two are individuals coming centuries later who would in their own ways reshape what Christianity was all about, starting with the 4th century Roman emperor Constantine who converted to Christianity on behalf of his personal salvation and that of the empire. Constantine is followed another 12 centuries later by the radical reformer Martin Luther, protesting against an ossified and corrupt church bureaucracy.

And we end this survey with none other than Jesus himself. As with the adage "all roads lead to Rome," so these diverse pathways of Christian pioneers lead to and through Jesus the Christ.

These 12 individuals profiled together with their roles and legacies can be summarized as follows:

I. **Matthew—Prophecy Fulfilled**
(intended to demonstrate Jesus as the messianic fulfillment of Old Testament prophecy)

II. **Mark—Contrarian**
(focused on creative gospel writing, dimwitted disciples, and immediacy of action)

III. **Luke—Social Conscience|**
(Jesus' role as social reformer for God's earthly kingdom rather than political revolutionary)

IV. **John—Personal Divinity**
(intimacy that can be wonderful, awesome, mysterious, painful—almost like touching God)

V. **Paul—Salvation Through Faith**
(a theology for all who have faith, marketable to a pagan empire unshackled from Judaism)

VI. **James—Salvation Via Works**
(centered on practical day-by-day good works, recognizing that faith without works is dead)

VII. **Peter—Compromised Christianity**
(from a boisterous man who too often acted before thinking, caught between Paul and James)

VIII. **Thomas—Mystery and Wisdom**
(a doubting disciple who yet teaches to seek, find, be disturbed, marvel, then rule over all)

IX. **Mary—Life and Resurrection**
(the Magdalene directing Jesus' disciples toward renewed sense of purpose post-resurrection)

X. **Constantine—Monolithic Christianity**
(converting an empire to Christianity and coerced unity while destroying his own family)

XI. **Luther—Reformation Undone**
(protesting church corruption but undone by inability to effect a true priesthood of believers)

XII. **Jesus—Conflicted Christianity**
(bringing not peace but division as a means to also serve as pioneer and perfecter of our faith)

Each of these 12 chapters begins by providing an overview of the individual under consideration. This is followed by a discussion of the role and legacy that each pioneer has left in shaping Christian faith and practice. For some, there also are notes as to peculiarities or personal issues of the individual that may have affected or compromised their message. And each chapter closes with an overview of ongoing legacy—the good, bad and (sometimes) ugly.

Each pioneer profiled has been viewed—whether temporarily or longer term—as outside the mainstream of the religious and/or cultural orthodoxy of their time. Their heresies can be categorized as relating to belief versus practice, i.e., substance versus style. Substantive (or doctrinal) deviations have generally received the most attention. However, as will be discussed, matters of practice or style have at times proved to be of similar or greater significance.

While generally proceeding in rough chronological order, discussion of Jesus' role is placed last because his humanity and divinity can be considered as both shaping and mirroring the experiences of those who came later in the Christian chronology.

Rules of the Road

Before proceeding, it is useful to elucidate the approach taken to characterizing each pioneer, their distinctive roles and resulting legacy. Rules of the road—so to speak. For analytical purposes, these are summarized as follows:

1. Research and interpretations reflect both evidence- and faith-based considerations. The faith-based part assumes that if there is a God or similar divine presence, this entity can do anything whether or not it fits with present-day human evidence and scientifically based observation. However, even with the capacity to act as divinity so

pleases, the question of whether and how God does act is based primarily on review and interpretation of the evidence available.

2. Whenever possible, information is drawn from a broad range of sources. In addition to what is described in the New Testament (NT), attention is given to other sources including Old Testament (OT) prefiguration (as with prophecies as well as historic events shaping NT culture), also with post-resurrection documents including writings of early church patriarchs together with non-Christian writers.

3. Unless noted otherwise, quotations from the Old and New Testaments use the New Revised Standard Version (NRSV)—specifically the NRSVA traditional Anglican version. Quotations from the non-canonical Gospels are from the Scholars Version (SV) or other translations as noted. Other versions as cited on occasion include the traditional King James Version (KJV), New King James (NKJV), and English Standard Version (ESV). Except where noted otherwise, quotations or other text in italics or boldface are for emphasis on my part.

4. The Bible and other historical documents may reflect varying degrees of literal narrative, metaphorical and poetic genres—as well as some mix of the above. Where applicable, observations are offered as to whether an alternative genre does or does not fit with the writings or actions of the 12 pioneers considered.

5. There are a number of instances where findings of archaeological excavations bear on interpretations of Christ's ministry and post-resurrection experience. Included is summary information as known or surmised about cultural experiences and influences of the eras considered.

6. At the end of each chapter is a short supplement, hopefully providing added background and context of interest for the individual being profiled.

7. Each pioneer profiled stands alone, considered on his or her own merits, largely independent of the character of those with whom they interact. However, there clearly are significant interactions between various groupings of our subjects and their respective non-mainstream objectives. Key interactions (or spillover effects) of note are those between the three gospel synoptics—Matthew, Mark and Luke. Also

as between Paul with Peter and James, Constantine with Luther (though centuries removed), and Jesus with Peter, John and Mary. The only one missing, one who seemingly stands apart, is Thomas.

8. Differences between sources as well as points of agreement are of note, especially with regard to the major contributions made by each of the dozen personalities profiled. Where information conflicts within or between varied sources, what is of most importance is to understand the nature and potential significance of the conflict—in some cases suggesting a resolution, in other cases not—as may be reasonably discerned from the Biblical and other evidence available.

9. As noted earlier, there are tradeoffs to be made with taking one action versus another or one doctrine versus another. This is assumed to apply to strategic moves by all of the principals profiled. So this book seeks to identify pros and cons of the various courses that each have taken—whether by a political leader like Constantine or by the Savior himself. Also considered are potential implications of paths not taken. Primary reliance is placed on the narrative, with theological or practical results important only to the point supported by the narrative.

10. And after reviewing all 12, I end with an epilogue: asking what does all this mean? Following the caution of Stevan Davies, tentative conclusions are offered for consideration. In all cases, the opportunity is offered for readers to reach their own conclusions. But retain the flexibility to modify conclusions based on new or re-considered evidence that may yet emerge from known as well as yet unexcavated archives.

I. Matthew—Prophecy Fulfilled

Look, the virgin shall conceive and bear a son,
and they shall name him Emmanuel.
Matthew 1:23, quoted from Isaiah 7:14 (Septuagint)

Pioneers can come in many forms. To a 21st century audience, Matthew's gospel is often characterized as the "greatest story ever told." But, to first-century Judaism, a tax collector turned Jesus follower named Matthew uttered words of heresy to the Jewish leaders of his day. Matthew proclaimed Jesus as Messiah—as prophecy fulfilled. [4]

As lead-off gospel to the New Testament, Matthew's purpose of prophecy fulfilled is made clear right at the outset. The author begins his gospel story this way, as:

> ...an account of the genealogy of *Jesus the Messiah*, the son of David, the son of Abraham.[5]

The prime thesis of Matthew's gospel is to demonstrate that Jesus is not a blasphemer intent on overthrowing Judaism. Rather, Jesus makes it clear that he did not come "to abolish the law or the prophets; I have come not to abolish but to fulfill."[6]

---

[4] A wide variety of authors have been quick to note Matthew's interest in prophecy fulfilled. An example is Robert M. Grant, *The Formation of the New Testament,* (New York: Harper & Row, 1965), 13. Grant states that." the evangelist Matthew depicts important events in the life of Jesus as taking place so that particular prophesies, carefully quoted, might be fulfilled."

[5] Matthew 1:1.

[6] Matthew 5:17.

More on this subject is yet to come. But first, turn to a brief review of what is known and not known about the time when this gospel was written, the author, and the audience.

Background of Matthew the Gospel

While Matthew is generally believed to be addressed to a Jewish audience, all of the currently known early versions of this gospel were compiled in Greek. However, early traditions reference a document that may have been written in Hebrew or Aramaic. Though scholars feel that the work contains at least some Semitic language influence, today the Greek version of Matthew generally is not viewed as a straight-across translation from the Aramaic—which may be problematic. (See the Supplement at the end of this chapter for more detail.)

However, this was not necessarily the early church view. As one of the leading authorities of the late first/early second century church, a bishop named Papias from Hierapolis (in Asia Minor) proclaimed that:

Matthew compiled the sayings in the Aramaic language, but everyone has translated them as best he could.[7]

There is some confusion as to whether this statement as reported by the 4th century church historian Eusebius of Caesarea is best translated as "Aramaic" (as indicated above) or as being written in "Hebrew," for example, as indicated by the more recent translation of Eusebius by Paul L. Maier.[8]

The confusion doesn't necessarily end here. A 20th century scholar offers this interpretation about the above noted statement by Papias:

---

[7] Eusebius, *The History of the Church,* 3.39. Unless otherwise indicated, references to this 4th century work of Eusebius of Caesarea and to the translation by G.A Williamson (1885–1892) is provided together with subsequent revisions/edits in 1989 by Andrew Louth. This volume of Eusebius is also often referred to as *Ecclesiastical History.*

[8] Paul L. Maier, *Eusebius—The Church History: A New Translation* (Grand Rapids: Kregel Publications, 1999), 3.39.

This enigmatic sentence (1) refers not to sayings of Jesus *(logoi)* but to Old Testament predictions *(logia)* and (2) suggests that various Greek writings similar to one another and probably ascribed to Matthew are in circulation.[9]

In any event, if the account of Papias is correct, there should an early Aramaic or Hebrew version of Matthew that predates the earliest available and extant manuscripts in Greek. Similarly, Eusebius quotes the renowned third century theologian Origen who had offered a similar view, specifically that:

> I accept the traditional view of the four Gospels which alone are undeniably authentic in the Church of God on earth. First to be written was that of the one-time exciseman who became an apostle of Jesus Christ— Matthew; it was published for believers of Jewish origin, and was composed in Aramaic.[10]

Like Papias, Irenaeus of the late second century and Origen of the third century, all describe Matthew as the first gospel to be written.[11] In contrast, the modern scholarly opinion more often centers on Mark as first of the gospel accounts.

So to summarize, we learn two key points from these early patriarchs which are at variance with most contemporary scholarship. Matthew is described by the patriarchs as the first gospel to be written. And this gospel is cited by early church patriarchs as originally composed in Aramaic or Hebrew, not Greek.

What are we to make of this divergence in opinion between those closer in time to the action than modern day scholars? This question is again explored in yet more detail and in the context of an alternative perspective as provided by the next chapter focused on Mark's gospel.

---

[9] Robert Grant, *Formation of the New Testament,* 71.

[10] As quoted from Origen's *"Commentary on Matthew"* by Eusebius in *The History of the Church,* 6.25. In contrast with G.A. Williamson's 1965 translation, Paul Maier's more recent 1999 translation indicates the gospel was written in Hebrew (not Aramaic).

[11] Origen, *Commentary on Matthew,* as cited by Eusebius, *The History of the Church,* 6.25.

Gospel Dating. As with the other Gospels, there is no clear consensus as to where or when Matthew was written. By tradition, Matthew is often viewed to have originated perhaps in Syria.

Dates suggested range from the early 50s to a time as late as 80–90 AD. The first-century Bishop Ignatius provides the earliest documented example of a person who appears to have cited Matthean passages as early as 110 AD.

Modern scholars including liberal theologians are more likely to posit a date for the composition of Matthew's gospel that is post-70 AD—after Jerusalem was destroyed.[12] More fundamental theologians lean toward a pre-70 date of composition (making the Jewish temple's destruction as the subject of prophecy rather than reporting on an event already occurred).

Authorship. Answers to the question of who actually wrote Matthew also tend to split along theological lines. More fundamental theologians note that early church patriarchs were virtually unanimous in holding that Matthew, one of the 12 disciples, was the author of this Gospel. Since at least the time of second-century Christian leader Irenaeus, the first gospel has been ascribed to the apostle Matthew.

The early church historian Eusebius of Caesarea wrote that:

> Matthew had begun by preaching to Hebrews; and when he made up his mind to go to others too, he committed his own gospel to writing in his native tongue, so that for those with whom he was no longer present the gap left by his departure was filled by what he wrote.[13]

As noted, Papias and Origin had much earlier offered similar views, specifically that Matthew was written by the tax collector of the same name.

Recent scholarship tends toward a different view of authorship for this and other Gospels influenced, in part, by dating the time of writing beyond the likely life spans of Jesus' 12 apostles. Modern scholarship views authorship as often being claimed in the name of an early disciple but by later adherent(s).

The Tradition of Matthew. Matthew (also identified as Levi) was a tax collector who left a vocation reviled by Jewish society to follow Jesus. His

---

[12] Jesus' lament over the *prophetic* destruction of Jerusalem is found at Matthew 23:37–39.

[13] Eusebius, *History of the Church,* 3.24.

name translated means "gift of the Lord." In the Gospels of Mark and Luke, Matthew is referred to as Levi.

Eusebius of Caesarea articulated the view that Matthew's mission was primarily oriented to a Jewish audience. Various church traditions indicate that he was martyred—possibly in "Ethiopia, in Persia, or in Pontus on the Black Sea."[14]

Prophetic Fulfillment

The theme most distinctive to Matthew's gospel is of Old Testament prophecies described as being fulfilled by the life and message of Jesus. Of the four New Testament gospel writers, Matthew makes the greatest use of Old Testament (OT) prophecy. A total of 14 prophetic fulfillments are quoted by Matthew, most introduced with a statement to the effect that:...*all* this took place *to fulfill*...

Isaiah is the prophet of the Hebrew Scriptures most widely cited by Matthew. There also are references to prophetic fulfillments of OT passages from the Hebrew scriptures of Samuel, Psalms, Jeremiah, Hosea, Micah and Zechariah.

The Matthean fulfillment statements typically are followed by an account of Jesus casting out spirits and healing the sick. For example, the author of Matthew writes this as a post-script to his description of a healing by Jesus:

> This was to fulfill what had been spoken through the prophet Isaiah, 'He took our infirmities and bore our diseases.'[15]

A Virgin Birth? Matthew's drive to demonstrate that Jesus' earthly sojourn represents prophetic fulfillment leads him into dangerous (if not erroneous) applications of Old Testament prophetic Scriptures. We begin with perhaps the most controversial example of Matthean overreach—with what this New Testament author describes as a prophecy from Isaiah of the *virgin birth* of Jesus, stated by Matthew as follows:

---

[14] Robert Brownrigg, *Who's Who in the New Testament* (New York: Oxford University Press, 1993), 176.
[15] Matthew 8:17, from Isaiah 53:4.

"Look, the *virgin* shall conceive and bear a son, and they shall name him Emmanuel," which means, "God is with us."[16]

An initial problem with this interpretation is that Chapter 7 of Isaiah is directly addressing an immediate challenge for Ahaz (an OT king of Judah) to fend off invasion from a coalition of northern Israel and Syria (Damascus). Isaiah records that God spoke directly to Ahaz requesting that the king ask for a sign of pending success or failure. Ahaz responds by saying "I will not put the Lord to the test."[17]

The question is: does Isaiah's prophetic pronouncement refer to birth of a son to King Ahaz (of Judah) at the time of Isaiah's encounter with Ahaz? Or is the prophecy intended to refer to a much longer lead time extending well beyond Isaiah's lifetime (not specifically stated but retrospectively understood by Matthew as referring to Jesus the Messiah)?

In the historical setting of Chapter 7, Isaiah lets the king know that he will receive a sign whether Ahaz wants it or not. If this is a near term prophecy, the son possibly refers to Hezekiah as the successor to Ahaz who would serve as Judah's next king, one who would restore Judah to God and (temporarily) save Jerusalem from destruction.

The prophecy may also be seen as a sign for Ahaz that the lineage of King David would be preserved.

If Isaiah is referring to a future Messiah separate from or possibly in addition to a coming son for Ahaz, a second and more significant question arises—this time placed directly on the shoulders of Matthew. This question is whether Matthew has misinterpreted the Hebrew term *almah* which generically means a young woman or whether in this instance the woman might be appropriately considered as a virgin (i.e., not yet had intercourse).

As noted, Matthew's quotation of Isaiah likely comes as the result of an apparent mistranslation of the Old Testament from the original Hebrew to the Greek Septuagint (which occurred in about the third century BC). While the Matthean account cites correctly from the Septuagint, in the process this New Testament author appears to wittingly or unwittingly misrepresent the words

---

[16] Matthew 1:23 (NRSV), as adapted from Isaiah 7:14 per the Septuagint and not a Hebrew text. The KJV translates the underlying Hebrew term *almah* in Isaiah as "virgin," the NRSV as "young woman."

[17] Isaiah 7:12.

and the meaning of the original Hebrew manuscripts (from which the Septuagint was translated).

The term appropriated by Matthew from the Greek Septuagint is *parthenos,* specifically meaning a virgin. However, the term used from the original Hebrew of Isaiah 7:14 is *almah,* more appropriately translated as maiden, young woman or unmarried woman.

As noted, the term *almah* is not definitive as to whether the young woman has or has not experienced sexual intercourse. The Hebrew does have another term *bethulah* that is more narrowly defined as a virgin, a term that is used repeatedly throughout the Old Testament. However, *bethulah* is not the word that is used by earliest Hebrew manuscripts of the Isaiah passage.

The term *almah* is used several other times in the Hebrew Scriptures—referring to women ranging from older children to those being seduced or forced to have sexual relations before marriage. In some of these cases, it is unclear whether the use of *almah* is intended to be a general reference simply to a young woman or more specifically to a young woman who is also a virgin.

Perhaps the most graphic depiction of a less than virginal passage is to be found in the Proverbs:

Three things are too wonderful for me;
four I do not understand:
the way of an eagle in the sky,
the way of a snake on a rock,
the way of a ship on the high seas,
and the way of a man with a girl *(almah).*[18]

In effect, Matthew's citation best illustrates the far-reaching consequences of a potential overreach—an insult or heresy to those steeped in the traditions

---

[18] Proverbs 30:18–19 (NRSV). Per *Young's Analytical Concordance*, other uses of the Hebrew term *almah* are found in Genesis 24:43 (describing when Isaac first met Rebekah as a young woman at the well), Exodus 2:8 (referring to Miriam sister of Moses), Psalms 68:25 (referring to damsels playing their tambourines), Song of Solomon 1:3 (referring to one whom maidens love), and Song of Solomon 6:8 (some variants of which describe "sixty queens and eighty concubines, and maidens [almah} without number").

of Judaism. This is because the *virgin* described by Isaiah is not necessarily a virgin, but *an unmarried young woman*—virginal or otherwise.

Matthew's misquotation of Isaiah does not necessarily mean that there is no virgin birth. Luke's gospel provides a similar account of Mary's virgin birth without reference to Old Testament accounts—prophetic or otherwise. In fact, Luke's description describes the visit to Nazareth of the angel Gabriel "to a virgin (*parthenos*) engaged to a man whose name was Joseph, of the house of David. The virgin's name was Mary."[19]

Luke does not feel the need to inject an ostensibly prophetic statement from six centuries earlier to support the case for Mary's virginity. While not directly stated, the implication from Luke is that her virginity was maintained from the time of becoming engaged to Joseph to at least the time of Jesus' birth.

What is one to make of this apparent Matthean overreach? Four summary observations are noted:

- Assuming an all-powerful God, the issue at stake is not whether God (or the Holy Spirit) could disrupt the natural order for a woman to become pregnant without intercourse. All is possible with God. Rather, the question is of a historical nature. Did the all-mighty, in fact, cause Mary to conceive via divine (non-human) intervention? Or did Mary conceive via the normal human route of human sexual intercourse?
- Matthew sees the opportunity and/or feels the need to reach back to a prophecy by Isaiah to make or strengthen the case for a virginal birth—in part by using a sloppy Septuagint translation together with disregarding the immediate implications of Isaiah 7 for then King Ahaz and his son Hezekiah. In contrast, Luke's gospel is comfortable stating the facts of Mary's virginity at engagement without the need to bolster the case with a prophetic re-interpretation.
- Whether or not Matthew was aware of the difference between the original Hebrew and the Greek translation is indeterminate based on the information available. However, the resulting implications for Christian authenticity are unfortunate—casting doubt on an item

---

[19] Luke 1:27.

viewed as consequential yet not necessarily essential to Christian faith and practice.
- Even more questionable is a pattern of emphasizing Jesus' fulfillment of varied prophecies that runs throughout Matthew's gospel—retrospectively re-interpretating OT prophecies from times gone by into a first-century context as a means to validate or reinforce the messianic role of Jesus.

Other Examples of Prophetic Overreach. A sampling of other prophecies cited by Matthew as being fulfilled by Jesus life and ministry includes the following:

- Matthew refers to statements in Samuel and Micah that a ruler of Judah will emerge from Bethlehem. The original citation in Samuel is that of a forerunner to the kingship of David, not Jesus. It is not clear whether the subsequent statement in Micah is looking back to David or forward to someone who is yet to come.[20]
- Upon his return from Egypt (after King Herod's reputed slaughter of the innocents), Matthew refers back to the statement of the prophet Hosea that: "Out of Egypt I have called my son."[21] However, Hosea's use of the term son clearly refers to the entire nation of Israel rather than to an individual (i.e., Messiah). The full text of the verse in Hosea is: "When Israel was a child, I loved him, and out of Egypt I called my son."
- In describing Herod's massacre of the young males of Bethlehem, Matthew recalls Jeremiah: "A voice was heard in Ramah, wailing and loud lamentation, Rachel weeping for her children; she refused to be consoled, because they are no more."[22] However, Ramah is not Bethlehem, but most likely a town situated north rather than south of Jerusalem.[23] Jeremiah is writing of the exile of the Northern tribes of

---

[20] From Matthew 2:6. Sources are 2 Samuel 5:2 and Micah 5:2.
[21] Matthew 2:15, from Hosea 11:1.
[22] Matthew 2:18 quotes from Jeremiah 31:15.
[23] The Ramah referred to by Jeremiah is believed to be situated five miles north of Jerusalem. Other places in Palestine have had the name Ramah meaning "hill." Along with Bethlehem (south of Jerusalem), Ramah is cited as a potential place of burial or

- Israel to Assyria, with Ramah potentially a site for deportation of those being deported.
- Regarding the use of parables rather than a more straightforward message delivered to the masses, Matthew's Jesus once more quotes Isaiah: "You will indeed listen, but never understand."[24] Again, Isaiah does not appear to have been writing of a future time, but of a message that Isaiah was to take to his contemporaries. However, centuries later, Matthew has Jesus (perhaps erroneously) suggesting a direct prophetic link, quoting Jesus as saying: "With them indeed is fulfilled the prophecy of Isaiah…" Jesus appears to be re-interpreting a malaise of Isaiah's day to 1st century Israel, as well.
- In remorse for betraying Jesus, Judas returns the thirty pieces of silver he was paid back to the chief priests. Matthew reports that the priests use the money to buy a potter's field as a place to bury foreigners. This is in fulfillment of a prophecy made by Jeremiah: "And they took the thirty pieces of silver, the price of the one on whom a price had been set, on whom some of the people of Israel had set a price, and they gave them for the potter's field, as the Lord commanded me."

Matthew is mistaken; there is no directly similar verse in Jeremiah. Rather, Matthew's quote appears to be a very loose paraphrase of a verse in Zechariah.[25]

Fulfillment of Torah Law. Matthew saw Jesus not only as a fulfillment of specific events foretold by Jewish prophets of the Scripture. Jesus also serves as a fulfillment of Jewish teaching—and more specifically of Judaic law or the *Torah.*

Of the four gospel writers, Matthew is the only one to refer repeatedly to the "law and the prophets." For example, in Matthew's account of the *Sermon on the Mount,* Jesus asks the crowd:

---

memorial for Rachel (Jacob's wife)l. Precise locations are a subject of some dispute.

[24] Excerpted from Matthew 13:14–15 which is referencing Isaiah 6:8–10.

[25] Matthew 27:9–10. Zechariah 11:13 indicates that this prophet "…took the thirty shekels of silver and threw them into the treasury in the house of the LORD." Any reference to Jeremiah would be much more oblique, perhaps to Jeremiah 19:1–13, 18:2–12, or 32:6–9 (including references to the valley of Hinnom-Gehenna) and potter's house.

> Do not think that I have come to abolish the law or the prophets; I have come not to abolish but to fulfill. For truly I tell you, until heaven and earth pass away, not one letter, not one stroke of a letter, will pass from the law until all is accomplished.[26]

More so than with the other Gospels, Matthew's account is particularly critical of the Jewish sect known as the Pharisees. As a first-century movement, the Pharisees were intent on assuring devoted adherence to all forms of Jewish law—including customs built up over the centuries—particularly so since the return of exiles from Babylonian captivity starting in the 6th century BC.

While Matthew's Jesus is highly critical of the Pharisees, the criticism does not appear to be focused on the fine details of the law. Rather, Jesus' criticism is that in prescribing detailed rules (as for tithing and other matters), the Pharisees had "neglected the weightier matters of the law: justice and mercy and faith."[27]

Jesus as Messiah. A final theme of fulfillment important to Matthew's gospel relates to Jesus' role as the Messiah or *Anointed one* of God. As noted, Matthew makes known his view of the messiahship of Jesus right from the outset of his gospel. In verse 1 of chapter 1, Matthew states his purpose as: "An account of the genealogy of Jesus *the Messiah...*" (*emphasis* mine)

Beyond the Obvious. There is one other possible explanation for Matthew's apparent misinterpretations or extrapolations of Old Testament prophetic pronouncements. This is raised by the possibility that Jesus and other New Testament writers were, in fact, legitimately re-interpreting OT Scripture as applying not only during OT times but also in a New Testament (NT) context.

For example, the authors of a book titled *Beyond the Obvious* observe that:

> It becomes increasingly clear the more we pursue this issue that there are several instances where the New Testament interprets the Old in strange and varied ways, and surely not in a literal way.[28]

---

[26] Matthew 5:17–18.
[27] Matthew 23:23.
[28] James DeYoung and Sarah Hurty, *Beyond the Obvious* (Gresham, Oregon: Vision House, 1995), 47–48. The difference between the scriptural author's literal intent and later spirit-led re-interpretation is what the authors of this book describe as the

In effect, the Spirit of God may have intended a meaning for Scripture beyond that of the original author. Divine intent may have applied not only historically but also prospectively. This more liberal approach could include reshaping the narrative to reflect what would become the unfolding kingdom of God or New Covenant purposes.

Acceptance of Matthew. Early Christian literature indicates that Matthew was generally accepted as the first of the New Testament Gospels by the early 2nd century AD. As would later be recounted by the 4th century church historian Eusebius of Caesarea, the late first/early second century patriarch Papias of Hierapolis in Asia Minor preferred an "oral gospel" but attested to the Gospel of Matthew stating:

> Matthew compiled the sayings in the Aramaic language, and everyone translated them as well as he could.[29]

During this same time period, Polycarp who was bishop of Smyrna and reputedly a disciple of the apostle John also quotes or references passages found in the Gospel of Matthew.[30] As the 2nd century bishop of Lyons, Irenaeus is perhaps the last of the early church patriarchs to rely extensively on oral tradition. He also is first to list the current four Gospels and 13 Pauline letters as accepted. Irenaeus quoted from Matthew, Mark, Acts, I Corinthians, I Peter, Hebrews and Titus.

Eusebius also offers a more extensive quote from the 3rd century theologian Origen, stating:

> I accept the traditional view of the four Gospels which alone are undeniably authentic to the Church of God on earth. First to be written was that of the one-time exciseman who became an apostle of Jesus Christ—

---

difference between existential and essential meaning. The authors also note that "the divine Author's meaning may go beyond the human author's, unknown to him." (p. 303). Less certain is whether and to what degree the same license of reinterpretation extends beyond Christians of the first century.

[29] Eusebius, *History of the Church,* 3.39.

[30] Polycarp, *The Letter to the Philippians,* http://ntcanon.org/Polycarp.shtml, accessed March 25, 2024.

Matthew; it was published for believers of Jewish origin, and was composed in Aramaic.[31]

Some Jewish Christian congregations such as the Ebionites who emigrated to Transjordan after the first Roman destruction of Jerusalem (in 70 AD) reportedly preferred or "admitted only the authority of Matthew."[32] In effect, Matthew's acceptance as authoritative was generally but not completely endorsed by the early church.

As with other Gospels, Matthew was rejected by the 2nd century Gnostic Marcion. The gospel also was opposed by the late 2nd/early 3rd century Ebionite Symmachus, author of a Greek version of the Old Testament who favored a return to Jewish law.

Even among those accepting the gospel, some caveats are noted. For example, the 2nd century theologian Clement of Alexandria notes that that Matthew added several phrases to the Beatitudes.[33] The most important outstanding questions continue to center on the language in which the book was originally written and whether it is written first, as early church patriarchs indicate.

Matthew in Summary

Matthew's gospel has been widely cited down through the last two millennia as the primary source for *the greatest story ever told*. However, as noted in this chapter, the evidence available suggests that the story as told by this first of the Christian pioneers may be, in fact, too good to be true. An alternative viewpoint might be that if Matthew overstates his case, it is to make a point consistent with his overall objective of portraying Christ as prophecy fulfilled.

Matthew endeavored to weave a narrative that would serve to keep a nascent Christianity within the folds of Judaism. For Matthew, Jesus

---

[31] Eusebius, quoting Origen's "Commentary on Matthew," *History of the Church,* 6.25.

[32] As cited by Williston Walker, et al, *A History of the Christian Church,* 4th ed. (New York: Charles Scribner's Sons, 1985), 74.

[33] Robert Grant, *Formation of the New Testament,* 166.

represented a righteous form of Judaism in contrast to the retrograde Judaism practiced by Jewish leaders of the day—scribes, Pharisees and Sadducees.

In the end, this gospel as we now have it—including with possible additions and redactions—may have over-reached. Whether by malevolent design, sloppy homework or simple exuberance, Matthew clearly reaches beyond what the original Old Testament authors may have originally intended. Another possibility is that this re-interpretation and application of prophecy both in the moment and prospectively is in fact justified, if recognized as spirit-led and consistent with other Scripture.

To the extent viewed as heretical for 1st century Judaism, Matthew's heresy can be viewed primarily as a matter of substance. This gospel writer presents an alternative paradigm of belief. This was a change from considering how prophecy was to be interpreted in the context of an OT prophet's world view versus projected forward to a fulfillment in Jesus that may or may not have been intended with the prophecy as originally articulated.

Despite these difficulties, Matthew's grand purpose was served. By repeatedly portraying Jesus as a fulfillment of OT prophesies, Matthew carved a niche for a Christianity that could be broadcast not only for Jewish consumption, but also for a broader Gentile audience. This would be evidenced with Peter's sermon at Pentecost and more generally by Paul the apostle in his exhortations to Gentile as well as Jewish audiences.

There may be a price to be paid for such exuberance. To his own contemporaries and to succeeding generations, Matthew's overreach raises doubts not only as to the legitimacy of the prophetic claims offered, but as to the integrity of the rest of this gospel. If the author stretched to reinterpret history in one portion of the gospel for which he is named, might he have done so elsewhere?

As the first of our dozen pioneers of the faith, Matthew serves a vital purpose for the church that was to be. For Matthew, Jesus is the **bridge** between the old order and the new. Through Matthew, the Christian church was not just an upstart sect, but a full-fledged religious movement rooted both in history and looking forward post-resurrection.

To the Jewish establishment of the first century, Matthew's gospel was *in your face.* Corrupt Judaism was to be replaced by a new Judaism—through Jesus as the fulfillment of those whom the prophets had spoken.

Matthew's pioneering role was critical to the flowering of a church that could leave behind the old for the new. However, in his ultimate mission, Matthew may have fallen short of the mark.

Rather than reforming Judaism from within, Matthean *overreach* served instead to help drive Christianity out from the Judaic fold—separating and embittering people who nonetheless have continued to worship the same *Yahweh* for two succeeding millennia.

As this chapter illustrates, there is both an upside and a downside to the endeavors of Matthew. This pattern of tradeoff—of a price to be paid for advancement of Christianity—is a recurring theme played out in multiple ways across the eleven other pioneers of the faith profiled through the chapters which follow.

Supplement — Hebrew, Aramaic or Greek?

Communicating within one's native language is never as precise as one might want but nonetheless can lead to miscommunication. This is especially the case in situations where a specific term may have multiple meanings, for example, depending on the context in which it is used. The risk of incorrect interpretation and miscommunication becomes greater when translation between languages is involved.

For first-century Palestine, three languages are of particular importance to understanding the Bible—both Old and New Testament:

- **Hebrew** is the language in which the Old Testament was largely written. Whereas the typical American has command of perhaps 50,000 words (at high school level), the Hebrew vocabulary comprised about 4–5,000 terms—obviously with more meanings possible for a given term than in English today. An additional challenge was that by the time of Christ, evidence indicates that old Hebrew was no longer in widespread use, making readings as from the Torah more problematic.[34]
- **Aramaic** had become the most prevalent language of everyday use for Jewish written and oral communication by about the 3rd century BC.

---

[34] Britannica, *Hebrew Language*, https://www.britannica.com/topic/Hebrew-language (accessed February 2, 2024).

Jewish religious texts such as the Mishnah and Talmud would be written in Aramaic. While the earliest extant manuscripts of the New Testament are written in Greek, Aramaic words and phrases are found, especially in the Gospels, attesting to the use of Aramaic among the population of Jesus' day. There also is evidence including quotations from the late first/early 2nd century bishop Papias that Matthew was initially written in Aramaic or Hebrew—though confirming documentation is no longer available.

- **Greek** most likely was not the dominant language across Judea, Samaria and the Galilee but is generally acknowledged as being the language of the ruling elites as with Herodians and Romans.

Greek also was used in trade and commerce, especially in larger urban centers such as Jerusalem, Sepphoris (near Nazareth) and Tiberias (when Herod Antipas relocated his capital from Sepphoris to be on the Sea of Galilee). Educated urban communities were often bilingual as evidenced by historic accounts including the influence of Greek philosophy with elites such as the ruling Sadducees in Jerusalem.

While these are general tendencies, it is largely unknown as to whether, where and when Jesus spoke in Aramaic or Greek. To the extent that Jesus made extensive use of Aramaic, there is increased likelihood of mistranslations by writers whose earliest extant New Testament works are preserved only in Greek.

This issue is perhaps most problematic for Matthew, especially if the initial manuscript was composed in Aramaic—whether or not later redacted as well as coupled with further translations from Hebrew and Aramaic to Greek. Mistranslation coupled with loose interpretation also surfaces as a potential issue for the other three Gospels as noted with the chapters on Mark, Luke and John which now follow.

II. Mark—Contrarian

So they went out and fled from the tomb, for terror and amazement had seized them; and they said nothing to anyone, for they were afraid.
Mark 16:8

The Gospel according to Mark represents a conundrum for theologians, scholars, clergy and parishioners. Compared to the other Gospels, Mark is short on sayings (or theology) as articulated by Jesus. It is considerably shorter, more concise and fast-paced than its synoptic counterparts Matthew or Luke.

To the early church and continuing today, Mark's path can be characterized as a tale of the *dimwitted dozen*—twelve male disciples characterized by ineptitude, carelessness and even avarice. For this gospel writer, the tragicomedy begins but does not end with Jesus' chosen twelve.

Similar characterizations are extended to cover both followers (including women followers as noted above) and also enemies of the Son of Man. Whether by design or not, Mark's skewering of Jesus' twelve closest disciples and others around him helps set the post-resurrection stage for two upstarts to subsequently claim the mantle of Christianity—Jesus' brother James and then the self-appointed apostle Paul.

Who was this "Son of Man" as depicted by Mark? One can look back to similar terminology with Daniel of the Old Testament, arguing that "Son of Man" means "one like a person," because he has a human face.[35] His humanity can be sharply contrasted with the beastly emanations around God's throne—notably a lion, bear, leopard, and horned beast. In Mark's gospel, "Son of Man" is used as an indirect title for Jesus himself.[36]

---

[35] See Daniel 7:1–13. NRSV translates what the KJV terms as "son of Man" to "one like a human being."

[36] See, for example, John Dominic Crossan in *The Historical Jesus: The Life of a Mediterranean Jewish Peasant* (New York: Harper Collins, 1991) for a detailed

On the surface, Mark's gospel of the Son of Man comes across as a relatively innocuous narrative. Mark's Jesus is a man of action, abruptly and "immediately" moving from one event to another.

When he speaks, Mark's Jesus conveys his thoughts in short burst phrases or sentences rather than multi-paragraph discourses. Consequently, the message of Mark tends to be transmitted via the action—including the rapid-fire interactions occurring with those around him. It is from this action video that the message of Mark's Jesus emerges—often jarring, at times seemingly contradictory. The message is directed to friends and foes alike—all of whom *just don't get it.*

The fast-paced action of "immediately" moving from one event, one crisis to another can be uncomfortably jarring. A major hypothesis of this review is that, of the New Testament writers, Mark comes across as *the contrarian*—in some cases perhaps unwittingly but in others most intentionally.

In this self-appointed position of contrarian, Mark also plays a pivotal role in the never-ending Christian struggle to reconcile seemingly conflicting gospel accounts, especially as between his gospel and the two other synoptic Gospels of Mathew and Luke. This review addresses Mark's contrarian role from two perspectives:

- Portrayal of the disciples (and others) as *dimwitted,* not grasping what Jesus is about.
- A *contrarian* personality affecting creation of seemingly divergent gospel accounts—all with an unceasing and driving sense of urgency.

But before traveling to these themes, it is useful to begin with an overview of Mark and his gospel.

Background of Mark the Gospel

To believers of both the early and modern church, Mark's gospel receives lesser notice. Most of Mark (plus yet more) is also found in the other synoptic accounts of Matthew and Luke. And Mark's abruptness causes many to prefer other less confrontational New Testament accounts of Jesus and his ministry.

---

discussion. Crossan argues that: "It was Mark, therefore, and Mark alone, who created the suffering and rising Son of Man," (p. 259)

To the 20th/21st century scholarly community, Mark has taken on greater importance because this gospel is now widely viewed as the first to be written, not Matthew. If true, Matthew and Luke might then be considered as reactions to possible excesses and omissions of the Markan account. However, there is still a case to be made for the opposite view—that Mark's gospel was written after Matthew and/or Luke.

Gospel Dating and Authorship. While the author is never directly identified, the widespread view shared by the early Christian church and most fundamentalist churches today is that this gospel account was written by John Mark. From the vantage point of identified first to fourth century Christian leaders and writers, Mark generally was generally considered as the second of the four Gospels to be written.

However, a considerable number of modern scholars have taken exception to the early tradition, concluding that Mark actually may be the first of the currently available New Testament gospel composed. With this amended view, Mark is seen as being rooted in the period between emperor Nero's persecution of Christians (64 AD) and the Jewish revolt against Rome (70 AD)—or just after.

Less discussed is the decidedly non-mainstream perspective that Luke may have been one of the first Gospels to be written. One advocate of this theory points out that, of the four Gospels, the Greek of the earliest manuscripts found in Luke is the most readily translated back to an earlier and more colloquial, spoken Aramaic form. If this is the case, then Mark may have drawn from either or both of early but no longer extant accounts of Matthew and Luke—just presented in Mark's more abbreviated and fast-paced form.

In effect, one advocate of this theory makes the case for an unconventional Gospel of Mark, observing that:

> Mark's methods may be very foreign to us but once we catch the playful spirit he displays in dealing with texts we can sit back and enjoy the somewhat amusing performance of a writer who delights in change for little other reason than his love of change.[37]

---

[37] Robert Lisle Lindsey, *A New Approach to the Synoptic Gospels* (Jerusalem: Dugith Publishers, Baptist House: 1971), 21.

The first reference to young Mark as the gospel's author may come from the writer himself. At the arrest of Jesus in the Garden of Gethsemane, only this gospel includes the following brief note:

> A certain young man (Mark?) was following him (Jesus), wearing nothing but a linen cloth. They caught hold of him, but he left the linen cloth and ran off naked. [38]

Could this have been John Mark's first (but not last) encounter with the Son of Man?

Role in the Early Church. The John Mark of the New Testament appears to come from a family of some wealth. As early leader of the post-resurrection church, the apostle Peter is arrested, then delivered from prison—coming to the home of the mother of John Mark. The home is described as large enough to accommodate a maid and a number of Jesus followers who were inside praying.[39]

Mark traditionally has been viewed as a disciple of Peter. This view is buttressed by the statement attributed to Peter that:

> Your sister church in Babylon, chosen together with you, sends you greetings, and so does *my son Mark*.[40]

Mark played a central role as foil to two of the main protagonists of the early church—Peter and Paul. In some ways, the traditional affiliation of Mark with Peter seems a bit odd given: (a) the strong criticism that Peter receives from Jesus in the Gospel of Mark; and (b) Mark's on/off relationship with the apostle Paul.

Mark accompanied Paul and Barnabas on their first missionary journey. However, Mark apparently deserted them at Perga (in Pamphylia on the southwestern coast of Turkey), returning to Jerusalem—for reasons not fully stated in the account given by the New Testament book of Acts.

---

[38] Mark 14:51–52. The anonymity of the reference suggests that the subject was the author. As the outer garment is generally made of wool, the linen garment indicates that the youth likely was from a wealthy family.
[39] Acts 12:12–13.
[40] 1 Peter 5:13.

Paul's subsequent unhappiness with Mark was considerable. The writer of Acts (likely Luke) indicates that Paul severed his working relationship with Barnabas when Barnabas proposed taking Mark (his cousin) on a second missionary trip. Paul and Barnabas parted company, with Barnabas taking Mark on a subsequent mission trip to Cyprus.[41]

While not describing why or how, by the end of Paul's life Mark appears to have regained Paul's approval. This is made clear in at least three of the NT epistles commonly attributed to Paul.[42]

Historical Accounts. Mark and his gospel attracted attention from subsequent patriarchs of the early church. As early as the turn of the first century, Clement of Rome appears to have some knowledge of Mark's work as that of an evangelist at Rome.[43] Polycarp of Smyrna also refers to a passage unique to Mark's gospel where Jesus refers to himself as a "servant of all."[44]

The late first/early second century church patriarch Papias offers more detailed comments, based on what he had heard from someone named John the presbyter:[45]

> Mark, who had been Peter's interpreter, wrote down carefully, but *not in order*, all that he had remembered of the Lord's sayings and doings. For he had not heard the Lord or been one of His followers, but later, as I said, one of Peter's. Peter used to adapt his teachings to the occasion, without making a systematic arrangement of the Lord's sayings, so that Mark was quite justified in writing down some things just as he remembered them. For he had one purpose only—to leave out nothing that he had heard, and to make no misstatement about it.[46]

The late 2nd century philosopher-theologian Clement of Alexandria offers additional information on the composition of this gospel. Clement's

---

[41] This rift is recounted in Acts 13:13 and Acts 15:36–39.
[42] Colossians 4:10, Philemon 24, and 2 Timothy 4:11.
[43] Robert Grant, *Formation of the New Testament,* 166.
[44] http://ntcanon.org/Polycarp.shtml. The passage referenced is Mark 9:35.
[45] John the presbyter (or elder) is arguably distinct from the apostle John and is possibly the author of Revelation rather than John the "beloved disciple."
[46] Papias, as quoted by Eusebius, *History of the Church,* 3.39.

comments are paraphrased by the fourth century church historian Eusebius this way:

> He (Clement) used to say that the earliest Gospels were those containing the genealogies, while Mark's originated as follows. When, at Rome, Peter had openly preached the word and by the spirit had proclaimed the gospel, the large audience urged Mark, who had followed him for a long time and remembered what had been said, to write it all down. This he did, making his gospel available to all who wanted it. When Peter heard about this, he made no objection and gave no special encouragement.[47]

Third century theologian Origen also commented on the circumstances of Mark's composition, noting that Mark: "followed Peter's instructions in writing it."[48] Eusebius also suggests that Mark may have written his gospel under a bit of duress:

> So brightly shone the light of true religion on the minds of Peter's hearers that, not satisfied with a single hearing or with the oral teaching of the divine message, they resorted to appeals of every kind to induce Mark (whose gospel we have), as he was a follower of Peter, to leave them in writing a summary of the instruction they had received by word of mouth, nor did they let him go till they had persuaded him, and thus became responsible for the writing of what is known as the Gospel according to Mark.[49]

Eusebius further notes that Mark served as Bishop of Alexandria in Egypt, around whom a large following of men and women was established, practicing "an extremely severe rule of life."[50] This may have planted the seeds of divergent practices between later ascetics versus a more pragmatic and orthodox church leadership. In this comment, we sense the paradox presented by Mark and his Jesus—with elements both of action and mystery.

---

[47] Eusebius, 6.14.
[48] Origen, *Commentary on Matthew,* as cited by Eusebius, *History of the Church,* 6.25.
[49] Eusebius, 2.15. Eusebius notes that this story comes from Clement who bases his account on Papias of Hierapolis.
[50] Eusebius, 2.16.

Dimwitted Disciples

The first sentence of Mark's gospel introduces Jesus as the Anointed (or the Christ), the Son of God. The remainder of the gospel is dedicated to describing how few of those who met or followed Jesus understood who he really was and is.

There are at least a couple of dozen interactions between Jesus and his disciples that Mark records. In all but one instance, Jesus is portrayed by Mark as dismissive—if not demeaning—in attitude toward his own chosen twelve.

On an occasion which occurs at the outset of his ministry, Simon Peter and companions search for Jesus, letting him know that a crowd of "everyone" is looking for him. In a way, Jesus affirms and reinforces the initiative taken by his disciples. But in a way, he sidesteps, saying:

Let us go on to the neighboring towns, so that I may proclaim the message there also, for that is what I came out to do.[51]

From this point on, the disciples are presented in substantially less flattering terms. Consider an interaction that occurs just after Jesus has fed a crowd of 4,000 from just seven loaves of bread. Mark records that:

They forgot to bring any bread and had nothing with them in the boat except one loaf. Then he (Jesus) started giving them directives: "Look," he says, "watch out for the leaven of the Pharisees and the leaven of Herod!"

They began looking quizzically at one another because they didn't have any bread. And because he was aware of this, he says to them: "Why are you puzzling about your lack of bread? You still aren't using your heads, are you? *You still haven't got the point, have you? Are you just dense? Though you have eyes, you still don't see, and though you have ears, you still don't hear!*"[52]

---

[51] Mark 1:38.

[52] Mark 8:14–18 (SV). Quoted is the more pungent translation of the Scholars Version.

A parallel passage to this account from Mark can be found in Matthew's gospel. But, as is typical, Mark's Jesus piles on the abuse—with the added vitriol (as *italicized above*) found only in Mark.

In contrast, Matthew's Jesus is prompt to give the disciples the benefit of the doubt. For example, after this interchange about bread, Matthew states that the disciples finally "understood that he (Jesus) was not talking about guarding against the leaven in bread but against the teaching of the Pharisees and Sadducees."[53] Unlike Matthew, Mark's gospel provides no indication that the disciples ever figured out what Jesus was talking about.

There are several such incidents where the accounts of Matthew or Luke suggest a more positive view of the disciples than does Mark. Another noteworthy example is provided by Jesus' response to the disciples' request for a private interpretation of the Parable of the Sower. Alternative versions of Jesus' response as told by each of the three synoptic writers follow:

Mark. Do you not understand this parable? Then *how will you understand all the parables?*[54]

Matthew. To *you it has been given* to know the secrets of the kingdom of heaven, but to them it has not been given.[55]

Luke. To *you it has been given* to know the secrets of the kingdom of God; but to others I speak in parables.[56]

In other words, while Mark's Jesus is critical of the disciples' question, Matthew and Luke portray a Jesus who is pleased to share secrets of the kingdom with his select dozen.

Mark's Jesus comes across as dismissive not only toward his disciples but also his larger public audience.

For example, Mark has Jesus saying that he talks in parables in part so that those "outside":

---

[53] Matthew 16:12 (SV).
[54] Mark 4:13 (NRSV).
[55] Matthew 13:11.
[56] Luke 8:10.

...may indeed look, but not perceive, and may indeed listen, but not understand, *so that they may not turn again and be forgiven.*[57]

Luke's gospel excludes the hardened (above *italicized*) portion of Jesus' statement.

Jesus' response to a group of children and their parents provides an added example. All three synoptics have Jesus asking the children to come to him. Only Mark also reports that Jesus was indignant with the disciples for trying to keep the children and their parents away.[58]

Hard-Edged Criticisms Unique to Mark. In some instances, the other two gospel writers will agree with Mark—also criticizing the disciples involved. But in most cases, Mark offers a harsher assessment of the disciples' understanding and capacity for spiritual discernment.

Two other examples are noted of Jesus dressing down his disciples, not recorded by the other Gospels:

- Jesus walks on water, the disciples are terrified. All three synoptics record that Jesus called out "Take heart, it is I; do not be afraid." Only Mark adds the editorial note: "And they (the disciples) were utterly astounded, for they did not understand about the loaves, but their *hearts were hardened.*"[59]
- In response to an argument among the disciples as to who is the greatest, Jesus answers both philosophically and cryptically: "Whoever wants to be first *must be last of all and servant of all.*"[60]

And the Women. A final example occurs at the conclusion of Mark's gospel—which ends before the risen Jesus even re-establishes contact with his disciples. The earliest extant manuscripts of this gospel end with an angel telling the women who visited the tomb:

---

[57] Mark 4:12.
[58] Compare Mark 10:13–16 with Matthew 19:13–15 and Luke 18:15–17.
[59] Mark 6:50–52.
[60] Mark 9:35. Compare this response with Matthew 18:1–5 and Luke 9:46–48.

But go, tell his disciples and Peter that he is going ahead of you to Galilee; there you will see him, just as he told you.[61]

Subsequently, the women:

...went out and fled from the tomb, for terror and amazement had seized them; and they said nothing to anyone, for they were afraid.[62]

And so Mark's gospel account (in its earliest form) abruptly ends—with the women, the disciples and the rest of us left to figure out the meaning on our own.

The longer version of Mark (verses 9–20) offers a more positive conclusion—including Jesus commissioning the disciples and then ascending to heaven. This extended conclusion to Mark's gospel comes across as more consistent and compatible with the other Gospels; it's just not included in the current oldest and still extant manuscripts.

Mark the Contrarian

Now switch to Mark's attachment to immediacy. Then move on to the challenges associated with dating of the synoptics and their interrelationships.

...And Immediately. Mark's brevity makes it possible for even a first-time reader to sense the fast-paced nature of this gospel compared to the more languid pace taken by Matthew, Luke or John. Just to make sure that no one misses the focus on action, Mark makes great use of his favorite transitional phase from one event to the next, with the simple introduction, "and immediately..."

Depending on the English translation, Mark uses the term translated as "immediately" up to nearly forty times. In the Greek, the primary though not only term translated as immediately is *eutheos* or *euthus*. Mark uses this term more than twice as many times as the books of Matthew, Luke or Acts. John's Gospel uses the term on only a couple of occasions.[63]

---

[61] Mark 16:7.
[62] Mark 16:8
[63] For example, in the NRSVUE, translation to "immediately" occurs 67 times throughout the New Testament, including 26 times in Mark, as compared with 12 each

This repetitive use of "immediately" is immediately recognizable as what appears to be a writing quirk of Mark. It's a willingness to play with terminology in a way that contrasts sharply with the other gospel accounts. And while most obvious, this non-conventional (or contrarian) approach to his gospel is not limited just to an immediacy fetish. It shows up in other stylistic quirks or willingness to play with gospel language further throughout Mark's narrative. But before going there, let's now consider Mark's potentially fundamental contribution to the current day misunderstanding surrounding the seeming complexities of gospel formation.

Complexities of Gospel Formation. The tradition of the early church patriarchs was that the three synoptic Gospels were composed first by Matthew, then Mark, then Luke. Today, the modern consensus among both liberal and conservative theologians is that the more likely chronology is Mark first, then Luke and Matthew (both also drawing from a hypothetical but unproven Q sayings document comprising material not contained in Mark).

A third and lesser known alternative has been presented by Robert Lisle Lindsey who for years pastored at a church in Jerusalem, Israel.[64] This is the hypothesis that either Matthew (or a proto-Matthew) document was composed first. This proto-Matthean account then served as a primary source for Mark's gospel but with Mark's focus primarily on the actions rather than sayings of Jesus. Mark's version was then used by Luke together with sayings material as also used earlier by Matthew.

With less detail than provided by Lindsey, I would summarize the logic of his case roughly as follows:[65]

---

in Matthew and Luke and 14 times in Acts. The ESV uses "immediately" 77 times in the New Testament including 35 occasions in Mark versus 14 in Matthew, 12 in Luke and 13 in Acts.

[64] Robert Lisle Lindsey, also see *A Hebrew Translation of the Gospel of Mark,* 2nd ed. (Jerusalem: Dugith Publishers, Baptist House, 1973). Lindsey came into possession of an authentic Dead Sea Scrolls jar in payment for a debt. Due to a donation from the Lindsey family, the jar currently is in possession of the Lanier Theological Library in Houston as the only such Dead Sea Scrolls jar in private hands in the United States.

[65] Robert Lisle Lindsey, *A New Approach to the Synoptic Gospels* (Jerusalem: Dugith Publishers, Baptist House, 1971). This listing summarizes 12 points provided by Lindsey at pp 3–5 of this tractate. Where quotes are indicated, they are from the pages noted.

- Extensive portions of the three synoptic Gospels appear to be derived from literal translations of an unknown Hebrew document including both events of Jesus life and his sayings (possibly via a Q-type or proto-Matthean document). Much or almost all of Luke can be back-translated "word by word to idiomatic Hebrew and the same is true for the non-Markan portions of Matthew."
- Matthew and Luke do not appear to be "acquainted" with each other's writings but both are acquainted with "another source" than Mark which turns out to also be a source via Luke on which Mark depends for much of his gospel.
- Mark normally follows the order of pericopae (or manuscript extracts) that form Luke's gospel but in the process also changes more than 50% of Luke's wording.
- Matthew as we currently know it apparently does not know of Luke's gospel "but closely follows" the pericope ordering of Mark's gospel, although in many cases changes the wording of the "highly redacted text" to more closely fit other early source documents (e.g., Q or proto-Mathew) to which both Mark and Luke are privy.
- One-on-one comparisons of Mark's literary style with that of Matthew and then Luke reveal that Mark's style includes "constant repetition of stereotypic terminology, frequent redundancy, homolyzing, and other dramatizations, and other oddities which suggest that the author (Mark) may well be the evangelist responsible for the unceasing and deliberate verbal change..."
- Detailed analysis of the entire text of Luke and the non-Markan portions of Matthew makes it possible for a Hebrew translator "to reconstruct most of the details of the Hebrew text from which our earliest Greek sources were derived." While the unique Markan insertions can be disconcerting and have confused questions surrounding dating of the Synoptics, the overall conclusion is that "the basic story in our Gospels is textually sound and there is no reason to deny its essential historicity."

An added and more quantitative supporting observation as noted by Lindsey is that:

In other words, if we study the (36) pericopae that Matthew and Luke share without Mark we find that their wording is often *exact for whole sentences and even paragraphs.* But if we study the (78) stories they share with each other and with Mark we find that Matthew and Luke occasionally agree on small words against Mark *but never agree for more than a few words with each other* even when Mark has the same text.[66]

Lindsey concludes that:

The problems of all pericope and verbal disparities (between the three synoptics) revolve around the presence of Mark. Take Mark out, and Mathew and Luke show unity of approach. Put Mark in and the whole picture changes. The clue to the Synoptic Problem lies in Mark's redactive activity as the middle man between Matthew and Luke.[67]

Markan Behavior. At this point, we circle back to what can be gleaned as to the character of John Mark from this analysis of Mark's role in gospel formation and how he is described at various points throughout the New Testament. What we know from these NT accounts is that:

- John Mark was the son of a woman named Mary who apparently was a person of some means with a substantial house in Jerusalem that was the home "where many had gathered and were praying" and to which the apostle Peter immediately went after his release from prison and was answered at the door by a "maid named Rhoda."[68]
- Mark joined with Paul and Barnabas when they returned to Antioch after delivering relief for "the brethren" in Jerusalem suffering during a great famine.[69] Mark (who is later cited by Paul as a cousin of Barnabas) travels with Paul and Barnabas "to assist them" in Cyprus. But when Paul sails from Paphos in Cyprus to Perga in Pamphylia

---

[66] Lindsey, *A New Approach to the Synoptic Gospels,* 16. Italics are those of Lindsey.
[67] Lindsey, 21.
[68] Acts 12: 12–14.
[69] Acts 12:25 for reference of Mark's traveling with Barnabas and Saul (as then named).

(southern Turkey), John (Mark), however "left them and returned to Jerusalem" for reasons largely unstated.[70]

- Mark then shows up after the Church Council in Jerusalem as Paul and Barnabas prepare a follow-up visit to cities in which they had previously ministered. Barnabas wanted Mark to come along. "But Paul decided not to take the one who had deserted them in Pamphylia and had not accompanied them in the work." The disagreement is so heated that Paul and Barnabas part company. Barnabas takes Mark back to Cyprus while Paul chooses Silas and travels through Syria and Cilicia.[71]
- Sometime later and likely toward the latter part of Paul's missionary journeys, there is an apparent reconciliation between Paul and Mark. Writing to the church at Colosse, Paul notes that "Mark the cousin of Barnabas" sends his greetings to the Colossians. And Paul asks that if Mark comes to Colosse, "welcome him."[72]
- And then finally in writing to his younger partner Timothy from a Roman prison, Paul notes: "Only Luke is with me. Get Mark and bring him with you, for he is useful in my ministry."[73]

Mark Having Fun? We now come back full cycle from what is undisputedly said about Mark in the New Testament to two additional observations that help solidify Mark's personality as that of a contrarian—having fun along the way—involving Mark as first as a youth and later as a gospel writer.

Begin with a mysterious gospel account that says much but without clear identification of the person involved. An unusual incident occurs at the time of Jesus' betrayal and arrest in the Garden of Gethsemane. As previously noted and recounted only in Mark's gospel, it is at this point that:

---

[70] Acts 13:4–13.

[71] Acts 15: 36–41 describes the split between Paul and Barnabas over the behavior of Mark.

[72] Colossians 4:10.

[73] 2 Timothy 4:11. Some contemporary scholars question whether Paul is the actual author of the Colossians and Timothy letters.

> A certain young man (Mark?) was following him (Jesus), wearing nothing but a linen cloth. They caught hold of him, but he left the linen cloth and ran off naked.[74]

Could this be anything but a slightly disguised autobiographical note? Could this be anyone other than an impetuous, perhaps spoiled kid named John Mark?

If so, do the character traits which define Mark as a youth carry over to his continued impetuous behavior as an adult—whether as a sometimes assistant in Paul's ministry and as author of his own similarly fast-paced gospel? And would it be surprising that an upstart Mark would team up with a similarly impetuous and sometimes hot-headed disciple named Simon Peter as a major source of the independent material used in his gospel?

As recounted by Papias:

> Peter used to *adapt his teachings* to the occasion, without making a systematic arrangement of the Lord's sayings, so that Mark was quite justified in writing down some things just as he remembered them.[75]

This love of irreverence, literary creativity, and plain contrariness shows up in multiple forms in the gospel attributed to Mark. It accounts for Mark's willingness to intersperse his love of immediate action and willingness for word play in deviating from the proto-Matthean and the Lukan gospel accounts.

What's remarkable is Mark's ability to shift the language but without impairing the basic purpose and conduct of Jesus' earthly ministry. Here's how Lindsey describes the verbal disparity between what Luke wrote and how Mark rephrases Luke's account:

> This verbal divergence is so great that it is even amusing, If Mark uses *ek* (out of), Luke will use *apo* (from). If Luke uses *ek,* Mark will use *apo.* If Mark uses "how," Luke will often use "what." If Luke uses "how," Mark will use "what." If Luke gives "teach," Mark will use a synonym. There are dozens of examples of this kind of synonymic interchange.

---

[74] Mark 14:51–52.

[75] Papias, as quoted by Eusebius, *History of the Church,* 3.39.

Obviously, the only explanation of this phenomenon is that one writer is changing the text of the other for no more serious a reason than his own love of change.[76]

Mark in Summary

Christian writers of the early church up to the present tend to give less play to Mark than other NT Gospels. Not only are most of the events recounted by Mark also found in the lengthier synoptics of Mathew and Luke, but Mark is also less favored as a text because it appears to be doctrinally *light*. Specifically missing from Mark are the extensive discourses (or sayings) of Jesus that offer more insight into the savior's views or theology.

Dimwitted Disciples? At first blush, Mark's Jesus appears strong on action, weak on substance. Yet this quick conclusion would miss the carefully if not slyly crafted narrative, clearly meant to leave certain impressions on the reader. To his readers, Mark appears to have intentionally conveyed the sense of a man of action and mystery, albeit surrounded by adherents (both men and women) who just never quite seem to get it. But yet, have a bit of fun along the way.

Far from being a simple narrative, Mark's terse gospel is carefully crafted, generating powerful undercurrents pushing their way up through the last two millennia. Mark's Jesus is a man set within yet apart from the milieu of the last decades of temple Judaism.

Jesus is routinely misunderstood by what are routinely portrayed as *dimwitted disciples.* If his disciples don't understand, how much less so will he be understood by the general public—to whom Jesus deliberately speaks in parables to be sure they won't get it.

While it is unclear whether Mark's gospel was written before or after the writings of Paul, Mark's gospel does provide useful cover for the teachings of Paul. As an outsider, Paul's ministry depends on confronting and ultimately superseding the influence of Jesus' original disciples.

With inept disciples, it is Jesus' brother James and then Paul the convert who step in to fill an emerging leadership void post-resurrection. And subsequent to the execution of James, Paul is essentially granted an unchallenged license to interpret (or reinterpret) the message of Jesus as he sees fit.

---

[76] Lindsey, *A New Approach to the Synoptic Gospels,* 18.

While not directly claiming divinity for Jesus, Mark's portrayal of the disciples goes a long way to set the Son of Man apart from mere mortals. Mark's God is a task-oriented deity—but accommodating of human fetishes and frailties. This is divinity focused on delivery of "good news"—aimed at preparing humans for the kingdom of God.

And paradoxically this is a God whose own son beseeches the almighty God in endearing terms even nearing betrayal, trial and death—recorded only by Mark overhearing the prayerful cry on the cross by Jesus to "Abba (or Daddy), father…"[77]

A Contrarian Account? For better or worse, Mark's stands in odd juxtaposition to the more theologically oriented synoptics of Luke and Matthew. For some, this has fostered confusion and uncertainty about authenticity of Jesus' earthly sojourn down through the last two millennia. Could this be what a godly Father and Son intended for Mark to accomplish? Layering in one individual's impetuosity albeit mixed with some form of divine inspiration?

To sum up, Mark's deviation from orthodoxy is more a matter of style than substance. As an action-oriented narrative, he largely avoids the teachings of Jesus, essentially eliminating the possibility of doctrinal heresy. Where he does deviate is in the manner of his presentation—action-focused and with seemingly carefree initiative taken to wordsmith his gospel more creatively—creating the illusion rather than the substance of conflict with other NT accounts.

Pros and Cons. If there is an *upside* to the pioneering nature of Mark's gospel, this is it. The church of believers is not to place full reliance in other earthly leaders—even those closest to Jesus. And for those willing to discern and follow the way, don't expect a contemplative route only but rather a sojourn of immediacy, action and adventure.

If Robert Lisle Lindsey is correct in his analysis, there is an added upside from a theological perspective. It is that while "Mark's methods may be very foreign to us:"

---

[77] Mark 14:36. "Abba" is the Aramaic term for "father."

Of far more importance, however, is the fact that when we comprehend the synoptic relationships in this way we have no further need to apologize for the seeming shakiness of the basic gospel account. The story is sound.[78]

Conversely, the potential downside imparted by Mark's impetuous gospel is that the message of those closest to the Son of Man could readily be swept aside by other upstarts who had little or no direct contact with the earthy Jesus.

We are left with an unknown. If early post-resurrection church leadership would have remained in the hands of the remaining 11 disciples, what might be different about the Christianity we know and practice today?

Supplement — Where and How Does Mark End?

The 1611 King James Version (KJV) and subsequent traditional English versions end at Mark 16:20 in a manner similar to that of the other synoptics—with Jesus exhorting his followers to take up Great Commission. As Mark's gospel tells it:

> So then the Lord Jesus, after he had spoken to them, was taken up into heaven and sat down at the right hand of God. And they went out and proclaimed the good news everywhere, while the Lord worked with them and confirmed the message by the signs that accompanied it.[79]

A Shorter Ending? However, the earliest extant Greek manuscripts of this gospel end at Mark 16:8 with the women at the tomb being told by an angel that Jesus has risen from the dead, urging Mary Magdalene and Mary the mother of James and Salome to:

> "...*go,* tell his disciples and Peter that he is going ahead of you to Galilee; there you will see him, just as he told you." So they went out and fled from the tomb, for terror and amazement had seized them, and they said nothing to anyone, for they were afraid.[80]

---

[78] Lindsey, *A New Approach to the Synoptic Gospels,* 21–22.
[79] Mark 16:20.
[80] Mark 16:7–8. A so-called intermediate ending of Mark adds the following statement to Mark 16:8. "And all that had been commanded them they told briefly to those

By ending at verse 8, Mark's shorter gospel would not include reference to Jesus' initial appearance to Mary Magdalene, Jesus' encounter with two followers (on the road to Emmaus), Jesus' parting command to the disciples of the Great Commission, and the subsequent ascension of Jesus to heaven. In effect, ending Mark's gospel at 16:8 leaves the women confused and afraid, not clear as to how the message of resurrection would be communicated to the male disciples, and feeling both "in terror and amazement" about the future.

As stated by the NRSV Study Bible regarding the longer ending:

Though known as early as the late second century C.E., the longer ending is missing from the earliest, most reliable Greek manuscripts and seems to mix motifs from the other Gospels.[81]

Despite its early appearance in some manuscripts, the longer version of Mark also is missing from two of the three most significant complete bibles extant from the 4th century—the Codex Sinaiticus and Codex Vaticanus which are considered as among the earliest, most reliable intact versions of the Greek Bible—comprising the majority of both Old and New Testament writings.[82]

Which is More Likely? Two millennia after the writing of Mark's gospel, as yet there is no scholarly consensus as to whether the shorter or longer ending of Mark represents the more authentic original.

Advantages of the traditionally accepted longer version are that it better harmonizes with the two other synoptic accounts, doesn't leave the reader abruptly hanging as to what happens next, and more completely as well as favorably describes the role of the women in communicating the resurrection message to their male counterparts.

Conversely, a stylistic disadvantage of the longer version is that there are differences in vocabulary, syntax and theological emphasis as compared with the rest of Mark's gospel—suggesting the possibility that this ending was written or added later by a different author.

---

around Peter. And afterward Jesus himself sent out through them, from east to west, the sacred and imperishable proclamation of eternal salvation. Amen."

[81] Provided as notes to the *NRSV Study Bible*, 1952.

[82] The other significant 5th century and largely extant whole Bible is the *Codex Alexandrinus*.

The primary advantage of the shorter version is that it aligns well with the contrarian views and abrupt transitions characteristic of Mark's writing style throughout this gospel. Who other than Mark would delight in leaving his audience hanging? As is the case throughout his account, Mark seems more than content to let his readers fill in the blanks.

III. Luke—Social Gospel

Blessed are you who are poor, for yours is the kingdom of God.
Jesus, as quoted by Luke 6:20

Like Matthew, the gospel of Luke presents a sweeping account of the life and message of Jesus. Both Gospels describe a virgin birth, both present a genealogy, both give accounts of great teachings such as the Sermon on the Mount.

However, Luke is written *for different reasons* than Matthew. In some pivotal respects, Luke's Jesus stands diametrically in opposition to the Jesus of Matthew. Or as indicated by the preceding chapters, it is probably more accurate to say that Matthew is written for different reasons than Luke.

As one example, Luke's view of the Pharisees contrasts with the picture presented by Matthew. Luke's gospel portrays Jesus as having standing among the Pharisees, while Matthew depicts the relationship as one of open conflict.

However, it is Luke's portrayal of the *social conscience* of Jesus that offers the sharpest contrast with his New Testament counterparts—from Matthew to Mark to John and Paul. Matthew's Jesus is concerned with poverty of the spiritual rather than material realm.

Luke's Jesus is attuned to earthly economic and social justice; Luke's Jesus is a social reformer.

Of the four New Testament Gospels, Luke stands alone with a heightened concern for the poor and underprivileged in society. This sense of social conscience extends to others with lesser status in first-century Jewish society—including women and non-Jews.

In this respect, Luke provides a linkage between Jesus as the radical first-century reformer in an isolated land and Jesus as the hope of all peoples. This reformer offers hope for those struggling for recognition, social justice and equality extending yet today into the early years of this third millennium.

Background of Luke the Gospel

Both this third gospel and the Acts of the Apostles are traditionally attributed to a physician named Luke. Taken together, these two books provide the most sweeping NT-based historical account of early Christianity from the genealogy and birth of Christ through to the arrest and confinement of the apostle Paul in Rome. The focus of this chapter is on Luke's perspective of Christ's earthly sojourn, less so on the history of the subsequent post-resurrection church.

Gospel Dating and Authorship. Two time frames are commonly suggested as dates for the writing of Luke's gospel: the period from 59–63 AD versus later in the 70s or 80s. Support for earlier composition is provided by the oldest known partial fragmentary evidence of a Lukan manuscript—the Paris Papyrus (P4) dated not much later than about 66 AD (prior to destruction of the Jerusalem Temple). An earlier date is also more likely if Luke were to have been written before the other extant synoptic Gospels of Mark and/or Matthew.

Most (though not all) early and contemporary scholars believe that Luke was written subsequent to both Matthew and Mark. This position is buttressed by the introduction to the gospel itself, wherein the author writes:

> "Since many have undertaken to set down an orderly account of the events that have been fulfilled among us, just as they were handed on to us by those who from the beginning were eyewitnesses and servants of the word, I too decided, after investigating everything carefully from the very first, to write an orderly account for you…" [83]

Less discussed is the decidedly non-mainstream view that Luke may have been one of the first Gospels to be written. One advocate of this theory points out that, of the four Gospels, the Greek (of the earliest manuscripts) found in Luke is the most readily back-translated to an earlier and more colloquial, spoken Aramaic form. Perhaps Luke draws from an earlier manuscript, for example, the hypothetical Q document or an earlier version of Matthew written in Hebrew or Aramaic (although there currently is no extant manuscript of either such document).

---

[83] Luke 1:1–3.

As detailed in the prior chapter on the Gospel of Mark, in the 1970s and after extensive research, Jerusalem pastor Robert Lisle Lindsey came to the conclusion that of the extant synoptic Gospels, Luke was written first (based on some earlier but no longer available account). Lindsey posits that Luke was followed by Mark and Mark was followed by Matthew.

Having initially subscribed to the widely accepted view of Markan priority, Lindsey describes his surprise at coming to a different conclusion as follows:

> Having long supposed that Luke, as the non-Jewish companion of Paul, had tended to modify his text to make it more understandable to Greeks of pagan background I was even more surprised to note that the Lukan text was almost always easier to translate to idiomatic Hebrew than was Mark. After several more years of study in which this observation has been confirmed again and again, I today find my earlier supposition amusing, but the point is that I was quite unprepared to suppose that of all the Synoptists Luke should prove to be the best in preservation of earlier texts.[84]

From these introductory remarks, it is evident that: (a) there were one or more earlier accounts available from which Luke could draw; and (b) there is apparent concern by Luke's author that some earlier written account(s) may not have been wholly reliable, therefore serving as a stimulus for writing his own more authentic version of a New Testament gospel.

Just as Matthew (as currently available) emphasizes prophecy fulfilled and Mark comes at his gospel with an improvised, fast-paced narrative, so Luke's version should be viewed as driven by goals of reliability coupled with reaching out to a Roman world comprised of a largely non-Jewish audience.

Authorship. Both Luke and Acts are addressed to the same person, the unknown Theophilus. The Acts of the Apostles also begins with a reference to "my former book."[85] Even today, most (though not all) scholars believe that the same author writes both books.

Neither volume explicitly identifies Luke as the author. However, certain sections in Acts use the pronoun "we," suggesting that the author was with

---

[84] Robert Lisle Lindsey, *A Hebrew Translation of the Gospel of Mark*, 2nd ed. (Jerusalem: Dugith Publishers, Baptist House, 1973), 12.
[85] Acts 1:1 (NIV).

Paul for many of the events being described. This was certainly the case for Luke.

Perhaps the earliest known reference to Luke's gospel is a citation from Polycarp's early 2nd century *Letter to the Philippians* where he quotes the Lukan version of the beatitude "blessed are the poor."[86]

Interestingly, while Eusebius quotes the early church patriarch Papias as commenting on the writings of Matthew and Mark, he does not reference any statement of Papias regarding Luke's gospel. However, in his writing of early church history, Eusebius does go on to quote 3rd century Origen as stating that after Mark' gospel: "Next came that of Luke, who wrote for Gentile converts the *gospel praised by Paul*."[87]

Luke's gospel authorship also is supported by the testimony of other early Christian documents including the Muratorian Canon, circa 170 AD and the works of Irenaeus, c. 180. Irenaeus states that "Luke, the follower of Paul, set down in a book the gospel preached by him."[88]

The late 2nd/early 3rd century church historian and polemicist Tertullian also attests to Lukan authorship of this gospel. And as noted, Origen offered a similar view.

Fourth-century historian Eusebius appears to go a bit further, indicating that the apostle Paul may himself have had a hand in writing this gospel. This is what Eusebius thinks Paul means when he refers to "my gospel" in several of his epistles.[89] Eusebius states that:

> It is actually suggested that Paul was in the habit of referring to Luke's gospel whenever he said, as if writing of some Gospel of his own: "According to my gospel."[90]

The Tradition of Luke. Luke is known by the title given by Paul as "the beloved physician."[91] In a short letter to a slave owner named Philemon, Paul

---

[86] Polycarp, *op cit,* quoting Luke 6:20.
[87] Eusebius, *History of the Church,* 6.25.
[88] Irenaeus, *Against Heresies,* III.1.1.
[89] See Romans 2:16/16:25, and 2 Timothy 2:8.
[90] Romans 16:25.
[91] Colossians 4:14.

describes Luke along with Mark and two others as "my fellow workers."[92] So, Luke was a co-traveler with at least one other gospel author.

Luke may well have been a Gentile by birth, certainly well-educated and versed in Greek culture. Luke accompanied Paul at various times beginning with Paul's second missionary journey. As later indicated by Paul's writing to Timothy, Luke was one of a handful who remained with Paul after others deserted. Interestingly, at the close of the Timothy letter, Paul notes that:

> Only Luke is with me. Get Mark and bring him with you, for he is useful in my ministry.[93]

So, Luke clearly is connected with Mark. Both of these two gospel writers are linked via a common affiliation with Paul the apostle, often traveling together with Paul. This relationship raises interesting questions as to the particular *spin* given to each of these two Gospels by their reputed respective authors.

By tradition, Luke is identified as a member of the church at Antioch. He is believed to have written his gospel in Greece—and for a Greek speaking audience. Little to nothing is known of Luke's status and later life after his completion of the Acts of the Apostles which concludes with Paul in prison at Rome during the reign of emperor Nero. However, traditions cited in multiple documents suggest that he died unmarried at about age 84 toward the end of the first century BC.[94]

The Jesus of Social Conscience

Matthew's Jesus is concerned with poverty of the spiritual rather than material realm. Luke's Jesus is attuned to earthly economics; his Jesus becomes a social advocate and reformer. Luke's presentation of Jesus as a man of *social conscience* and action comes across in several ways: Christian charity, care for the poor, economy of the kingdom, outreach to women,

---

[92] Philemon 1:24.
[93] 2 Timothy 4:11.
[94] Ronald Brownrigg, *Who's Who in the New Testament,* 2nd ed. (London: Oxford University Press, 1993) 151.

possible role as borderline social revolutionary, intimidated by his own home town crowd, and disdainful of local and region-wide politics.

Christian Charity. At the Sermon on the Mount (or possibly a separate similar occasion), it was Luke's Jesus who proclaimed: "Blessed are you who are poor."[95] Matthew's text suggests a far different meaning with Jesus saying: "Blessed are the poor *in spirit.*"[96]

Of the four New Testament Gospels, Luke stands alone in with a heightened concern for the poor and underprivileged in society. This sense of social conscience extends to others with lesser status in first-century Jewish society—including women and non-Jews.

Another comparison comes from what are known as the Beatitudes:

Luke's version—Blessed are you who are hungry now, for you will be filled.[97]

Matthew's version—Blessed are those who hunger and thirst *for righteousness,* for they will be filled.[98]

Luke's Beatitudes are aimed at earthly, present-day material needs; Matthew's version is pointed toward the spiritual—a heavenly kingdom.

Altogether, Luke's version of the Beatitudes consists of only four affirmative sayings, while Matthew comprises a total of eight blessings. Then, following the positive affirmations, Luke issues four condemnations that have no counterpart in Matthew:

But woe to you who *are rich*, for you have received your consolation.
Woe to you who are *full now*, for you will be hungry.
Woe to you who are *laughing now*, for you will mourn and weep.
Woe to you when *all speak well of you*, for that is what their ancestors did to the false prophets.[99]

---

[95] Luke 6:20.
[96] Matthew 5:3.
[97] Luke 6:21.
[98] Matthew 5:6. Here and throughout this listing, *Italics* are my emphasis unless otherwise indicated.
[99] Luke 6:24–26. See the supplement to this chapter to a comparison of beatitudes between Matthew and Luke.

Each of these denunciations appears directly aimed at the *haves* of first-century Jewish society. Luke's Jesus condemns the rich, those who are well fed, those who laugh, and those who are otherwise respected members of their respective communities.

This distinctive emphasis that Luke places on righting social and economic inequities also comes through in a variety of other events and sayings. These actions and comments by Jesus have no counterpart in the other NT Gospels, as indicated by the following summary listing:

- In Nazareth, Jesus reads Isaiah in the synagogue: "The Spirit of the Lord is upon me, because he has anointed me to bring good news *to the poor.*"[100]
- To an inquiry from disciples of John the Baptist, Jesus replies: "Go and tell John what you have seen and heard: the blind receive their sight, the lame walk, the lepers are cleansed, the deaf hear, the dead are raised, *the poor have good news brought to them.*"[101]
- In response to a lawyer who asks what he must do to inherit eternal life, Jesus tells the parable of the *good Samaritan*—the only one to render aid to a man of a despised ethnicity robbed, beaten and left to die.[102]
- Jesus relates the parable of the rich man whose life is taken after building bigger barns to illustrate the moral: "Be on your guard *against all kinds of greed*; for one's life does not consist in the abundance of possessions."[103]
- To his disciples, Jesus discusses the need to "not worry about your life." He further directs: *"Sell your possessions, and give alms."*[104]
- Jesus tells the story of "the rich man" and the *"poor man named Lazarus."* In Hades, the deceased rich man asks Abraham for mercy. Abraham's matter-of-fact response: "Child, remember that during your lifetime you received your good things, and Lazarus in like

---

[100] Luke 4:18.
[101] Luke 7:22.
[102] Luke 10:30–37.
[103] Luke 12:15.
[104] Luke 12:22,33.

manner evil things; but now he is comforted here, and you are in agony."[105]

- Jesus spots a despised tax collector named Zacchaeus in a tree, and invites himself to the home of this Zacchaeus, who there proclaims: "Look, half of my possessions, *Lord, I will give to the poor...*" Jesus responds: "Today salvation has come to this house."[106]

With the exception of Jesus' reply to the disciples of John the Baptist, none of the above incidents relating to the poor have any counterpart in the other synoptic Gospels of Matthew or Mark. For Luke, Jesus' sympathies lie with the poor and the social outcast. If one experiences the misfortune of wealth, the apparent remedy is to sell what one has and distribute the proceeds to the have-nots.

Always the Poor? Perhaps most telling are the contrasting accounts provided by all four gospel writers of a woman (or separate women?) who anoint Jesus. In the versions provided by Matthew, Mark and John, the anointing takes place at Bethany. Onlookers complain that the ointment could have been sold and the money given to the poor (their one common show of charity).

All three of the non-Lukan Gospels record that Jesus dismissed these complaints with the comment that "you always have the poor with you." Just to make sure no one misses the point, Jesus further notes that you will "not always have me."[107]

Luke takes a different tack. An anointing takes place in a Pharisee's house (at an unspecified location) by "a woman in the city, who was a sinner." The Pharisee says to himself: "If this man were a prophet, he would have known who and what kind of woman this is who is touching him—that she is a sinner."[108]

In response, Luke's Jesus presents a story (or parable) to his critics about two debtors, then gets to the point: "Therefore, I tell you, her sins, which were many, have *been forgiven*; hence she has shown great love. But the one to

---

[105] Luke 16:25.
[106] Lk 19:8–9.
[107] John 12:8.
[108] Excerpted from Luke 7:37–39.

whom little is forgiven, loves little." He then says to the woman: "Your faith has saved you; go in peace."[109]

In effect, three of the gospel writers (including John) have picked an incident where the punch line is that a luxury gift for a special occasion can be (on at least some occasions) a more important priority than helping the poor. In contrast and despite his normal approach of using material in common with Matthew and Mark, in this instance Luke selects a seemingly similar account (albeit in a different setting), but with the emphasis shifted from matters of economics to priority placed on forgiveness.[110]

Only Luke avoids the statement (and the resulting admission) that the poor will always be with us. This is not surprising since Jesus' seemingly more cynical acceptance of poverty's inevitability as expressed in the other gospel accounts stands in sharp contrast with Luke's generally consistent praise for Jesus as advocate for the poor and oppressed.

Economy of the Kingdom. Of the four gospel writers, Luke is most clearly interested in Jesus' views regarding not only the social but also economic order. The R*obin Hood* tone of Luke is set early on, with Jesus' mother Mary proclaiming in her *Magnificat* prior to Jesus' birth: "…he has *filled the hungry with good things, and sent the rich away empty.*"[111]

Passages found only in Luke appear to advocate a fairly radical form of what might be considered as redistributionist economics. For this gospel writer, wealth and spirituality are inherently incompatible. Only Luke's gospel records Jesus as commanding:

- "Whoever has two coats must share with anyone who has none; and whoever has food must do likewise."[112]
- "Give to everyone who begs from you; and if anyone takes away your goods, do not ask for them again."[113]

---

[109] Excerpted from Luke 7:47–50.

[110] Whether or not Jesus was the beneficiary of one or two anointings during the course of his ministry is immaterial.

[111] Luke 1:53.

[112] Luke 3: 11.

[113] Luke 6:30.

- "If you lend to those from whom you hope to receive, what credit is that to you? Even sinners lend to sinners, to receive as much again."[114]

This passion evident in Luke's gospel extends well beyond sympathy for the less fortunate to a more activist role for economic redistribution. Only Luke tells us about tax collector Zacchaeus, who has a remarkable *come to Jesus* experience. At the conclusion, Zacchaeus offers to make substantial amends for past misdeeds, telling Jesus:

Look, half of my possessions, Lord, I will give to the poor; and if I have defrauded anyone of anything, I will pay back four times as much.[115]

This passage implies a very active role for the economic oppressor to assure restitution *above and beyond* the bare minimum.

Champion of Women. In all four New Testament Gospels, Jesus has comparatively little directly to say about distinctions between (or expectations of) women versus men. However, implied differences are evident.

The twelve disciples all are men. Virtually all of the authority figures identified (Romans, priests, etc.) are men. This is not surprising, since both the Jewish and Roman cultures of the 1st century AD were essentially patriarchal in character.

However, women are integral to the Jesus story, first, as individuals who interact with Jesus. Second, women figure in a significant number of the parables. Of the three synoptics, Luke provides the most coverage of activities and events involving women. Consistent with his views on other forms of social reform, it is not surprising that Luke's Jesus appears as the greatest advocate for addressing the social and economic inequities faced by the women of first-century Palestine.

We can learn a fair amount about Luke's views by focusing on passages unique to this gospel:

---

[114] Luke 6:34.
[115] Luke 19:8.

- Luke's gospel provides details about the conception of Mary's cousin Elizabeth and chronicles the visit between the two prior to the birth of her son.[116]
- Only Luke describes the role of the prophetess Anna and Mary's motherly admonishment to Jesus at age 12. Luke records that Jesus speaks the need to be in his Father's house, but also returns home to Nazareth and "was obedient" to his parents.[117]
- Luke notes that "some women" took the initiative and "provided for them (meaning Jesus and his disciples) out of their own resources."[118]
- Luke's Jesus admires persistence and attentiveness in women; he is less charitable toward impatience and busy work.[119]
- While sympathetic toward women with children, Luke's Jesus appears especially supportive of women who are single (e.g., widows).[120]

Yet while sympathetic, the Jesus of Luke remains somewhat aloof from the women with whom he interacts on a regular basis. There is a clear sense of social activism but little of the intimacy that one finds between Jesus and women, for example, as would be recorded by John's Gospel.

Social Revolutionary? Of the themes that emerged in the late 20th century quest for the *historical Jesus,* one of the more popular has been that, as a product of an oppressed Jewish society, the message of Jesus was that of a social or political revolutionary. However, the evidence from this New Testament gospel suggests a more nuanced perspective. The Jesus of Luke is portrayed as a social reformer and perhaps advocate—but not as a revolutionary seeking earthly political regime change.

Those who advocate the view of Jesus as a revolutionary tend to do so from either (or both) of two perspectives: (a) as a political revolutionary (e.g. zealot) who sought the overthrow of Roman authority and return to Jewish home rule; and/or (b) as a radical social reformer representing the interests of the poor and outcast members of Jewish society against the ruling elites—whether those elites be Jew or Gentile.

---

[116] Luke 1:39–45.
[117] Luke 2: 36–48.
[118] Luke 8:2–3.
[119] See, for example, the story of sisters Mary and Martha, Luke 10:38–42.
[120] Luke 21:3–4.

Of the four Gospels, Matthew clearly presents Jesus as a man reaching out to social outcasts, but not as an advocate for societal reform or more sweeping social revolution. Mark's gospel portrays Jesus in similar fashion to Matthew; however, Mark aims more of his social critique at the Jewish scribes while Matthew focuses on the Pharisees. And John's Jesus avoids political and social critique, instead elevating Jesus' interests away from earthly concerns to a higher spiritual plane.

In effect, the New Testament case for Jesus as social revolutionary rises or falls largely on material presented in Luke's gospel. The verdict depends on one's view of Lukan social interactions, in many (but not all) of which Jesus serves as an advocate for the *poor and underprivileged.*

The passion of Luke's gospel extends beyond sympathy to encompass a more activist role for social if not going further to advocate economic redistribution. As noted, only Luke tells the story of Zacchaeus, a man willing to give half of his possessions if he has defrauded anyone of anything, This passage implies a very active responsibility assumed by an acknowledged economic oppressor to assure restitution extending well above and beyond the bare minimum.

In another situation, noticing how guests to a party or formal dinner often choose their seats, Luke's Jesus advises: "do not sit down at the place of honor, in case someone more distinguished than you has been invited by your host But when you are invited, go and sit down at the lowest place..." Then, to the host, Jesus suggests that rather than inviting friends or relatives or rich neighbors, "invite the poor, the crippled, the lame and the blind."[121]

Home Town Crowd. The first public act of Jesus' ministry (recorded in detail only in Luke) is of Jesus' rejection in his hometown of Nazareth. Quoting from Isaiah, Jesus reads from the synagogue scroll:

The Spirit of the Lord is upon me, because he has anointed me to bring good news *to the poor.* He has sent me to proclaim release to the captives and recovery of sight to *the blind*, to let *the oppressed go free*, to proclaim the year of the Lord's favor.[122]

---

[121] Excerpted from Luke 14:7–13.

[122] Luke 4:18–19, quoting from portions of Isaiah 61:1–2 and 58:6.

In effect, Luke immediately puts his readers on notice that the mission of Jesus is to the poor, the captives, the physically challenged and the oppressed. Luke's Jesus goes on to make clear that today represents the fulfillment of this prophecy, a claim that at least initially goes down surprisingly well with the audience—despite its audacity.

Jesus then ups the ante by commenting that "no prophet is accepted in his hometown."[123] The mood of the audience changes to "rage" moments later when Jesus uses the example of the former prophet Elisha to indicate that his message of "good news" may go to a broader audience than just the immediate Jewish population. The final comment Jesus offers before the local audience drives him out of town relates to a leper being healed in the time of Elisha being not an Israelite, but Naaman the Syrian.

Consistent with disdain for those of wealth and power, Luke's Jesus is critical of those who also present themselves as authorities. But when the discussion turns toward the prospect of a non-Jewish audience, Jesus can be more accommodating.

Like Matthew, Luke's Jesus is critical of the Pharisees—the most conservative and traditional of 1st Jewish sects. Unlike Matthew, Luke opens the door far more to the possibility of *Gentiles* also participating in the kingdom of heaven.

Luke also details several unique accounts of interactions with Samaritans. As *half-breeds* of only partial Jewish blood due to intermarriage with pagan populations, the Jewish establishment and much of the broader Jewish community disparaged residents of Samaria.

In the first Lukan reported encounter, residents of a village in Samaria refuse to receive Jesus. The disciples ask:

Lord, do you want us to command fire to come down from heaven and consume them.[124]

Jesus rebukes the disciples; they then travel on to another village. Later as recounted by Luke, while traveling to Jerusalem Jesus cleanses ten lepers. Only one of the lepers returns to thank Jesus. Luke notes: "And he was a Samaritan." In return, Jesus asks:

---

[123] Luke 4:24.
[124] Luke 9:54.

Were not ten made clean? But the other nine, where are they? Was none of them found to return and give praise to God except this foreigner?...Get up and go on your way; your faith has made you well.[125]

After this initial encounter with Samaritans (in Luke 9), Jesus moves on to offer a *culturally radical* message to would be followers. One *wannabe* desires to follow Jesus but bury his father first. Jesus says:

Let the dead bury their own dead; but as for you, go and proclaim the kingdom of God.[126]

Another prospect is interested but wants to say farewell to those at home. To this 2nd person, Jesus states:

No one who puts a hand to the plow and looks back is fit for the kingdom of God.[127]

After sending 70 of his followers to go in pairs to towns to bring peace and healing, the 70 return and Jesus rejoices with them. This festivity is disrupted by a lawyer who comes to test Jesus. In response to the lawyer's question of "who is my neighbor," Luke is the only gospel writer who recounts the powerful and well-known parable of the Good Samaritan.[128] Building from his continuing theme of social reform, Jesus' answer is that neighborliness depends not necessarily on who is perceived as most righteous or offering the best connections, but on showing mercy to whomever is in need including social and cultural outcasts.

Jesus and Politics. Despite clear efforts to steer clear of Jewish and Roman politics, circumstances intervene to test Jesus' resolve. Unique to Luke are accounts of two catastrophic events with *political overtones:* Galileans whose "blood Pilate had mingled with their sacrifices" and 18

---

[125] Luke 17:11–19.

[126] Luke 9:60.

[127] Luke 9:60–62. The first part of the encounter is also recorded by Matthew. The second statement given to further emphasize Jesus' point appears solely in Luke.

[128] Luke 10:29–37.

people killed by the collapse of the tower of Siloam. Regarding the first event, Jesus comments:

> Do you think that because these Galileans suffered in this way they were worse sinners than all other Galileans? No, I tell you; but unless you repent, you will all perish as they did.[129]

Then, regarding the collapsing tower, Jesus rhetorically asks:

> ...do you think that they were worse offenders than all the others living in Jerusalem? No, I tell you; but unless you repent, you will all perish just as they did.[130]

The message this time: no special favors even for the seemingly righteous. What matters is not one's political orientation but rather his or her repentance before God.

As in Matthew, Luke's Jesus weeps over Jerusalem and its future. Luke has Jesus render an even more graphic prophetic depiction of Israel's current condition and fate:

> *If you, even you,* had only recognized on this day the things that make for peace! But now they are hidden from your eyes. Indeed, the days will come upon you, when your enemies will set up ramparts around you and surround you, and hem you in on every side. They will crush you to the ground, you and your children within you, and they will not leave within you one stone upon another; because you did not recognize the time of your visitation from God.[131]

The prophetic message embraced by Luke is that the mantle of divine favor will pass—from the favored elites to the repentant (including those previously considered spiritually disenfranchised).

Not surprisingly, Luke is the only gospel writer to note that the non-religious political establishment was taking notice of Jesus. After the disciples

---

[129] Luke 13:2–3.
[130] Luke 13:4–5.
[131] Luke 19:42–44.

return from teaching in villages, the Galilean ruler Herod Antipas is reported to observe:

> John I beheaded; but who is this about whom I hear such things?[132]

Luke then indicates that Herod actually tried to see Jesus; however, the outcome of this initiative is not described.

As he nears the final days of earthly ministry, ramped up political intrigue does not lead Jesus to violent action. Shortly after Jesus is arrested and a disciple cuts off the right ear of the high priest's slave. Jesus responds: "No more of this!"[133] And unlike the other two synoptics, Luke states that Jesus then touched and healed the wounded ear.

Luke does record a subsequent audience of Jesus before King Herod, taking place after his arrest.[134] Consistent with his earlier reference to Antipas, Luke states that:

> When Herod (Antipas) saw Jesus, he was very glad for he had been wanting to see Jesus for a long time, because he had heard about him and was hoping to see him perform some sign. He questioned him (Jesus) at some length, but Jesus gave him no answer.[135]

And finally, Luke provides an intriguing political aside—regarding the role that Jesus may have had in cementing a relationship between the Jewish ruler Herod and the Roman procurator Pilate. Luke observes:

> That same day Herod and Pilate became friends with each other; before this they had been enemies.[136]

If Luke's gospel clearly and consistently presents a portrait of Jesus as social reformer, there is little evidence that Luke's Jesus goes beyond his

---

[132] Luke 9:9.
[133] Luke 22:51.
[134] This is Herod Antipas, tetrarch of the northern regions of Galilee and Perea, who was probably in Jerusalem for the Passover.
[135] Luke 23:8–9.
[136] Luke 23:12.

divine mission to also assume a role of political revolutionary, despite what some modern liberation theologians have suggested. Rather, Luke's Jesus is revolutionary for a message of both social and personal but not necessarily for political redemption or regime change. Prophetic, yes. Political revolutionary, no.

Luke in Summary

And so ends this tour of what has been called the *most beautiful book ever written*—the only gospel that definitely can be attributed to a Hellenist—whether Jew or Gentile. A man of apparent professional training. Well-learned and with a heart for those less fortunate.

Acceptance of Luke. While not explicitly mentioned in the extant writings of at least one early 2nd century patriarch (Papias), Luke's gospel appears to have won ready acceptance among Christian patriarchs and churches by at least the mid-second century. This was the only gospel accepted (albeit with significant edits) by the 2nd century Gnostic heretic Marcion—due largely to Luke's affiliation with the apostle Paul.

Pros and Cons. Luke has presented Jesus as a man of *social conscience* and action. This comes across in Jesus' views regarding the importance of charity toward the poor, economy of the kingdom, outreach to women, and arguably as borderline social revolutionary.

Luke's deviation from NT orthodoxy can be considered as a matter of both substance and style—but leaning more to a difference in the practical application of Jesus' gospel. Of the 12 Christian pioneers profiled in this book, Luke and James are the two that place priority on social and collective justice in this world as opposed to personal spiritual accountability.

This is a very different Jesus than is portrayed by the other three NT Gospels. To Matthew, Mark and John, Jesus offers a message of *personal* hope and redemption. With Luke, the emphasis is more *collective* than individual. His is the only gospel aimed toward redressing societal evils—of mitigating poverty, redistribution of wealth, and improved status for women.

Not surprisingly, it is Luke who describes a merciful God. But Luke's God is also more distant, experienced more through intermediaries rather than personally. Ironically, while this gospel writer rails against class divisions on a material level, he seemingly upholds hierarchical distinctions on a spiritual level.

Luke's God is patrician, regal in character. As expressed by the Mary of Luke's gospel in her formal Magnificat, "holy is his name."[137]

A Jesus' of social conscience represents a new idea for the early Christian church—advanced by no other New Testament writer than Luke. This then is Luke's contribution to Christendom and his heresy.

Over two millennia, the benefit of Luke's role as fellow missionary traveler and author has been the recognition that the *good news* of Christianity is not only for the next world after this life, but also for the here and now. The social activism of Luke's Jesus has animated Christian reformers from Augustine to the liberation theologians of the last century—from the communal post-resurrection church to mainline congregations in the wake of the "God is dead" theology of the mid-20th century.

Luke provides a linkage between Jesus as the radical first-century reformer in an isolated land and Jesus as the hope of all peoples—including those struggling for recognition, social justice and equality at the dawn of the third millennium.

If there is a drawback of Lukan theology, it has been the de-emphasis of a personal relationship and individual accountability before the divine—the diminished opportunity for realizing intimacy in this life with a crucified and risen Savior.

---

[137] Luke 1:49.

Supplement — Beatitude Comparison

What follows is a comparison of the Beatitudes as provided by Matthew as compared with Luke.

Boldface items denote differences between the most comparable blessings.

Matthew 5:3–10	Luke 6:20–26
Blessings:	**Blessings:**
Blessed are the **poor in spirit**, kingdom of heaven.	Blessed are you who are **poor**, for yours is the kingdom of God.
Blessed are those who **mourn**, **comforted**.	Blessed are you who **weep** now, for you will **laugh**. *(comes after hungry in Lukan text)*
	Blessed are the meek, for they will inherit the earth.
Blessed are those who **hunger righteousness**, for they will be	Blessed are you who are **hungry now**, for you will be filled.
Blessed are the merciful, for they will receive mercy.	--
Blessed are the pure in heart, for they will see God.	--
Blessed are the peacemakers, for they will be called children	--
Blessed are those who are **persecuted for righteousness' sake**, for theirs is the kingdom of heaven. 'Blessed are you when people revile you and persecute you and utter all kinds of evil against you falsely[b] on my account. Rejoice and be glad, for your reward is great in	Blessed are you when **people hate you**, and when they **exclude you, revile you**, and **defame you** on account of the Son of Man. Rejoice on that day and leap for joy, for surely your reward is great in heaven; for that is what their ancestors did to the prophets.
	Condemnations:
--	But woe to you who are rich, for you have received your consolation.
--	Woe to you who are full now, for you will be hungry.
--	Woe to you who are laughing now, for you will mourn and weep.
--	Woe to you when all speak well of you, for that is what their ancestors did to the false prophets.

IV. John—Personal Divinity

Jesus wept.
At the tomb of Lazarus, John 11:35 (KJV)

Matthew, Mark and Luke are called the *synoptic* Gospels because they present a *common view* of Jesus. These first three Gospels are remarkably similar, particularly in the events chronicled—albeit with varied nuances with each writer as discussed in previous chapters.

The Gospel of John represents a radical departure from the synoptic gospel formulation. This gospel clearly appears to rely fully or in large part on different sources of information. John's account of the ministry of Jesus contains substantial information found in no other gospel. And by comparison with the synoptics, John is also significant for its omissions.

Unlike the synoptics, John makes virtually no use of parables. There is no hint of Jesus as a social reformer or revolutionary.

John's Gospel contains only three descriptions of healing miracles, none of which are found in the synoptics. John also describes five nature miracles, only one of which (the feeding of 5,000) can also be found in the synoptics. And unlike the synoptics, John's Jesus makes virtually no reference to any form of hell (whether termed as Gehenna or Hades) for those condemned—though he does speak of some unspecified form of future judgment.

Modern scholars often simply do not know what to make of John. Some place less emphasis on John as an historically reliable representation of the teachings and actions of the historical Jesus. For example, the work of the post-modern *Jesus Seminar* articulates the "diminished role the Gospel of John plays in the search for the Jesus of history."[138]

This rejection of John's Gospel is nothing new. There is a reason, essentially rooted in a heresy that packs as much punch today as in the early

---

[138] Funk, Roy W. Hoover and The Jesus Seminar, *The Five Gospels*, 10.

church. In short, the heresy of John's Gospel is that of a divine Jesus who gets *up close and personal*—over and over and over again.

Matthew's Jesus speaks of a new religious order that represents a fulfillment of history. Mark's Jesus is earthy but also portrays a Savior often contemptuous of even his closest associates. Luke's Jesus becomes a sort of divine social worker. But in all three synoptics, Jesus cannot and does not get too close to those he came to save, to heal, to comfort.

John's Jesus is different. The first words uttered by Jesus in John comprise a question aimed at two who were following him: "What are you looking for?" They reply: "Rabbi, where are you staying?" Right off, Jesus gets up close and personal, with a simple invitation: "Come and see."[139]

John presents a Jesus who tells a wealthy Pharisee and Jewish ruler (Nicodemus) that he must be "born again." And early on, John also portrays a Jesus who interacts in a deeply personal way with a Samaritan woman at a well, including a recounting of her five past marriages and current live-in partner.

As acknowledged by the writings of 2nd century Clement of Alexandria and summarized by Eusebius in the 4th century:

> …aware that the physical facts had been recorded in the (other) Gospels, encouraged by his pupils and irresistibly moved by the Spirit, John wrote a spiritual gospel.[140]

Background of John's Gospel

More so than with the synoptic writers, scholars have widely divergent perspectives on the dating, authorship and tradition of John the beloved disciple of Jesus.

Gospel Dating. John's account of the life of Jesus is generally (though not universally) recognized as the last of the canonical Gospels to be written. Yet paradoxically, one of the earliest known manuscript fragments attributable to any New Testament book comes from John—with two fragments dating to the

---

[139] John 1:38–39.
[140] Eusebius, *History of the Church,* 6.14.

second century. The earliest near complete manuscript of John is Bodmer Papyrus II (Johannine Codex P66), dating to about 200 AD.[141]

The late 2nd century Christian apologist Irenaeus makes clear that John was penned after Matthew, Mark and Luke. He writes:

> Lastly John, the disciple of the Lord, who had leaned back on His breast, once more set forth the gospel, while residing at Ephesus in Asia.[142]

A composition date of 80–90 AD is often suggested by scholars of the last two centuries. In part, this is due to accounts of hostile relations between Jewish leaders and Jewish followers of the Jesus movement (also known as the Way). Jewish Christians became subject to expulsion from synagogues—an event coinciding with the growing rift between adherents of a nascent Christianity versus regrouping Jewish society in the wake of Roman destruction post 70 AD.

Adding insult to injury was the abandonment of Jerusalem and its remaining residents by Jewish Christians, relocating to Pella east of the Jordan prior to Roman destruction of the holy city.

As noted, late 1st century dating of John's Gospel is supported by the late 2nd century theologian, Clement of Alexandria. Clement writes that: "Last of all, aware that the physical facts had been recorded in the Gospels, encouraged by his pupils and *irresistibly moved by the Spirit*, John wrote a spiritual gospel."[143]

Some (typically evangelical) scholars have suggested an earlier date, perhaps as early as the 50s and certainly no later than 70 AD. An argument for this position is the statement in that there "is" (rather than "was") a Sheep Gate suggests a time before 70 AD when Jerusalem was destroyed.[144]

---

[141] For dating on ancient biblical papyri containing portions of the Gospel of John, see the web site: *The Johannine Literature Web,* "*Papyri and Manuscripts related to the Gospel and Epistles of John,* https://catholic-resources.org/John/Papyri.html, (accessed February 20, 2024).

[142] Irenaeus *Against Heresies,* III.1.1.

[143] Eusebius, *The History of the Church,* 6.14. Eusebius also quotes Origen as writing that: "Last of all came John's," 6.25.

[144] John 5:2.

Authorship. The traditional view is that John, the "disciple whom Jesus loved," authored this gospel.

However, the author is never explicitly identified by name in the text.[145]

Early Christian writers such as Irenaeus (c. 140–203) and Tertullian (c. 160–225) attest to John as the author. Few of the extant early writers suggest authorship of this gospel by anyone else—with the exception of some who suggest John was written by the Jewish-Gnostic heretic Cerinthus.[146]

The Tradition of John. This apostle was the brother of James the apostle and son of a fishing entrepreneur named Zebedee. The case has been made that John may have been a first cousin of Jesus. The mother of John was Salome, who appears to have been a sister of Jesus' mother Mary (based on a composite reading of Matthew, Mark and John (further detailed as a supplemental addendum to this chapter).

Of Jesus' 12 disciples, John and his brother James had perhaps the best access to the ruling authorities of 1st century, possibly extending up to the time of the Jewish revolt starting in 66 AD:

- Father Zebedee's family appears to have run a flourishing fishing business at Capernaum on the Sea of Galilee. What's today known as *Peter's Fish* was typically salted and shipped as a delicacy to elites stationed and living throughout the Roman empire.
- Zebedee was no isolated self-employed fisherman. At the very least, his sons John and James worked in the family business. Peter and his brother Andrew—from Bethsaida at the northern end of the Sea— were employed or possibly partners fishing together with other hired men also employed by the Zebedees.
- Situated on the western shore of Galilee, Capernaum was well connected to nearby fish processors as at Magdala, to trade routes north, west and south and to the Galilee's capital (post 18 AD) relocated from Sepphoris (near Nazareth) to Tiberias on the Sea of Galilee.

---

[145] References of this type are found in several places in John's gospel at 13.26, 19:26, 20:2, 21:7,20.

[146] As cited in J. Stevenson, *A New Eusebius* (London: William Clowes and Sons, Limited, 1957), document 138. Another early legend was that the resurrected Lazarus was the author of this gospel.

- Despite being a smaller community on the Sea of Galilee than Tiberias or Magdala and in addition to being Jesus' adopted home town, Capernaum had enough fishing and other trade activity to warrant on-site stationing of a tax collector. This was none other than Matthew (aka Levi) working from "the tax booth"—one who would be called to be a fellow disciple with others from Zebedee's family and work crew well-known in the Capernaum community.[147]
- Most notably, John not only had access to the Galilean authorities but also to at least some of the elites in Judea as well. This is evident based on his ability to have immediate access to the home of high priest Caiaphas after Jesus' arrest. Peter was only able to gain access into the courtyard of Caiaphas by request from John who was already on the premises and could request that a servant let Peter in.

The apostle John has been widely though not universally considered as the author of the Books of 1/2/3 John—as well as Revelation. Whether John the apostle and John the Elder as identified simply as "John" in Revelation actually are one and the same person is a matter of long-standing debate.[148]

While authorship of Revelation is directly attributed right from the start of this last book of the New Testament book to "his servant John," there has long been scholarly and theological confusion as to who this John really was. In the third century, Dionysius, the Bishop of Alexandria stated the conundrum thusly:

That the writer (of Revelation) was John he himself states, and we must believe him.

But which John?[149]

---

[147] Matthew 9:1, 9:9.

[148] As early as the third century, an African bishop named Dionysius advocated the view that a John the Presbyter was author of Revelation, not the apostle John. This conclusion was based, in part, on a comparison of the language, style and substance of the gospel versus that of the Apocalypse.

[149] Eusebius, 7.25.

Fourth century historian Eusebius writes that, as early as the second century, Papias, the Bishop of Hierapolis, considered the confusion as resulting from two distinctly different Johns who had been buried in Ephesus—the apostle John and another Christian leader known as John the Elder (or Presbyter).[150] The author of NT books of 2 and 3 John, in fact, refers to himself as "the elder."

Papias also wrote that both the apostle John and the Presbyter John were considered as those that "taught the truth."[151] Of all the early Christian writings, Revelation was among the last books and the "most enigmatic" to be accepted as part of the current New Testament canon.[152]

The traditional view has been that, of the original disciples, perhaps only John lived a long life—ending with exile on the island of Patmos. However, this tradition requires that the disciple John also serves as author of Revelation, for it is in Revelation that a John's residence on Patmos is specifically identified.[153] Supporting information is provided by Eusebius of Caesarea in the fourth century who writes that John was "sentenced to confinement" on the island of Patmos during the reign of emperor Domitian.[154]

---

[150] 2 John 1:1, 3 John 1:1.

[151] As quoted by Eusebius, *History of the Church,* 3.39. Eusebius also states that according to Papias, "two men in Asia had the same name," i.e. John.

[152] Robert M. Grant, A Historical Introduction to the New Testament, "Chapter 15, The Book of Revelation," https://www.religion-online.org/book-chapter/chapter-15-the-book-of-revelation/ (accessed February 20, 2024). Also see Grant's *Formation of the New Testament,* 169–178. This indicates that Dionysius of Alexander wrote in *On Promises* to show that an apostle composed the Gospel of John and another John wrote Revelation. As late as 962 AD, a listing from Gregory of Nazianzus at the Council of Constantinople does not include Revelation with the canonical books of the New Testament. At the eastern edge of the Christian world, there continued to be considerable doubt regarding the Apocalypse, though it became more generally accepted by about the sixth century. Irenaeus, Clement and Origen provide attestation for John the apostle as author. And Justin Martyr is quoted as stating that Revelation was written by "John, one of the disciples of Christ." Per Grant, 136.

[153] Revelation 1:9.

[154] Eusebius, 3.18.

A contrasting viewpoint is offered by second-century writers Polycrates and Irenaeus—who indicate that John died at Ephesus. Polycrates states that John was martyred, Irenaeus that he died of natural causes.[155]

A related perspective is that John's Gospel was written in a locale where an earlier gospel (notably Mark) was not known, perhaps in Palestine, or where Mark was so accepted that there was no need for John to relate to it.[156]

In any event, the focus of this discussion is on the gospel attributed to John. There is less emphasis on other writings that have been attributed at various times to John. In large part, this is because our primary attention is on the experience of Jesus during the period of his earthly ministry—as reflected through his relationship with a son of Zebedee, John the disciple.

Getting Intimate with Divinity. John's Gospel is all about *God becoming human*. But John goes further. In the form of Jesus, God becomes eminently approachable, even intimate with humankind. This sense of intimacy represents a breakthrough both from representations of a less approachable God in the Jewish Scriptures and similarly with an even more distant God the Father of the New Testament synoptics. Rather, Jesus makes it clear that he is now the intermediary and that "no one comes to the Father except through me."[157]

The very first words uttered by Jesus in John's Gospel come shortly after his baptism. Two disciples of John the Baptist turn to follow Jesus, who also turns and directly asks: *"What are you looking for?"*[158]

The two disciples ask where Jesus is staying. Jesus replies simply: "Come and see." The author of John's Gospel goes on to state that: "They came and saw where he was staying, and they remained with him that day."[159]

The Case of Nicodemus

There are numerous paths that could be taken to better understand John's take on Jesus and his deeply personalized approach to human interaction.

---

[155] Yet another theory that has been advanced is that John the apostle was martyred with his brother James.

[156] This possibility is referenced by Robert Grant, *Formation of the New Testament*, 28.

[157] John 14:5.

[158] John 1:38.

[159] John 1:39.

Chapter 3 provides the best-known and most distinctive passage in John's Gospel—derived from several perspectives via a secretive visit by a respected Jewish leader to interview Jesus—discussing his divine role, eternity, salvation and condemnation.

The narrative starts with the Pharisee Nicodemus coming to visit Jesus at night. The meeting most likely takes place in Jerusalem at the time of the annual Passover festival at a place not identified. Nicodemus shows the utmost respect for Jesus, starting the conversation by saying:

Rabbi, we know that you are a teacher who has come from God; for no one can do these signs that you do apart from the presence of God.[160]

Born Again or From Above? Jesus does not give Nicodemus the benefit of asking what he has come for, but at once interrupts. Jesus immediately elevates the discussion to a different level—directed both personally and spiritually—with Jesus interjecting:

Very truly, I tell you, no one can see the kingdom of God without being born *from above*.[161]

Or did he say than one cannot see the kingdom unless being "born again" as frequently translated from the Greek term *anothen* by many traditional New Testament versions such as the King James Version (KJV)?[162] Nicodemus gets confused as he interprets what Jesus said as be being "born again" and so responds to Jesus with the query:

How can a man be born when he is old? Can he enter a second time into his mother's womb and be born?[163]

---

[160] John 3:2.

[161] John 3:3, per one common translation of the Greek term *anothen*.

[162] The Greek *anothen,* used twice in the discussion at John 3:3 and 3:7, has been translated both as born "again" and "from above"—as well as in other ways elsewhere in the New Testament given the multiple meanings with which this Greek term is associated.

[163] John 3:4.

In the ensuing conversation, Jesus shows both sympathy and frustration at Nicodemus' lack of understanding about the concept of spiritual birth. In a more sympathetic moment, he lets Nicodemus know that entry to the kingdom of God is predicated on being born both of water and Spirit, reinforced by saying:

> Very truly, I tell you, no one can enter the kingdom of God without being born of water and Spirit. What is born of the flesh is flesh, and what is born of the Spirit is spirit. Do not be astonished that I said to you, "You must be born from above." The wind blows where it chooses, and you hear the sound of it, but you do not know where it comes from or where it goes. So it is with everyone who is born of the Spirit.[164]

At this point, and not surprisingly, the conversation gets a bit testy. Nicodemus asks Jesus, 'How can these things be?' Jesus answered him, 'Are you a teacher of Israel, and yet you do not understand these things?'[165]

Jesus then pivots back to an even more elevated spiritual level, letting Nicodemus in on God's intent for sending his only son in order that humankind need nor perish but have eternal (i.e., age-long) life. More on this momentarily. But first address the question: How did Jesus and Nicodemus get into such confusion over semantics?

The answer appears to depend, in part, on a further question of semantics. As noted, the term used at John 3:3 and 3:7—variously translated as born "again" versus "above"—is the Greek word *anothen*. In the New Testament, this Greek term appears at least 11 other times in contexts including twice translated as "from above," once as "again," five times as "from the beginning" or "from the very first," once as "from the top," and twice as "from top to bottom" (used in reference to splitting of the temple veil at the time of Jesus crucifixion).[166]

---

[164] John 3:5–8.

[165] John 3:9–10.

[166] *Greek New Testament Concordance,* "Greek New Testament concordance of the adverb avrnOsv [Str-509], which occurs 13 times in the New Testament" https://www.abarim-publications.com/Concordance/I/c-509–1.html (Accessed for *anothen,* February 20, 2024).

Relevance of the Spoken Language. If Jesus and Nicodemus were conversing in Greek, the confusion is understandable, maybe even intentional on Jesus' part, made possible by the multiple and diverse ways in which the word *anothen* might reasonably be interpreted. As a man of great learning including contacts among the Judean elite, partial or full fluency in Greek is certainly possible for Nicodemus, maybe likely. There is circumstantial evidence Jesus also may have been fluent in Greek as well as Aramaic (as described in the supplement to the Chapter 2 review of Mark's gospel).

But look closely at the other options, starting with *other Greek terms* for "above" and "again." There are about a dozen Greek terms (in addition to *anothen*) that have been translated, for example, by the KJV as "above." Even in English these variations on "above" can have a range of meanings—such as above a certain number, superior to, from a height, and so on. Each of the dozen or so terms are used fairly sparingly in the New Testament—with none being the dominant Greek word translated as "above."

A different situation occurs with optional term "again." There is one Greek word, *palin,* which is repeatedly used throughout the New Testament and consistently translated into English as "again." *Palin* is used 140 times in the New Testament including 45 times in John.[167] So, if Jesus and Nicodemus were conversing in Greek, Jesus could easily have made clear a statement about being born "again" by using the Greek word *palin* rather than *anothen.* But that's not what happened, at least as recorded within early Greek manuscripts of John's Gospel.

What if They Weren't Conversing in Greek? What if Nicodemus and Jesus were speaking in the more common Semitic language of Aramaic (recognizing that its predecessor of classical Hebrew was no longer in common use in the first century AD)?

While likely not relevant to 1st century Palestine, start with the Hebrew option. Unlike the Greek *anothen* which can and has been translated into widely varied English terms, there are very distinct Hebrew words for above versus again that are employed in the Old Testament. Virtually the only Hebrew term consistently translated into English as "above" is the Hebrew

---

[167] *Greek New Testament Concordance,* "Greek New Testament concordance of the adverb naliv [Str-3825]," which occurs 140 times in the New Testament" https://www.abarim-publications.com/Concordance/IV/c-3825–1.html (Accessed for *palin* February 20, 2024).

word *maal*. Hebrew analogues for "again" are the terms *shub* or, less likely, *yasaph,* more closely meaning "to add."[168]

The other and more likely alternative to Jesus and Nicodemus conversing in Greek would be in Aramaic, the common language spoken by Jews and other Semitic peoples of the 1st century. The Aramaic equivalent for "above" is pronounced in English as *wann*. The equivalent for "again" is *mshiha*.[169] So, an Aramaic discussion could have led to more distinction in meaning that would have made it easier for Nicodemus to understand that Jesus was talking about being born from above rather than being born again.

While not definitive, consideration of the language options potentially available would appear to be most consistent with a conversation in Greek. And because there were different Greek terms other than *anothen* available to distinguish "above" from "again," this also suggests that Jesus may have intentionally been confusing or testing Nicodemus—leading this Jewish leader through a rugged Socratic process to understand what this concept of spiritual birth was all about.

Not surprisingly, this approach to what might be considered as disingenuous or even demeaning behavior on the part of Jesus as teacher (or Rabbi) also fits with other similar situations of Jesus intentionally baiting those with whom he interacted. Examples would include the Samaritan woman of many husbands at the well, a response to the wealthy young ruler who wanted an easy route to heaven, and healing at the insistence of a non-Jewish Canaanite (or Syro-Phoenician) woman.

Salvation and Condemnation. Assuming that the miscommunication over "above" versus "again" is at least partially resolved, Jesus moves on to disclose the purpose of his earthly mission to Nicodemus. He pivots to this topic by comparing himself to the Hebrew icon Moses, noting that:

> …just as Moses lifted up the serpent in the wilderness, so must the Son of Man be lifted up, that whoever believes in him may have eternal life.[170]

---

[168] Definitions are per Microsoft Bing search, accessed January 16, 2024, per Strong's Hebrew.

[169] Terminology translations provided as result of ChatGPT inquiries, January 16, 2024.

[170] John 3:14–15.

There's a bit of a catch here. The term "eternal" used by translations such as the NRSV or "everlasting" by other versions as with the KJV is the English version of the Greek *aionios* literally meaning "age-long." In other words, an era or age (literally "eon") represents a long but finite period of time. The corresponding Hebrew term translated as everlasting or eternal is *olam,* also meaning age-lasting.

Jesus goes on to provide a bit more clarity in both positive and negative terms, beginning with what is probably the best-known verse in the Bible:

> For God so loved the world that he gave his only Son, so that everyone who believes in him may not perish but may have eternal life.[171]

Of even greater significance, Jesus concurrently appears to at least partially discount the opposite outcome for non-believers as follows:

> Indeed, God did not send the Son into the world to condemn the world, but in order that the world might be saved through him. Those who believe in him are not condemned; but those who do not believe are condemned already, because they have not believed in the name of the only Son of God.[172]

Taken at face value, it may appear as though John's Jesus is contradicting himself. On the one hand, he is clearly saying that God is not willing to condemn anyone. In effect, a divine imperative to condemn would represent defeat to God's purpose for humanity on earth. If anyone ends up being condemned, Jesus' mission may also be considered a failure.

But then Jesus lays the responsibility for salvation or condemnation not at God's feet but at the doorstep of rebellious human(s). In effect, this is a self-executing judgment—albeit defined somewhat weirdly with Jesus wrapping up his conversation with Nicodemus as follows:

> And this is the judgment, that the light has come into the world, and people loved darkness rather than light because their deeds were evil. For all who do evil hate the light and do not come to the light, so that their deeds may

---

[171] John 3:16.
[172] John 3:17–18.

not be exposed. But those who do what is true come to the light, so that it may be clearly seen that their deeds have been done in God.[173]

What seems to be missing from this view of *judgment* is some clarity as to the resulting consequences. For Jesus, the judgment is more about each individual's preference being realized (albeit to that person's detriment) than to any specifically divinely ordained consequence. This is a judgment that is both self-executing and self-imposed for a time period that effectively may be both self-determined and finite in duration.

What are the mechanics of how all this takes place? No further details of Jesus' views on implementation are provided by John's account. The only way out would appear to be for salvation to be made available through belief and repentance whether during a person's lifetime or beyond. This approach is highlighted, for example, in allegorical terms by C. S. Lewis' 20th century tale of *The Great Divorce.*

Lewis illustrates the options by describing a bus ride from heaven to hell. The passenger discovers that it is possible to transition from hell to heaven by repenting and believing. But few do. For too many:

The choice of every lost soul can be expressed in the words, "Better to reign in Hell than serve in Heaven."[174]

Echoing John's Gospel, Lewis writes:

Never fear. There are only two kinds of people in the end: those who say to God, "Thy will be done," and those to whom God says, in the end, "Thy will be done." All that are in Hell, choose it. Without that self-choice there could be no Hell. No soul that seriously and constantly desires joy will ever miss it. Those who seek find. To those who knock it is opened.[175]

Of the four Gospels, John is unique in that there are virtually no references to any of the Hebrew or Greek terms for Hell (Gehenna or Hades). However, even without using these terms, John's Jesus is forthright about the

---

[173] John 3:19–21.

[174] C. S. Lewis, *The Great Divorce—A Dream* (New York: Harper One, 2000), 71.

[175] Lewis, *The Great Divorce,* 75.

condemnation awaiting unbelievers. While God wills otherwise, the condemnation is effectively self-determined both in terms of its start and completion.

After his encounter with Nicodemus and in discourse with his disciples, Jesus warns that both believers and non-believers also face consequences from non-productivity. This is illustrated by analogy about the vine and the branches, with Jesus observing that:

> Whoever does not abide in me is thrown away like a branch and withers; such branches are gathered, thrown into the fire, and burned.[176]

With this gospel writer, we have an anomaly. Condemnation of some sort, yes. A *hell* of never-ending and inescapable torment, no.

And so there we also have it with Jesus and Nicodemus—perhaps the keynote chapter of John's Gospel. The conversation starts with a misunderstanding over semantics. Then proceeds to a much more intimate revealing of God's purpose for Jesus' earthly mission. Then ending with explication of the self-executing though not necessarily unchangeable results for believers versus those who choose not to acknowledge and follow the savior. All documented by a beloved disciple who offers this peek into the divine purpose and will that none perish but have unending opportunity for ultimate salvation.

Divinity Personalized

We have explored the interaction of Jesus and Nicodemus in some detail as illustrating issues of interpersonal communication at the human-divine interface. There are numerous other examples of divinity personalized that could be considered from John's Gospel. One is the story of Lazarus as representing the interaction of Jesus with a family deeply committed to Jesus' saving power. This is followed by the interactions of Jesus with his 12 disciples at the event of his earthly last supper.

Lazarus. This is the story of the death and resurrection of Lazarus— brother to Martha and Mary. As with the other accounts noted, Jesus'

---

[176] John 15:6.

interaction with Lazarus and his sisters can be described as intensely intimate. This one vignette conveys:

- The readily apparent and oft repeated affection between Jesus and the entire family of Lazarus, Martha and Mary.
- The way in which this affection moved Jesus—literally to tears as "Jesus wept."[177]
- The deliberate decision of Jesus to delay his arrival at their home due to an ulterior motive—to demonstrate the ultimate healing power of the divine, the victory of life over death.
- The intimacy of the connection between Jesus and the Father to whom he prayed—apparently a model for the multi-faceted relationships between Jesus and his earthly flock.

Last Supper. John's focus on *divinity personalized* also is evident by contrasting varied events as described in the fourth gospel with similar events as reported by the synoptics. This is perhaps best illustrated by the divergent accounts offered of the interactions between Jesus and his disciples around the time of the last supper.

Only John's Gospel speaks of the "love" Jesus has for his disciples on their last evening together. Only John then records Jesus getting up from the table, taking off his outer robe, tying a towel around himself, pouring water into a basin, washing the feet of his disciples, then drying them with the towel.

The uniquely intimate and personalized nature of John's account is apparent from what follows – in Jesus' up close interaction with Judas. Note: phrases in *italics* are as exclusively recorded by John.

> The disciples looked at one another, uncertain of whom he was speaking. *One of his disciples—the one whom Jesus loved—was reclining next to him; Simon Peter therefore motioned to him to ask Jesus of whom he was speaking. So, while reclining next to Jesus,* he asked him, 'Lord, who is it?' Jesus answered, 'It is the one to whom I give this piece of bread when I have dipped it in the dish.' So when he had dipped the piece of bread, he gave it to Judas son of Simon Iscariot. *After he received the piece of bread,*

---

[177] John 11:35.

> *Jesus said to him, 'Do quickly what you are going to do.' No one at the table knew why he said this to him. Some thought that, because Judas had the common purse, Jesus was telling him, 'Buy what we need for the festival;' or that he should give something to the poor. So, after receiving the piece of bread, he immediately went out. And it was night.*[178]

Intimate and highly personalized details of two remarkably different scenes are offered only by John's version of the last supper. First is the snapshot of the disciple "whom Jesus loved" reclining next to Jesus. To ask a question, Peter who must be seated further away must interact not directly with Jesus but through this other disciple—John, the one whom Jesus loved.

Second is the personal connection of a very different, more painful sort. Jesus dips the bread, gives it to Judas as prospective betrayer, also sitting next to the master. Jesus knows what Judas plans and so advises:

"Do quickly what you are going to do."[179] This is an exchange shared by Jesus and Judas directly; the other disciples around the table, except for John, are left to second guess what is taking place.

Summary Themes. We could tell of other *up front and personal* encounters. Examples beyond those of Nicodemus, the Samaritan woman and the last supper include Jesus' call of Philip and Nathaniel, the manufacture of wine at wedding in Cana on behalf of his mother, dialogue with a Samaritan woman over "living water," the healing of a royal official's son, Jesus prayer for his disciples, interrogation by Pontius Pilate, handing over care of his mother to the beloved disciple while hanging on a cross, encounter with Mary Magdalene at the empty tomb, and post-denial restoration of Simon Peter.

And so it goes. Johannine themes indicated by these encounters recur throughout this gospel:

- Jesus is *very direct* in his questions and comments. His answers require direct involvement of the hearer—evidenced by encounters as diverse as those with Nicodemus and the Samaritan women.
- Jesus wastes no time to *interact* with those with whom he comes in contact. Unlike the sometimes dismissive Jesus whom the synoptic

---

[178] John 13:22–30.
[179] John 13:27.

writer Mark describes, John's Jesus is always trying to build upon the capabilities and insights of those around him. For example, when Andrew introduces his brother Simon to Jesus, the master greets this newcomer warmly: "You are Simon son of John. You are to be called Cephas" (which is translated as Peter or *rock*).[180]

- John's Jesus is ready to *offer opinions* about other people. The day after Andrew introduces Peter to Jesus, Philip is introduced to Jesus who then brings Nathaniel to meet Jesus. The first question posed by Nathanael to his friend is steeped in skepticism: "Can anything good come out of Nazareth?" Later, when Jesus sees Nathanael coming toward him, Jesus comments: "Here is truly an Israelite in whom there is *no deceit*." The sense of recognition is mutual, with Nathanael observing on this first encounter, "Rabbi, you are the *Son of God*! You are the King of Israel!"[181]

From the start to the finish of Jesus' ministry, John's Jesus is constantly in motion—moving from the elucidation of complex and at times bizarre spiritual concepts to personal, even intimate, interactions—and then back again. The Jesus of John's Gospel rarely speaks in third person voice, but rather in the first person ("I am") and the second person ("You…"). Unlike the synoptics who portray Jesus as uncomfortable with any disclosure of a possible divine role, in John's Gospel the special link of Jesus to the divine is openly acknowledged by many if not most of those with whom he comes in contact.

Acceptance of John. The Gospel of John would be accepted in some quarters but not necessarily or totally in all. The gospel was suspect at times because of its appeal to those of Gnostic persuasion. A secondary cause for concern was the generally assumed late dating of this gospel. However, it met the informal canonical criteria of widespread use and the tradition of being penned by an apostolic author.

---

[180] John 1:42.

[181] This statement is prompted by Jesus telling Nathanael, "I saw you under the fig tree before Philip called you." The encounter is excerpted from John 1:43–51.

John in Summary

This is a peculiar gospel. John's Jesus gets up close and personal. With an intimacy that can be wonderful, awesome, mysterious, transcendent, painful. Almost like touching God.

John's Jesus is divinity personalized, the Jewish Messiah, the word, the eternal "I am." This is no social revolutionary, but one who reaches out to interact on an up-close-and-personal level with both man and woman.

John's deviation from his NT counterparts can be considered as more a matter of substance or belief than style. His perspective is oriented more to the unfolding kingdom not just in this life but beyond. There is considerably less interest evident in terms of present-day application.

Jesus is a god-man who offers a carrot and carries a stick. The carrot is the promise of eternal life; the stick becomes the threat of judgment and condemnation, though apparently not to a place or state that John would term as an eternal hell, or in the vernacular of the day as "Gehenna."

The infamous passage of John 3:16 makes clear the options of perishing versus eternal life. But then John 3:17 goes on to clarify that "God did not send his Son into the world to condemn the world, but to save the world through him." The only way to resolve this seeming paradox is if, for time immemorial, the option of salvation always retains the capacity to trump death. This is the scenario in which God's will prevails is via the never-ending second chance—whether in this life or beyond.

And the next verse (18) goes on to further clarify that any condemnation is not God-inflicted but self-inflicted—whether of short or long duration.

In positioning Jesus as the "way, the truth and the life," God the Father takes on a more distant, hands-off role than in the Hebrew Scriptures of the Old Testament. The Father still is in charge, but leaves the often messy details of interacting with earthly humanity on a day-to-day basis with the Son—a responsibility subsequently passed on to and shared with the Holy Spirit.

Unlike the three synoptics, John's Jesus does not engage in denial or obfuscation of his messianic role. He speaks openly and directly—both as the "I am" and "Son of God."

No wonder that some readers—often scholars—have so much difficulty to deal with or simply reject this peculiar gospel. Others—particularly those of a deeply spiritual, evangelistic or charismatic bent—embrace this Jesus as one who is and is in all, one with God and one-on-one with humankind.

Supplement — John As Cousin of Jesus?

A careful reading of four disparate New Testament passages raises the possibility that John the beloved disciple may have been a cousin of Jesus. Consider the references and logic, as follows:

Mark: Immediately he called them; and they left their father Zebedee in the boat with the hired men, and followed him.[182]

Matthew: And many women who followed Jesus from Galilee, ministering to Him, were there looking on from afar, among whom were Mary Magdalene, Mary the mother of James and Joses, and *the mother of Zebedee's sons.*[183]

Mark again: There were also women looking on from afar, among whom were Mary Magdalene, Mary the mother of James the Less and of Joses, *and Salome,* who also followed Him and ministered to Him when He was in Galilee, and many other women who came up with Him to Jerusalem.[184]

John: Meanwhile, standing near the cross of Jesus were his mother, and *his mother's sister*, Mary the wife of Clopas, and Mary Magdalene. When Jesus saw his mother and the disciple whom he loved standing beside her, he said to his mother, 'Woman, here is your son.' Then he said to the disciple, 'Here is your mother.' And from that hour the disciple took her into his own home.[185]

Assuming the same set of individuals identified at the crucifixion as in Mark, Salome would be the same person as Jesus' mother's sister.[186]

---

[182] Mark 1:20. Note that Zebedee wasn't just some impoverished fisherman; he had hired hands and possibly partners, including Peter and Andrew working with the Zebedee organization.

[183] Matthew 27: 55–56 (NKJV). There is some uncertainty as to the identity of Joses. Based on the combined evidence of these four accounts, this Joses appears to be the son of a Mary who is married to Clopas or Alphaeus.

[184] Mark 15:40–41 (NKJV).

[185] John 19: 25–27.

[186] Salome is also identified as likely wife of Zebedee and other of apostles James and John by other sources. For example, see: Joan E. Taylor and Boaz Zissu, "The Cave of Salome: Tomb of Jesus Disciple," *Biblical Archaeology Review*, Spring 2024, 39.

Luke is the only gospel not providing added information on these familial relationships. So, now for the quasi-mathematical logic:

Mother of Zebedee's Sons = Salome = Jesus' Mother's Sister
Zebedee's Sons = James and John
Therefore: James and John = Jesus' Cousins

V. Paul—Salvation Through Faith

I wish those who unsettle you would castrate themselves.
Galatians 5:12

With Saul of Tarsus (later renamed Paul), the opportunity for spreading the good news of Christ reaches well beyond the original circle of Jesus' followers. Paul is a man who lived at the time of Jesus, yet most likely never met him *in the flesh*. This is a Jew who was not even from the homeland of the Jewish people but from Tarsus in present-day Turkey.

Yet Paul is the man who almost single-handedly propels Christianity from its status as a minor Jewish cult to eventual adoption as the religion of an empire. This is a tireless evangelist who relentlessly proclaims a theology of salvation through faith—available to the Gentile as well as the Jew. And this is a man who would take his message of a crucified and resurrected savior direct to Greco-Romans at the center of the empire, proclaiming:

> For I am not ashamed of the gospel; it is the power of God for salvation to everyone who has faith, *to the Jew first and also to the Greek.* For in it the righteousness of God is revealed through faith for faith; as it is written, 'The one who is righteous will live by faith.'[187]

In recognition of this initiative, Paul shapes Christian doctrine and practice largely as we know it today. But, to get there, Paul essentially severs himself from his cultural and theological roots.

---

[187] Romans 1:16–17.

Background of Paul and His Writings

As with our other gospel author pioneers, we begin with a bit of background. Saul (renamed Paul) of Tarsus is a complex person—quintessentially Jewish but ultimately the driving force behind the eventual separation of Christianity from Judaism.

The late 20th century author Allen F. Segal of *Paul the Convert* describes Paul as:

> ...one of only two Pharisees to have left us any personal writings. As the only first-century Jew to have left confessional reports of mystical experience, Paul should be treated as a major source in the study of first-century Judaism.[188]

To the Jews, Paul was what the author describes as "a first-century heresy."[189] However, Alan Segal goes on to note that:

> Although Paul met opposition from many Jews of his own day, because they believed Jesus to be neither Messiah nor God, his greatest battles were fought against other Christians, especially Jewish Christians.[190]

In short, Paul embodied the quintessential role of heretic—for traditional Jew and Jewish Christian alike.

Dating of Written Works. Paul apparently began writing what are now known as the Pauline epistles while traveling much of the Roman empire. Some scholars believe the epistle to the Galatians to be the earliest written work of the New Testament, dating from about 48–49 AD, just after Paul's first missionary journey and before the Jerusalem Council meeting.

An alternative view is that Galatians was written in the mid-50s, perhaps as late as 56 AD—consequently with 1 Thessalonians being written first, around 50–51. There is less dispute about the first letter to the Corinthians

---

[188] Alan F. Segal, *Paul the Convert: The Apostolate and Apostasy of Saul the Pharisee* (New Haven and London:
Yale University Press, 1990), xi.
[189] Segal, xiii.
[190] Segal, xiv.

which was written about 54 toward the close of a three-year residency in Ephesus. The epistle to the Romans likely was written shortly thereafter, about 56–57.[191]

The last extant epistle attributed (by some) to Paul is known as 2 Timothy, written from prison shortly before Paul's death in 66–67. It is to Timothy that Paul reportedly writes, *"…the time has come for my departure. I have fought the good fight. I have finished the race, I have kept the faith."*[192]

Authorship. Most modern scholars ascribe authorship of New Testament epistles Including Romans, both Corinthian letters, Galatians, Philippians, 1 Thessalonians and Philemon directly to the apostle Paul. Works most disputed (both historically and currently) include 2 Thessalonians and the pastoral letters to Timothy and Titus. Also questioned by some have been the letters to the churches at Ephesus and Colosse.

The Tradition of Paul. Originally called by his Hebrew name, Saul was born in the Cilician city of Tarsus—an intellectual and cultural center and a center of Greek Stoic teaching. In later life, Paul indicated that he was taught "at the feet of Gamaliel," a prominent Jewish teacher of the early first century.[193]

According to the New Testament book of Acts, Saul was present at the stoning of the early church deacon Stephen. Saul was not only present, but "approved of their killing him."[194] And Saul's murderous activities were not limited to one evangelist but quickly extended more widely.

After Stephen's death, Acts goes on, noting that:

> But Saul was ravaging the church by entering house after house; dragging off both men and women, he committed them to prison.[195]

---

[191] Wayne E. Meeks, ed., *The Harper Collins Study Bible—New Revised Standard Version,* 1st ed. Paperback (London: Harper Collins Publishers, 1993), 2113, 2182, 2218.

[192] 2 Timothy 4:6–7. Pauline authorship of both letters to Timothy is questioned by some scholars due to differences in style, vocabulary and teaching from prior letters.

[193] Acts 22:3. As a Pharisee, Gamaliel also is portrayed in Acts 5:34–39 as an advocate in the Sanhedrin of moderate treatment of the Christian apostles, waiting to see if the apostles' message will fail or if their work will persist as being of God.

[194] Acts 8:1.

[195] Acts 8:3.

Intense persecution caused Christians to flee for other parts of Judea and Samaria—and beyond. Saul then extended the geographic reach of his anti-Christian activity. At the time of his conversion, he was headed for the Syrian city of Damascus to arrest those who belonged to "the Way"—as early church followers were described. Subsequent to his conversion, Paul would confess:

> I persecuted this Way up to the point of death by binding both men and women and putting them in prison...

While dating is uncertain, it is around 34–35 AD that Saul experienced his vision of the risen Christ on the road to Damascus. Subsequently, he went to Arabia and the Nabatean kingdom situated east of the Jordan River.

Three years later, he appears to make his first post-conversion visit to Jerusalem, meeting with both Peter and James as elders of the Jerusalem church.

It has not been easy for scholars to reconcile the subsequent events of Paul's life based on the chronology of Acts vis-a-vis Paul's own account as provided by his letter to the Galatians.[196] However, it appears that Paul spent some time in Arabia preparing himself for subsequent ministry. He was introduced to the church in Jerusalem by Barnabas, a Hellenistic Jewish Christian who made his home on the Mediterranean island of Cyprus. The book of Acts records that Saul then:

> ...went in and out among them in Jerusalem, speaking boldly in the name of the Lord. He spoke and argued with the Hellenists; but they were attempting to kill him. When the believers learned of it, they brought him down to Caesarea and sent him off to Tarsus.[197]

For about a decade, Paul worked and ministered in Syria and Cilicia (on what is now the southeast Turkish coast). What occurred over this extended period of activity is not recorded in Acts but is referred to years later in Paul's

---

[196] A summary timeline of Pauline's life and major events is provided as a supplement at the end of this chapter.
[197] Acts 9: 28–30.

letter to the Galatians.[198] He was then brought to Syrian Antioch by Barnabas, which became Paul's base of operations for subsequent missionary journeys.

It was during his stay in Antioch that controversy over the applicability of Jewish customs (notably circumcision) first surfaced. Paul went to Jerusalem, a conference that would be recorded somewhat differently in Acts versus Paul's letter to the Galatians of Asia Minor.

According to the version in Acts, Paul appears to defer to the judgment of the Jerusalem Council chaired by James the brother of Jesus. However, to the Galatians he evidences clear disdain for the supposed authority of the mother church in Jerusalem. There also are differences between the two accounts as to which emissaries were to accompany Paul in a subsequent return trip to Antioch and as to the reasons for the subsequent split between Barnabas and Paul at Antioch following the Jerusalem Council meeting.[199]

At his prime, Paul would spend roughly a decade on three so-called *missionary* journeys:

- From about 46–48 AD, Paul took a relatively short journey from Antioch to Cyprus and through the closer regions of Asia Minor (now eastern Turkey)—followed by the Jerusalem Council.
- Subsequently to the Jerusalem Council and from 49–52, Paul's second journey took him to the western reaches of Asia Minor (including Ephesus) and from there to Macedonia and Greece (both Athens and Corinth).
- His third journey took place over much the same route as the second and lasted the longest, from 53–57 (with much of that time spent in Ephesus).

Each of the three missionary journeys would end in Jerusalem. Upon completion of his third journey, Paul was arrested in Jerusalem. He was brought before the Jewish ruling council of the Sanhedrin. However, as a Roman citizen he was protected from Jewish authority by Roman intervention, albeit being imprisoned in Caesarea for two years.

---

[198] Paul's time in Syria and Cilicia is briefly noted at Galatians 1:21.
[199] A more detailed discussion of differences between accounts in Acts and Galatians is found in the next chapter on James.

As noted, Paul successfully asserted his right to be tried as a Roman citizen before the emperor in Rome. After surviving two assassination plots, he journeyed to Rome about 59–60 where he lived at least two years under house arrest.[200] During this time Paul was free to receive guests, both friends and adversaries, all the while "proclaiming the kingdom of God and teaching about the Lord Jesus Christ with all boldness and without hindrance."[201]

Paul wanted to travel to Spain, but it is unclear whether he actually did. From Acts 28, it appears that Paul was released from Roman house arrest after two years in about 62 AD. The case for a fourth missionary journey to Spain is largely circumstantial, based on Paul's declared interest, a supporting implication by the fourth century Christian writer Eusebius, and statements from other early church patriarchs who attested to the early spread of the Christian gospel to Spain.[202]

In any event, Paul returned to prison under the reign of Nero. Though not recorded in the New Testament, the most common tradition is that Paul was executed at Rome about 64–68 AD—coincident with the early days of the Jewish insurrection against Rome.

Salvation and Grace

Paul's distinctive contribution to Christianity the doctrine *of justification by faith.* A salvation available not only to the descendants of Abraham, but to the pagan, non-Jewish world as well. It is also his heresy—as he was outside of the mainstream both of Judaism together with the gospel and practice of the early church leadership based in Jerusalem.

---

[200] The first assassination attempt occurred after Paul's arrest and questioning before the Sanhedrin, as recorded by Acts 23:12, when more than 40 Jews "joined in a conspiracy and bound themselves by an oath neither to eat nor drink until they had killed Paul." A second plan to ambush and kill Paul was hatched more than two years later when Festus replaced Felix as the Roman governor, per Acts 25:3.
[201] Acts 28:31.
[202] The declaration of Paul's Spanish interest is found in Romans 15:24, 28. Paul is definite about his interest, saying not "if" but "when" he would travel to Spain. The fourth century Christian historian Eusebius may imply a trip to Spain in his *History of the Church,* 2:22, indicating that Paul survived his first stay in Rome and was executed during a later return. And early statements about spread of the gospel to Spain are found in Clement of Rome's *Epistle to the Corinthians* and in the *Muratorian Canon.*

Writing to those in the Roman capital, Paul makes the declaration that proved to be the *cornerstone* of all his writings:

> For I am not ashamed of the gospel; it is the power of God for *salvation to everyone who has faith,* to the Jew first and also to the Greek. For in it the righteousness of God is revealed through faith for faith; as it is written, 'The one who is righteous will live by faith.'[203]

Paul had come on the scene at a propitious time for the spread and acceptance of Christianity. By the first century of the common era, Jewish populations and synagogues were spread as a diaspora throughout the Roman empire. Judaism was becoming more attractive to a more cultured society, in part because the notion of multiple pagan gods was proving increasingly anachronistic.

However, the legalistic practices of Judaism including blood sacrifice rituals, circumcision of foreskins and avoidance of certain meats were incomprehensible to the non-Jewish mind. What the Roman empire needed was a way for Gentiles to worship one god without the accompanying baggage of repugnant teaching and cultural customs unfamiliar throughout the Greco-Roman world. Paul was the one who made the message palatable—via a liberating theology of God's own son, Jesus Christ.

Paul's heresy is centered on four major premises, the latter three of which are not explicitly found elsewhere in the New Testament:

- There is salvation in Jesus.
- This salvation comes via the intangible expression of faith.
- Faith is a product of God's grace, not human performance.
- As newcomers to the faith like Paul, we also can be apostles with Christ.

In Paul's view, anyone can experience the godhead acting not from motives of *payback* but acceptance. Like children, we are becoming "joint heirs" with Christ as members of the household of God.[204]

Writing to the Galatians, Paul clearly states his case this way:

---

[203] Romans 1:16–17.

[204] From the passage at Romans 8:14–17.

...yet we know that a person is justified not by the works of the law but through faith in Jesus Christ. And we have come to believe in Christ Jesus, so that we might be justified by faith in Christ, and not by doing the works of the law, because *no one will be justified by the works of the law.*[205]

This is a man bold enough to buck not only Torah Judaism, but to also indict leaders of the early Christian movement for continued and often rigid adherence to religious traditions of yesterday. Lest anyone miss the point, Paul goes on to challenge his Galatian readers and perhaps warn his opponents:

I wish those who unsettle you would castrate themselves.[206]

Aggressiveness and persistence would pay off. Paul's characterization of Christian faith and practice would become a dogma to withstand the test of time.

Galatians Vs Jerusalem

No review of the driving message and pugnacious, single-minded character of the self-appointed apostle Paul would be complete without discussion of his letter to the Galatians—coupled with Paul's on/off relationship with the mother church at Jerusalem. As stated by an introduction to this letter in the NRSV Study Bible:

The bitterly polemical Letter of Paul to the Galatians reflects a critical moment in the early Christian movement's struggle to define its mission and identity.[207]

Of significance in this letter are Paul's views of his own apostleship, relationship to the recognized leaders of the early church, mix of combative and conciliatory viewpoint, and as a setup for the ensuing response from church leader James the brother of Jesus as covered by the next chapter to this book.

---

[205] Galatians 2:16.
[206] Galatians 5:12.
[207] *The Harper Collins Study Bible—NRSV,* 2181.

Introduction, Purpose and Credentials. Paul sets the stage for this confrontive letter to the Galatians right from the get-go:

> Paul an apostle—sent neither by human commission nor from human authorities, but through Jesus Christ and God the Father, who raised him from the dead—and all the members of God's family who are with me,[208]

As is apparent throughout the letter, Paul is letting the Galatian churches know that he is accountable to no church leader nor to any other "human being," but only to God "who had set me apart before I was born."[209] In effect, his credentials involve a prior record of persecuting the church, dramatic conversion and then avoiding contact with apostles in Jerusalem, only to interact with Peter (over 15 days) and with Jesus' brother James after a 3+/- year stay in Arabia and Damascus.

Confronting False Believers. Following this roughly 3+ year post-conversion preparation for the work ahead, Paul travels into the regions of Syria and Cilicia (in present-day southeastern Turkey). As noted, this is a decade-long time period about which little is documented. However, Paul would write to the Galatians acknowledging that Christ followers in Syria and Cilicia accepted this former persecutor and "glorified God because of me."[210]

It would be 15+ years from Paul's conversion to when Paul travels with Barnabas and Titus to participate in what would become known as the Jerusalem Council—including with the acknowledged church leaders of James and Peter. Based on his letter to the Galatians, Paul is clearly unhappy, feeling unduly constrained by the Jerusalem church.

And here Paul more fully vents his frustration, albeit temporarily mitigated by seeming acceptance from "acknowledged pillars" of the mother church. To the Galatians, he would let loose, explicitly stating that:

> But because of false believers secretly brought in, who slipped in to spy on the freedom we have in Christ Jesus, so that they might enslave us—we did not submit to them even for a moment, so that the truth of the gospel might always remain with you. And from those who were supposed to be *acknowledged leaders* (what they actually were makes no difference to me;

---

[208] Galatians 1:1–2.
[209] Galatians 1:15–16.
[210] Galatians 1:24.

> God shows no partiality)—those leaders contributed nothing to me. On the contrary, when they saw that I had been entrusted with the gospel for the uncircumcised, just as Peter had been entrusted with the gospel for the circumcised (for he who worked through Peter making him an apostle to the circumcised also worked through me in sending me to the Gentiles), and when James and Cephas and John, who were *acknowledged pillars,* recognized the grace that had been given to me, they gave to Barnabas and me the right hand of fellowship, agreeing that we should go to the Gentiles and they to the circumcised. They asked only one thing, that we remember the poor, which was actually what I was eager to do.[211]

There is a lot packed into this angry diatribe. Paul is troubled by "false believers" whom he does not identify but suggests they are "slipped in" (also not identified from where). However, at this point he still has church leaders on his side, having gained the support of "acknowledged pillars" of the church in James, Peter and John. However, that mutual trust does not last.

Differing Accounts. Often overlooked are differences between the accounts of Luke (in Acts) and of Paul (in Galatians) as to outcomes of the discussions at the Council. In Acts, Luke writes that it is James the brother of Jesus who presides and documents the conclusion of the council. James summarizes the outcome as follows:

> Therefore *I have reached the decision* that we should not trouble those Gentiles who are turning to God, but we should write to them to abstain only from things polluted by idols and from fornication and from whatever has been strangled and from blood.[212]

This judgment was codified by James with a letter carried by Judas (called Barsabbas) and Silas to the church in Antioch. Compare this with the account of what appears to also be the discussion with the Jerusalem Council, as recorded by Paul's above noted letter of explanation to the Galatians. The two recollections could hardly be more different.

The edict of James focuses on continued adherence to Jewish (Mosaic) law—about things (like food) polluted by idols, strangled animals and blood.

---

[211] Galatians 2:4–10.
[212] Acts 15:19–20.

To the Galatians, Paul mentions none of these but rather states that the only requirement was to remember the poor (which was not a stipulation of the council). In effect, Paul appears to have ignored James' edit and instead delivered an offering to relieve poverty in Jerusalem—a humanitarian gesture but not part of what James stipulated.

Insubordinate to Church Leadership? Does this amount to an act of insubordination to the acknowledged leaders of the early apostolic church? One cannot help but wonder.[213]

Sometime later (most likely after the Council of Jerusalem described by Acts 15). Peter is deputized by the church to Antioch where Paul is ministering. Paul's ire has shifted from "false believers" to at least two key leaders of the established church—Peter and James. Paul writes:

> But when Cephas (Peter) came to Antioch, I opposed him to his face, because he stood self-condemned; for until certain people came from James, he used to eat with the Gentiles. But after they came, he drew back and kept himself separate for fear of the circumcision faction. And the other Jews joined him in this hypocrisy, so that even Barnabas was led astray by their hypocrisy.[214]

So far, Paul's anger is focused on insistence by the Jerusalem church on adherence by Gentile believers to adhere to Jewish circumcision and dining customs. But now Paul widens the scope of his complaint about church practices to include the issue (or doctrine) of salvation via faith versus works. Paul argues that Jews also are not subject to traditional OT works of the law:

> We ourselves are Jews by birth and not Gentile sinners; yet we know that a person is justified not by the works of the law but through faith in Jesus Christ.[215]

---

[213] Unclear is whether the Council at Jerusalem occurred before or after Paul's letter to the Galatians. A pre-Council letter would indicate that Paul is trying to pre-empt and influence the Jerusalem meeting. Sending the letter after the Council seems more serious—a clear act of insubordination and non-compliance with what was agreed at Jerusalem.

[214] Galatians 2:11–13.

[215] Galatians 2:15–16.

And Paul emphasizes this point by concluding that: "if justification comes through the law, then Christ died for nothing."[216] As if Paul knows more about why Jesus died than Peter or James!

Liberty vs Bondage. Much of the remainder of the Galatian letter is devoted to a more drawn out exposition of justification by faith rather than continued adherence to the law. Paul uses the example of Abraham fathering one child by the maid servant Hagar (in bondage to the law) "according to the flesh" and another by being born according to Sarah (a freewoman of the promise) according to the Spirit. This argument would be countered by James (as addressed in the next chapter).

Enmity vs Reconciliation. Paul does an about face as he nears the conclusion of the Galatians letter. Shifting from his condemnations of a works theology to the importance of Christian charity and unity, he offers what would normally be considered as a plea for reconciliation.

But Paul can't quite extend the olive branch until he gets in a couple of parting shots directed toward the Jerusalem church. He reminds the Galatians that:

For freedom, Christ has set us free. Stand firm, therefore, and do not submit again to a yoke of slavery.[217]

And just to make sure no one misses the intensity of his perspective, Paul lets loose with one more all-encompassing zinger, as he rants:

I wish those who unsettle you would castrate themselves![218]

To whom is Paul referring? Well, the only ones mentioned earlier in Galatians are ostensibly "false believers" with the only ones identified by name being Peter, James and John. In this letter, Paul cannot let go of his personal animus.

Maybe in a moment of reflection before sending off his letter, Paul has second thoughts. He finally shifts from his condemnations of works theology to the importance of Christian charity and unity, writing:

---

[216] Galatians 2:21.
[217] Galatians 5:1.
[218] Galatians 5:12.

So then, whenever we have an opportunity, work for the good of all, and especially for those of the family of faith.[219]

Where does Paul really stand? Even to the end, the anger remains, only somewhat tempered by grace. His last two sentences betray the turmoil still residing within as Paul concludes:

From now on, let no one make trouble for me; for I carry the marks of Jesus branded on my body.

May the grace of our Lord Jesus Christ be with your spirit, brothers and sisters. Amen.[220]

Other Pauline Distinctives

Rightfully so, a major focus of this chapter has been on Paul's pioneering role and driving theme of salvation through faith coupled with his actions to position this at the center of Christian theology and practice. As we have seen, this spicy stew of faith and works is most dramatically illustrated by his letter to the Galatian churches.

However, there are a range of other actions, relationships and theological teachings distinctive to Paul. These characteristics all serve to support and implement his fundamental view of salvation through faith alone—not works. Topics briefly considered include Paul's:

- Relationship to Peter and James
- Linkage with John
- Self-view as apostle to Christ
- Experience with the Godhead
- No Hell for Paul
- Physical Infirmity
- Poverty and Social Justice
- Unity versus Conflict

---

[219] Galatians 6:10.
[220] Galatians 6:17–18.

- Submission to Authority
- Acceptance of Paul

Relationship of Paul to Peter and James. How is it that a person who was not with the Christ during his earthly ministry becomes the primary agent for Christian evangelization? After all, Jesus had labeled Peter as "this rock" on which "I will build my church."[221] And it was the brother of Jesus—James—who would become the recognized leader of the early post-Easter church at Jerusalem.

Yet Paul the apostle is the one who became the primary agent to shape Christian belief and practice from the first century forward. In part, this is because Paul is the most voluminous of the writers whose extant materials are contained in the canonized New Testament. Paul wins by sheer volume of material written—on matters ranging from the mysterious to mundane.

And in part, Paul emerges victorious because the legacy of potential competitors was largely extinguished. Paul's aggressiveness and his persistence paid off—his characterization of the Christian faith appears to be the one that has withstood the test of time over the last two millennia.

In contrast and despite his subsequent designation as the first in the line of papal succession, we really know very little about Peter's leadership role within the early church. The actions of Peter as church leader are recorded early in the book of Acts, and there are two short, relatively little cited New Testament books attributed to his name. However, beyond this, we know little. More to come in the chapters ahead.

The legacy of James the brother of Jesus ends with his illegal lynching at the hands of the Jewish leadership, followed by demise of the Jerusalem church with the Roman destruction of the city and temple in 70 AD. These events are not recorded in the New Testament but in other literature, notably the historical accounts provided by Jewish military leader, turned traitor turned author known as Flavius Josephus. However, James (or his followers) leave behind one important writing—the epistle of James which stands as a sharp counterpoint to the unstintingly and often provocative ministry of Paul the convert.

---

[221] Matthew 16:18.

Linkage of Paul and John. While John is mentioned along with Peter and James as among acknowledged leaders of the church—perhaps with presumed guilt by association—Paul has nothing specific to say about whether and how John was also in error with respect to Paul's view of salvation.

However, on a theological basis, it seems somewhat startling to realize that Paul may share more theology in common with John than any other gospel writer. Of the early church leaders, Paul and John are alone in their views as to the full divinity of Jesus, Jesus as the Christ/Messiah, disdain for hell, and use of terms around wisdom and the word.

For all his seeming practicality, Paul shared with John a sense of Jesus as more spiritual than physical.

Writing to the Galatians, Paul wrote of his conversion experience. In a line that often has been mistranslated, Paul is often quoted as saying that God was "pleased to reveal his Son to me."[222] In fact, the early Greek manuscripts of Galatians actually read "…in me" rather than "to me."

Lack of interest in the physical is indicated by Paul's almost complete disregard for Jesus' life and events of his earthly ministry. In other words, God's revelation of Jesus to Paul takes place not in a direct physical sense but indirectly, internally and spiritually.

Role as Self-Appointed Apostle to Christ. Paul is convinced that apostleship extends well beyond the realm of Jesus' initial twelve disciples. Far more than the gospel writers or James, the apostle Paul is unequivocal in placing the notion of a specific relationship in Jesus as Christ at the center of his message—over and over again.

Based on this highly personal sense of relationship, Paul declares himself to be an apostle—over and over again. As noted earlier, this is expressed in his introductory comments to the Galatians. Here is how he put it to the Romans:

> Paul, a servant of Jesus Christ, *called to be an apostle, set apart* for the gospel of God, which he promised beforehand through his prophets in the

---

[222] Galatians 1:15–16, translated by the NRSV as "to me." Footnotes to the NRSV Study Bible acknowledge that this is best translated from the Greek as." in me." Both the KJV and NIV translate the phrase as "in me." It has been argued that this mistranslation of a single preposition has led to a misunderstanding of Paul's personal experience of the resurrected Jesus in physical versus spiritual/visionary form, as per 1 Corinthians 15:8.

holy Scriptures, the gospel concerning his Son, who was descended from David according to the flesh and was declared to be Son of God with power according to the spirit of holiness by resurrection from the dead, Jesus Christ our Lord, through whom we have received grace and apostleship to bring about the obedience of faith among all the Gentiles for the sake of his name, *including yourselves* who are called to belong to Jesus Christ.[223]

Similar statements of greeting and introduction are made in Paul's first and second letters to the Corinthians as well as with intros to the epistles including those to the Ephesians, Philippians, and Colossians. Possibly due to critical questioning from disciples who had been with Jesus during his earthly ministry, Paul gets a bit defensive, evidenced by these remarks to the Corinthians:

Am I not free? Am I not an apostle? Have I not seen Jesus our Lord? Are you not my work in the Lord? If I am not an apostle to others, at least I am for you, for you are the seal of my apostleship in the Lord.[224]

And as further noted by his greeting to the Romans, he opens the tent to offer apostleship, in effect, to all "who are called to belong to Jesus Christ."[225]

Experiencing the Godhead, Personal and spiritual interaction via an overwhelming and blinding vision with divinity is the seminal event in the life of Saul—renamed Paul. Two items of are particular note.

First, as the conversion vision begins, Saul asks: "Who are you, Lord?" The question is not necessarily of God, but of a person that from the Greek could be translated as master or Sir. Second, the answer indicates that the source of the vision is not God the Father, but Jesus "whom you are persecuting."[226] Clearly, for Saul, this Jesus represents the supernatural, as the light (or source of the vision) is described as being "from heaven."

There is a third aspect to this initial encounter that would mark the entire ministry of Paul—the intensely personal nature of the interaction between the converted Saul and the Godhead. As noted, the first question posed to Saul by

---

[223] Romans 1:1–6.
[224] 1 Corinthians 9:1–2.
[225] Romans 1:6.
[226] Excerpted from Acts 9:3–5.

the Lord is: *"...why do you persecute me?"* As the writer of the Acts tells it, Saul's persecution of believers represents a personal affront to the person speaking through this vision. This personal connection comes to mark many of Paul's views of the Godhead.

Of added note, like John, Paul recognizes the respective distinct roles of God the Father and Jesus the Son—as part of Paul's introductory comments to the Galatians, saying:

> Grace to you and peace from God our Father and the Lord Jesus Christ, who gave himself for our sins to set us free from the present evil age, according to the will of our God and Father, to whom be the glory forever and ever. Amen.[227]

To summarize, for Paul the Father wills the actions of the Son. And to the Father is the glory ascribed.

No Hell for Paul? In contrast to the synoptics and James, neither John nor Paul make any use of any of the available Hebrew, Aramaic or Greek terms for hell. Both writers talk of judgment, but neither explicitly identifies hell as the result of that judgment.

The apostle Paul is not more helpful in describing his views of judgment (without any direct recourse to hell). For example, writing to the Romans, Paul states: "For we will all stand before the judgment seat of God."[228] Paul goes on to say that "every knee shall bow" and "every tongue shall give praise" but does not specify what happens to those who are judged harshly.[229] Similarly, to the Corinthians, Paul writes:

> For all of us must appear before the judgment seat of Christ, so that each may receive recompense for what has been done in the body whether for good or evil.[230]

---

[227] Galatians 1:3–5.
[228] Romans 14:10.
[229] Romans 14:11.
[230] 2 Corinthians 5:10.

Paul does not go on to explain with any greater specificity what may be in store for those who do evil. As an added example, to the Galatians Paul refers to judgment but with no specific detailing of consequence as he writes:

…if anyone proclaims to you a gospel contrary to what you received, let that one be accursed.[231]

In these passages, Paul can be direct in his condemnation, but comes across as somewhat evasive by *not detailing the consequences*—whether in the form of never-ending hell or otherwise.[232]

Physical Infirmity. Unlike other New Testament personalities, we know something of Paul's physical characteristics. By his own acknowledgment, Paul apparently was not a physically imposing individual. He came across as more authoritative in writing than in person. Writing to the Corinthians, Paul paraphrases his detractors like this:

For they say, 'His letters are weighty and strong, but his bodily presence is weak, and his speech contemptible.'[233]

Later in this same epistle, Paul writes that "a thorn was given me in the flesh, a messenger of Satan to torment me, to keep me from being too elated."[234] Nowhere does the New Testament directly reveal the nature of this infirmity.

However, speculation is that he may have been affected by mental or physical illness (such as epilepsy)—most likely a chronic condition. Lingering effects from Paul's blindness and conversion while on the road to Damascus

---

[231] Galatians 1:9. The NIV uses the stronger statement of "let him be eternally condemned." However, footnotes indicate that the Greek word (anathema) originally referred to a pagan temple offering in payment for a vow, which later came to represent a curse.

[232] 2 Thessalonians 1:5–9 may be an outlier in that it refers to "eternal destruction" for those who don't know God or obey the Lord Jesus. However, Pauline authorship of 2 Thessalonians is questioned based on, among other items, hints of forgery not found in other Pauline epistles.

[233] 2 Corinthians 10:10.

[234] 2 Corinthians 12:7.

are possible causes, as are the cumulative effects of multiple beatings from crowds and authorities while on his missionary journeys.

Poverty and Social Justice. The writers of the New Testament Gospels offer decidedly different views on the importance of meeting the needs of the less fortunate. Of the New Testament writers, Luke takes, by far, the most decidedly pro-social welfare position. However, Luke's views are far more tempered in the book of Acts than they are in Luke's gospel. A definite transition in thought and action is apparent.

At the outset of Acts, the believers live in a communal fellowship, sharing their material resources. When Saul (then Paul) appears on the scene, this Lukan emphasis on social justice fades to the background. Why? Because it appears to have been of little to no consequence for Paul.

Paul is at his most socially conscious behavior when he takes up an offering from Macedonia and Achaia to "share their resources with the poor among the saints at Jerusalem."[235] However, this appears to have been collected less from personal conviction and more from fulfilling a commitment he suggests was made at the Council of Jerusalem as recounted in his letter to the Galatians—even though this was not a requirement spelled out by James at the Council.

And to the Corinthians, Paul makes it clear that he is not commanding the offering; he asks that it be rendered "as a voluntary gift and not as an extortion." Those who give will reap rewards for "God loves a cheerful giver."[236]

The evidence indicates that, when in Jerusalem (or traveling thereto), Paul went out of his way to satisfy the church elders—whether in matters related to the issue of adherence to Jewish customs or offerings to the poor. When he was on the road elsewhere, Paul's priorities were something else.

With the notable exception of the collection for the church at Jerusalem, Paul's epistles otherwise provide little evidence of any overwhelming emphasis on addressing needs of the poor. Rather, the evidence available suggests that Paul takes a middle of the road position—somewhere between that of Luke and Matthew.

For Paul personally, riches and poverty are of little consequence. Paul writes that Christians may be treated "as poor, yet making many rich; as having

---

[235] Romans 15:26.

[236] 2 Corinthians 9:5,7.

nothing, and yet possessing everything."[237] Later, he goes on to extend this comparison to Jesus: "...that though he was rich, yet for your sakes he became poor, so that by his poverty you might become rich."[238]

And Paul on occasion would go further, lecturing on the value of one's work to make a living. For example, in his first letter to Timothy, Paul exhorts that "whoever does not provide for relatives, and especially for family members, has denied the faith and is worse than an unbeliever."[239] And Paul exemplifies this through his own work ethic, serving as a tentmaker even as he conducts his itinerant ministry.

To summarize, Paul seems to be saying that charity is important, but not necessarily the most important priority for the Christian. Higher obligations include working for one's own keep and maintaining love for others. As noted in his first letter to the Corinthians:

If I give away all my possessions, and if I hand over my body so that I may boast, but do not have love, I gain nothing.[240]

Unity versus Conflict. Few issues illustrate Paul's remarkable capacity to be "all things to all people" as evidenced by his seemingly contradictory views on the question of Christian unity. Writhing to the church at Rome, Paul exhorts:

If it is possible, so far as it depends on you, live peaceably with all.[241]

To the church at Corinth, Paul speaks more pointedly about the need for unity within the body of believers, i.e. the church, to wit:

But God has so arranged the body (of believers), giving the greater honor to the inferior member, that there may be no dissension within the body, but the members may have the same care for one another. If one member

---

[237] 2 Corinthians 6:10.
[238] 2 Corinthians 8:9.
[239] 1 Timothy 5:8.
[240] 1 Corinthians 13:3.
[241] Romans 12:18.

suffers, all suffer with it; if one member is honored, all rejoice together with it.[242]

This Paul who advocates "no dissension" is the same Paul who opposes the Lord's appointed apostle Peter to his face and even suggested castration for those so-called false believers who are troubling believing Gentiles across the region of Galatia. And this is the same Paul that openly scorns acknowledged church leadership, noting that:

"…from those who were supposed to be acknowledged leaders (what they actually were makes no difference to me; God shows no partiality); those leaders contributed nothing to me…"[243]

Here we have the picture of a man who wants to have it both ways. Confident enough to have his cake and eat it too.

When it suits Paul's purpose (of conformance to Pauline doctrine and practice), he urges unity—with common liturgy and hierarchical leadership. However, when Paul disagrees with others in Christian leadership, he is quick to suggest disdain and disregard for their ecclesiastic position.

Submission to Authority. The apostle Paul goes to great lengths to respect those in authority even when he disagrees strongly with their positions and actions. Paul shows no similar need to show deference to those whom he believes to be of lesser authority.

This sense of hierarchal structure comes through in Paul's treatment of others in the early church. He defers to James as leader of the church even though he violently disagrees with James' views on justification by works and adherence to Jewish custom. Conversely, Paul feels free to oppose Peter over differences on eating with Gentiles and circumcision. Paul views James as being in authority over him, but Peter—not so much.

Perhaps the clearest indication of Paul's delineation between those above versus below him in the social and ecclesiastical hierarchy is to be found in Paul's confrontation with the ruling Sanhedrin—after being arrested in Jerusalem. The event is worth recounting in its entirety:

---

[242] 1 Corinthians 12: 24–26.
[243] Galatians 2:6.

While Paul was looking intently at the council, he said, "Brothers, up to this day I have lived my life with a clear conscience before God." Then the high priest Ananias ordered those standing near him to strike him on the mouth. At this Paul said to him, "God will strike you, you whitewashed wall! Are you sitting there to judge me according to the law, and yet in violation of the law you order me to be struck?" Those standing nearby said, "Do you dare to insult God's high priest?" And Paul said, "I did not realize, brothers, that he was high priest; for it is written, 'You shall not speak evil of a leader of your people.'"[244]

Notice the sequence of events. Not realizing the authority of the person to whom he is speaking, Paul reacts both in anger and condescension after being struck on the mouth. Then after finally realizing whom he has just cursed, Paul comes as close to an apology as we see from him anywhere in the New Testament.

The closing chapter of Acts provides a final intriguing look at how Paul balances this desire for reconciliation with the need to speak boldly his view of the truth. Within three days of starting a period of house arrest in Rome, Paul calls the "local leaders of the Jews" to assemble at his "lodgings." The purpose: to explain that there is no basis for his arrest under either Jewish or Roman law.

The writer of the Acts goes on to report that: "Some were convinced by what he (Paul) said, while others refused to believe." Paul cannot resist one last dig at authorities who do not measure up to his standard. To the Jewish leadership in Rome, he quotes Isaiah on the hardness of hearts and ends by stating:

Let it be known to you then that this salvation of God has been sent to the Gentiles; they will listen.[245]

Acceptance of Paul. Of all the New Testament writings, Paul's have perhaps become the most widely read though not universally accepted, both by early Christian leaders as well as current scholars from a wide variety of

---

[244] Acts 23:1–5.
[245] Excerpted from the account at Acts 28:17–28.

persuasions. Core epistles most widely accepted as authentic—then and now—include Romans, 1 Corinthians, Galatians, 1 Thessalonians, and Philemon.

Others that have been more frequently debated—for reasons including authorship, assembly from multiple or fragmentary documents, stylistic considerations, potential forgery, and consistency with other Pauline letters include 2 Corinthians, Ephesians, Philippians, Colossians, 2 Thessalonians, 1/2 Timothy, and Titus.

Despite the apparent authenticity of core epistles and their acceptance as "Scripture," Paul's writings often were viewed even by the early church—including the apostle Peter—as "hard to understand."[246] The epistles of Paul and portions of Luke's gospel were the only New Testament writings accepted by the 2nd century Gnostic heretic Marcion, albeit conditionally.

By the time of church historian Eusebius in the early 4th century, all of the current Pauline epistles were widely accepted, though there were continuing doubts as to the authenticity of the epistle to the Hebrews (sometimes with authorship attributed to Paul). Interestingly, Eusebius also notes that, as of the 4th century, there was even a color portrait of Paul still in circulation.

Paul in Summary

This has been an attempt to sketch the times and pioneering if not at times heretical work of Paul the apostle. We have assessed the man who held the keys to formulating a set of Christian beliefs and doctrine that could endure for two millennia. An individual bold enough to buck not only Torah Judaism, but to also indict leaders of the early Christian movement for their rigid adherence to a hybrid Christianized Judaism more readily marketable to non-Jewish communities throughout the Roman empire.

As one might expect from a man as complex as Paul, his message and behavior is no less easy to understand—at least at first glance. Paul's logic often comes across as convoluted even as understood by Paul's sometimes dual nemesis in Peter and James.

Paul steps outside the mainstream of early Jewish Christianity in matters both of substance and style. Substantively, he takes a 180 degree turn from the notion of salvation via adherence to the law of Jewish orthodoxy. Stylistically

---

[246] 2 Peter 3:16.

or in practice, he eschews subordination to established early church authority—unless it's his own (Pauline) authority.

At its most basic, Paul is focused on a four-point message—of salvation in Jesus…manifest through the intangible expression of faith…a product of God's grace, not human performance…with opportunities for all to be apostles (or heirs) with Christ.

The challenge is to accept Paul's vision of humans reconciled to God not by our own attitudes or actions. Rather, in Paul's view, we experience the divine purely and solely by universal acceptance from a godhead acting not from motives of *payback* but acceptance. Like children, we are becoming "joint heirs" with Christ as members of the household of God.[247]

Paul counters James the brother of Jesus and leader of the Jerusalem church who states unequivocally that "faith without works is dead."[248] In sharp contrast, Paul declares that:

> …a person is justified not by the works of the law but through faith in Jesus Christ.[249]

Paul goes toe-to-toe not just against James but, as described in his letter to Galatian believers, also confronting the apostles Peter and John as those "who seemed to be pillars" of the church.[250]

The material benefit of Paul's teaching was the opportunity for the Gentile convert to come into the family of believers without also having to accept what are perceived as unnecessary trappings of Judaism. The disadvantage of the Pauline formulation was that it severed Christianity from its Jewish roots, creating ongoing and unnecessary enmity between the Jewish and Christian traditions—also thwarting Jesus' own message emphasizing both faith and works.

Like his pioneering counterparts of the 1st century and later, Paul's track record is one of sharply carved strengths and weaknesses. Unlike his counterparts, Paul fills a unique role in advancing the kingdom of God. No one before or since has been so uniquely qualified and timely placed to carry the

---

[247] Romans 8:17.
[248] James 2:20 (KJV).
[249] Galatians 2:16.
[250] Galatians 2:9 (KJV).

gospel well beyond its Jewish roots to a civilized world hungry for spiritual authenticity.

Supplement — Pauline Timeline

What follows is an approximate timeline for the life of the apostle Paul and key events.[251]

Year	Event(s)	References	Comments
5 AD	Birth in Tarsus of Cilicia	Acts 22:3/28 Phil 3:5	Israelite and Roman citizen
15–20	At school of Gamaliel in Jerusalem	Acts 22:3	Prominent Jewish teacher
32	Participant in stoning of Stephen	Acts 7:58, 8:1	Holds coats of assassins
33–34	Persecutor of the church	Acts 8:1–3, Phil 3:6	Scattering of believers
34	Damascus Road conversion	Acts 9:1–9	Sight recovered by Ananias
34–37	Trip to Arabia	Gal 1:17	Details unknown
37	Return to Damascus	Gal 1:17, Acts 9:20–25, 2 Cor 11:32–33	Due to plot to kill Paul, then exits city for safety
37	Travel to Jerusalem	Acts 9:26–29, Gal 1:18	Stays w/Peter, visits James
37–46	Travels to Tarsus, Syria/Cilicia (details unknown)	Acts 9:30	For safety, era of Antipas removal and Agrippa I death
47	Church in Syrian Antioch	Acts 11:25–26	Teaches with Barnabas
47	Travel to Jerusalem, then Cyprus	Acts 11:26,29–30,12:25, 13:2–4	Famine aid to church in Jerusalem, travel w/Mark

---

[251] Condensed/adapted from "Apostle Paul's Timeline—Study Resources." Blue Letter Bible. Accessed 9 Feb, 2024.
https://www.blueletterbible.org/study/paul/timeline.cfm (Accessed Feb. 9, 2024). Dates are approximate.

48	1st Missionary Journey (through Asia Minor)	Acts 13–14, Gal 2:1	Mark returns home. Paul, Barnabas and Titus(?) return to Antioch of Syria
48–49	*Letter to Galatians (Option 1)*	*Galatians 2*	*If written before Council*
49	Jerusalem Council	Acts 15:1–29, Gal. 2:1	Judas/ and Silas sent to Antioch to convey results
49	Separation of Paul and Barnabas	Acts 15:36–41	Barnabas and Mark to Cyprus, Paul and Silas to Syria
51–57	*Letter to Galatians (Option 2)*	*Galatians 2*	*If written after Council*
50–52	2nd Missionary Journey (including 18 months in Corinth)	Acts 16–18	Picks up Timothy, return thru Asia Minor to Macedonia and Greece
53	Return to Antioch	Acts 18:18–22	After stops in Ephesus, Caesarea and Jerusalem
53–56	3rd Missionary Journey (w/3 years in Ephesus)	Acts 18:23– Acts 21:14	Thru Asia Minor, Greece, back thru to Tyre/Caesarea
57–59	Arrest, Trial, Deportation	Acts 21:15– Acts 27:5	From plot on Paul's life to hearings before Felix, Festus and Agrippa, sailing for Rome
60–62	House arrest @ Rome	Acts 27–28	Preaches w/o hindrance
62–68	Release, 4th missionary trip, death	Writes 1/2 Timothy	Martyrdom under Nero

VI. James—Salvation Via Works

So faith by itself, if it has no works, is dead.
James 2:17

In the first century of the common (or AD) era, two concepts of Christian salvation contended for acceptance by a nascent church. One viewpoint was championed by none other than the titular leader of the first-century Christian church, James the brother of Jesus. This is the James who was also known to the early church as "the Righteous" or "the Just."[252]

In a short New Testament epistle bearing his name, James asks:

What good is it, my brothers and sisters, if you say you have faith but do not have works? Can faith save you?...*faith by itself, if it has no works, is dead.*[253]

James is writing to counter and correct an alternative viewpoint—as expressed by Paul the apostle. In his letter to the Galatians, Paul had declared that: "...we know that a person is justified not by the works of the law but through faith in Jesus Christ."[254]

These two alternative viewpoints vied for the hearts and minds of the early Christian church. James lost the first-century battle due in part to his own untimely execution and, later, crushing of the Jewish insurrection in Palestine by Rome. Paul's victory also was aided by his sheer persistence, the greater geographic breadth of his proselytization, prolific writing, and timing.

---

[252] Eusebius, 2.23. The translation by Williamson refers to James as the "Righteous" whereas Maier translates the name to the sobriquet of the "Just."
[253] James 2:14,17.
[254] Galatians 2:16.

Yet the message of James has continued to guide Christian behavior and experience—both officially and unofficially. The imperative of good deeds animated Catholicism of the middle ages to the point of widespread corruption. Luther rediscovered Paul's doctrine of faith by reading Galatians—prompting a reformation that affected both Catholic and Protestant sensibilities. Not surprisingly, assuming that Paul had access to James' short epistle as did Martin Luther centuries later, he would have thought little of it.

To churches of the 20th and 21st centuries, the debate remains as fresh as it was almost two thousand years ago. Fundamentalist, evangelical Christians typically put their doctrinal eggs in the basket of faith; mainstream churches including Roman Catholics emphasize works—often in the form of social action.

In the pantheon of Christian nobility, the significance of James to the early church and beyond often goes virtually unnoticed. Yet his influence at one time pervaded the early Jewish church. More so even than his half-brother Jesus, James also was viewed as an individual of political significance in the years leading up to the Jewish insurrection and resulting destruction of Jerusalem in 70 AD. Even today, the perspective of James lives on, prompting a more careful look at what we know about the man, his mission and political as well as eligious influence.

Background of James

Given the paucity of information that has been preserved, it is useful to look to the tradition of James including the writings of non-Christian sources as well as to the New Testament book commonly attributed to his authorship.

The Tradition of James. Paul and James are the first of our Christian pioneers who were not followers of Jesus during the period of his earthly ministry. However, James had one advantage over Paul as both became engaged in the post-resurrection church. For James was the half-brother (or possibly stepbrother) of Jesus—so the two undoubtedly got to know each other well growing up.

The person of James is mentioned several times in the New Testament Gospels, then in the Acts of the Apostles. In his hometown of Nazareth, Matthew identifies James as first in a list of four brothers and to unnamed, unnumbered sisters to Jesus:

Is not this the carpenter's son? Is not his mother called Mary? And are not *his brothers* James and Joseph and Simon and Judas? And are not all his sisters with us?[255]

To the writers of the New Testament, James appears to be regarded as the "brother" of Jesus. Many of the church patriarchs, including the 4rh century church historian Eusebius, viewed Joseph as Jesus' foster father, which would make James the Savior's stepbrother.[256] Yet later, from the time of Jerome forward, James was considered by much of Western tradition (including the Roman Catholic church) as a cousin of Jesus.[257]

In a similar passage, the writer of Mark's gospel identifies the same set of brothers.[258] While the Gospels make no other named references to James, he is implicated by association with Jesus family—in ways that suggest less than fully harmonious intra-family relationships. For example, Mark records that his family tried to restrain Jesus early in his ministry.

After all, as Mark's gospel states, "…people were saying, 'He (Jesus) has gone out of his mind.'" His family hears of it and tries to restrain Jesus. Shortly thereafter, his "mother and his brothers and sisters" again come calling. After Jesus is notified, he asks the crowd: "*Who are* my mother and my brothers?"[259]

Emergence of James as Early Church Leader. After Jesus' death and resurrection, James moves into a position of early post-Easter leadership within the nascent Christian movement. His ascendance is clearly in place by the time apostle Peter is imprisoned and then released. Peter shows up at the

---

[255] Matthew 13:55–56. The Roman Catholic church does not accept a full sibling relationship because it conflicts with a concept of the perpetual virginity of Mary.

[256] Eusebius along with Origen and the fourth century Epiphanius believed Jesus' "brothers" were sons of Joseph by an earlier wife before Mary, allowing the Lord's mother to remain a virgin.

[257] Commentators have noted that both James the Just and the disciple James the Less (son of Alpheus) had a mother named Mary. However, the Jewish historian Josephus records that James the Just was martyred at Jerusalem while historical tradition suggests James the Less was martyred at Ostrakine in lower Egypt.

[258] Mark 6:3.

[259] Excerpted from Mark 3:20–35.

house of John Mark's mother Mary, recounts the story of his deliverance from prison, then makes the request to: *"Tell this to James and to the believers."*[260]

The late first-century writer Clement of Alexandria describes James' ascendancy this way:

> Peter, James, and John, after the ascension of the Savior, did not claim pre-eminence because the Savior had specially honored them, but chose James the Righteous as Bishop of Jerusalem.[261]

While there has been preciously little open discussion in the church about brother James' quick rise to power, this has been a subject that has interested some investigators across subsequent centuries. More recently, a 21st century writer has explained what may have occurred in a fashion remarkably similar to that of the 1st century's Clement:

> The importance of Peter within the early church, particularly as a source of faith in Jesus' resurrection, has led to the understandable but careless conclusion that Simon Peter's vision is the only real source of belief that Jesus was raised from the dead. But it was James who took over Jesus' movement in Jerusalem. James—always more an ascetic than his famously carousing brother (Jesus)—practiced Nazarite vows of purity in a dedication to worship in the temple that made him a paragon among Jews as a whole, not only in the little movement that came to be called Christianity.[262]

When and how did James achieve this pre-eminence? The New Testament does not directly say. One theory is that James came over to Jesus' side toward the end of Jesus' ministry—when Jesus began to focus on sacrifice and purity of the temple in Jerusalem—as evidenced by his overturning the tables of the money-changers.

Another option is that James did not embrace his brother until after Jesus' resurrection. As the apostle Paul would later write, Jesus appeared to James,

---

[260] Acts 12:17.
[261] As quoted by Eusebius, *History of the Church*, 2.1.
[262] Bruce Chilton, *Rabbi Jesus: An Intimate Biography* (New York: Random House, 2000) 284.

and then *after that* to all the disciples. This might have occurred in the context of a post-resurrection reconciliation between the two brothers, much as occurred when Jesus forgave Peter for his three denials.

By the time of the first Council of Jerusalem, when Paul and Barnabas are brought before "the apostles and the elders," James is the one who replies to them. His response is authoritative: "My brothers, *listen to me.*"[263]

Much later, Paul returns one last time to Jerusalem. The writer of Acts comments that the day after his arrival, "Paul went with us *to visit James*; and all the elders were present."[264]

Whether for better or worse, the apostle Paul thinks enough of James to mention James four times in his letters. Writing to the Corinthians, Paul talks about the resurrection, stating that Jesus:

> …appeared to Cephas (Peter), then to the twelve. Then he appeared to more than five hundred brothers and sisters at one time, most of whom are still alive, though some have died. Then he appeared *to James*, then to all the apostles.[265]

Three times James is mentioned in Paul's epistle to the Galatians, though in less glowing terms than in Paul's later letter to the church in Corinth. First, describing his conversion on the road to Damascus, Paul writes that he went:

> …up to Jerusalem to visit Cephas and stayed with him fifteen days; but I did not see any other apostle *except James* the Lord's brother.[266]

Later, Paul would be directed to answer for his views on circumcision before "James and Cephas and John, who were acknowledged pillars of the church."[267] Paul agrees to abide by the rules (including circumcision), only to say much later that when Cephas (Peter) came to Antioch:

---

[263] Acts 15:13.
[264] Acts 21:18.
[265] 1 Corinthians 15:5–7.
[266] Galatians 1:18–19.
[267] Galatians 2:9.

I opposed him (Peter) to his face, because he stood self-condemned; for until certain people came *from James*, he (Peter) used to eat with the Gentiles. But after they (who apparently were sent by James) came, he (Peter) drew back and kept himself separate for fear of the circumcision faction.[268]

Exercising some caution, Paul is less willing to attack James directly, even as he frontally assaults Peter. But there is no doubt that James is in the line of fire, as the leader standing behind Peter—if not pulling the strings.

In his own epistle, James introduces himself as: "James, a servant of God and of the Lord Jesus Christ."[269] The even shorter letter of Jude offers a similar introduction: "Jude, a servant of Jesus Christ and brother of James."[270] James refers to his brother Jesus in respectful rather than more brotherly terms. As another brother in the savior's household, Jude clearly appears honored to refer to himself as a brother of James, the leader of the Jerusalem church.

It is James' epistle that counters the arguments made by Paul to the Galatians, aggressively asserting the primacy of faith over works (as recounted in the prior chapter). We get back to James' counter-argument in a few moments.

Significance of James to Early Church Leaders. Later patriarchs of the early church corroborate James' pre-eminent early church leadership position. For example, the fourth century church historian Eusebius maintained on the authority of the later first/early second century Clement of Rome that James had served as Bishop of Jerusalem. He quotes this Clement as saying:

Control of the church passed to the apostles, together with *the Lord's brother James*, whom everyone from the Lord's time till our own has called the Righteous, for there were many James, but this one was holy from his birth; he drank no wine or intoxicating liquor and ate no animal food; no razor came near his head; he did not smear himself with oil, and took no baths.

He alone was permitted to enter the holy place, for his garments were not of wool but of linen. He used to enter the Sanctuary alone, and was often

---

[268] Galatians 2:11–12.
[269] James 1:1.
[270] Jude 1:1.

found on his knees beseeching forgiveness for the people, so that his knees grew hard like a camel's from continually bending them in worship of God and beseeching forgiveness for the people. Because of his unsurpassable righteousness he was called the Righteous and *Oblias*—in our own language 'Bulwark of the People, and Righteousness'—fulfilling the declaration of the prophets regarding him.[271]

Not only was James clearly in charge of the early Christian movement, but he also appeared to have had the respect of other non-Christian Jewish leaders. In sharp contrast to his well-known brother who was accused of gluttony, James lived the life of an ascetic.[272]

Some have speculated that James may have been married. The apostle Paul seems to imply this in his letter to the Corinthians, asking: "Do we not have the right to be accompanied by a believing wife, as do the other apostles and *the brothers of the Lord* and Cephas?"[273]

For a period of more than a decade under James' direction, the post-resurrection church at Jerusalem was left essentially undisturbed. So long as Christians worshipped in the temple and the synagogue with their unconverted countrymen, there was no reason to form a separate community of their own—a movement that could be independent of Judaism.

The Death of James. With the death of a Roman procurator for Judea named Festus, the respectful relationship between Judaism and Christianity was about to change.[274] A portion of the Jewish leadership was clearly uncomfortable with the nascent Christian sect and its leader James.

The most complete and interesting description of James and his denouement comes from a secular, seemingly non-Christian source—the writings of the first-century Jewish historian Josephus. In his monumental work *The Antiquities of the Jews,* Josephus makes mention of three people associated with the Jesus movement—John the Baptist, Jesus and James. Of

---

[271] As quoted by Eusebius from Hegesippus, *The History of the Church,* 2.23.

[272] Jesus quotes others who refer to him as a "glutton and a drunkard" at Matthew 11:19 and Luke 7:34.

[273] I Corinthians 9:5.

[274] Festus was the procurator who previously was handed Paul's case and had him sent to Rome on Paul's appeal.

the three, the individual that Josephus views as most significant with changing political winds across Judea and the Galilee was James.

Here's how Josephus describes the undoing of James—as recounted in its entirety:

> *And now Caesar, upon hearing the death of Festus, sent Albinus into Judea, as procurator;* but the king deprived Joseph of the high priesthood, and bestowed the succession to that dignity on the son of Ananus, who was also himself called Ananus. Now the report goes, that this elder Ananus proved a most fortunate man; for he had five sons, who had performed the office of a high priest to God, and he had himself enjoyed that dignity a long time formerly, which had never happened to any of our other high priests: but this younger Ananus, who, as we have told you already, took the high priesthood, was a bold man in his temper, and very insolent; he was also of the sect of the Sadducees, who are very rigid in judging offenders, above all the rest of the Jews, as we have already observed; when, therefore, Ananus was of this disposition, he thought he had now a proper opportunity [to exercise his authority].
>
> Festus was now dead, and Albinus was but upon the road; so he assembled the Sanhedrin of judges, and brought before them *the brother of Jesus, who was called Christ, whose name was James,* and some others, [or, some of his companions]; and when he had formed an accusation against them as breakers of the law, he delivered them to be stoned; but as for those who seemed the most equitable of the citizens, and such as were the most uneasy at the breach of the laws, they disliked what was done; they also sent to the king [Agrippa], desiring him to send to Ananus that he should do no more, for that what he had already done was not to be justified; nay, some of them went also to meet Albinus, as he was upon his journey from Alexandria, and informed him that it was not lawful for Ananus to assemble a Sanhedrin without his consent; whereupon Albinus complied with what they said, and wrote in anger to Ananus, and threatened that he would bring him to punishment for what he had done; *on which king Agrippa took the high priesthood from him, when he had ruled but three months, and made Jesus, the son of Damneus, high priest.*[275]

---

[275] Josephus, *The Antiquities of the Jews,* Book 20, chapter 9 (20.197–203), as translated by William Whiston.

Three centuries later, church historian Eusebius would emerge to offer a slightly different version of James' death. He refers to the late first-century church leader Clement "who tells us that he (James) was thrown from the parapet (of the temple) and clubbed to death."[276]

However, Eusebius subsequently quotes from Clement, making clear that James was first thrown down. When James survived the fall from the Sanctuary parapet, he was then stoned.

When a member of a priestly family objected (noting that James was praying for his executioners even while being stoned), one of them:

> …a fuller, took the club which he used to beat out the clothes, and brought it down on the head of the Righteous one. [277]

In effect, James' demise appears to have come from being thrown from the height of a temple parapet, then stoned, then clubbed to death.

As told by Josephus, the execution of James in 62 AD created political havoc for both Jewish and Roman leaders in Palestine. The new high priest (the younger Ananus) had taken advantage of lack of Roman oversight to make a show of force, eliminating this competing religious figure of some repute by the name of James—leader of the Jewish followers of Christ.

The illegal nature of this act was so blatant that other citizens of the city complained vociferously both to the Jewish king (Agrippa) and the new Roman procurator (Albinus). The offense was deemed serious enough that the high priest Ananus was subsequently removed from office (after only a three-month term).

The death of James also set in motion a series of events leading to the Jewish insurrection and subsequent Roman destruction of Jerusalem in 70 AD. Immediately after his arrival, the new Roman procurator Albinus began a campaign to destroy the revolutionary *sicarii,* leading to kidnapping of the scribe of the temple governor and to internal fighting within the priesthood ("throwing stones at each other").[278]

---

[276] Eusebius, *The History of the Church,* 2.23.

[277] Ibid.

[278] Josephus, 20.204–213. The *sicarii* were the urban revolutionaries who would later stage the infamous last stand against the Romans at Masada.

The result was an increasingly disordered city, accompanied by the subsequent removal of the next high priest (Jesus son of Gamaliel). This leads to another transfer of the priesthood by King Agrippa to Matthias "under whom the Jews' war with the Romans took its beginning."[279]

History as cited by Eusebius identifies subsequent military actions of Roman General and future emperor Vespasian to quell the widening Jewish rebellion in Galilee and ultimately Jerusalem. Eusebius also quotes statements that crushing of the Jewish revolt served to avenge this unlawful execution of James.[280]

Had James lived, the story of Christianity might well have been different. The Christian movement would have been more clearly identified with Judaism (or at least with one portion of the 1st century Jewish leadership).

More emphasis would have been placed on good works (rather than faith alone) as integral to entering the kingdom of heaven, and we might have been left with a clearer heritage of a community and social (rather than primarily personal) gospel.

However, the way of James would not prevail. James died at the hands of in-town rivals, and the City of Jerusalem was leveled thereafter—leaving little legacy (including written material) as a counterpoint to the Pauline versions expressed in his letters regarding Christ and the Christian message. It is back to the letter of James—and his view of the substantive dispute with Paul—that we now turn.

James' New Testament Letter

Scholars of all persuasions generally assign a relatively early date to James' epistle. The letter typically is viewed as having been written pre-70 AD, possibly as early as the fifties. As noted in the last chapter, it is unclear whether James epistle was written before or after Paul's letter to the Galatians.

What arguably seems to be the case is that one party is directly responding to the other. What's not so clear is who's on first.

---

[279] Josephus, 20.223.
[280] Eusebius, 2.23. A similar statement is made by Origen (*Contra Celsum* 1.47). There is also reference to a similar statement attributed to Josephus, the authenticity of which is disputed.

Authorship and Audience. In the first verse of this New Testament epistle, the author is self-identified as James. The letter is addressed to the "twelve tribes of the dispersion," most likely meaning the Jewish people living outside of Palestine.[281] The first-century historian Josephus identifies James as the "brother of Jesus, who was called Christ,[282] indicating widespread religious and secular acknowledgement of their sibling relationship."

Acceptance of James' letter was not as readily accomplished as for other New Testament writings. Some early Christian patriarchs, notably the theologian Origen in the 3rd century, expressed doubt as to the authenticity of James' epistle. Eastern writers also voiced concern about the canonicity of the epistles ascribed to James (as well as Peter, John and Jude). And among the Latins of the western church, James (and 2 Peter) were relatively unknown and/or were rejected.[283]

The noted 4th century church historian Eusebius certainly expressed his doubts. After describing the manner of James' death, Eusebius goes on to conclude:

> Such is the story of James, to whom is attributed the first of the 'general' epistles. Admittedly its *authenticity is doubted,* since few early writers refer to it, any more than to 'Jude's,' which is also one of the several called general. But the fact remains that these two, like the others, have been regularly used in very many churches.[284]

A more contemporary source indicates that it "is not clear how James, Jude and 2 Peter were brought into the authoritative collections" leading to a generally accepted church canon.[285] Despite suspicions, the letter of James was accepted as canonical Scripture by the church in Alexandria in the third century AD, by the western church from about the fourth century, and by the Syrian church in the fifth century.

---

[281] James 1:1.
[282] Josephus, *The Antiquities of the Jews,* Book 20, chapter 9 (20.200)
[283] Neither book appears in the Muratorian Canon of the second century AD and both are noted as questionable or dubious both by Origen and Eusebius of Caesarea.
[284] Eusebius, *History of the Church,* 2.23
[285] Robert Grant, *Formation of the New Testament,* 182.

In more recent times, the reformer Martin Luther questioned the authenticity of the epistle attributed to James because it contradicted writings of Paul that Luther found to be of greater importance—notably the Pauline emphasis on salvation via faith.

Salvation Via Works

Among New Testament writers, James is significant due to his insistence that salvation comes primarily via works, not faith. This distinctive perspective of James is really two-fold: (a) undeterred adherence to Torah law; and (b) consequent insistence that Paul's gospel of faith alone is dead (unless accompanied by works).

Adherence to Torah Law. As the acknowledged leader of the Jerusalem church, James reflects a more traditional Jewish approach to upholding Torah law. The writer of Acts records that at the Council of Jerusalem, Paul and Barnabas were brought before the "apostles and the elders" to discuss the conflict Paul had with those who claimed that: "Unless you are circumcised according to the custom of Moses, you cannot by saved…"[286]

At this council, Peter steps forward to speak on Paul's behalf. However, James has the final word, referring to the remarks of Peter and to the prophets, then offering his own conclusion:

> Therefore *I have reached the decision* that we should not trouble those Gentiles who are turning to God (with circumcision), but we should write to them to abstain only from things polluted by idols and from fornication and from whatever has been strangled and from blood. For in every city, for generations past, Moses has had those who proclaim him, for he has been read aloud every Sabbath in the synagogues.[287]

Paul had won the victory, eliminating requirements of Judaism including the rite of circumcision as a pre-condition for Christian fellowship. However,

---

[286] Acts 15:1.

[287] Acts 15:19-21. The apostles and elders, with consent of the whole church, subsequently sent emissaries accompanying Paul and Barnabas with a letter to the believers of Antioch stating the edict of James.

James (at least at this point) retained the ultimate decision authority, including the appeal to Torah law.

Writing to the Galatians (as recounted in the last chapter) Paul gives a somewhat different account of this encounter(s) with the official church leadership. He describes the "acknowledged leaders" (identified as James, Peter and John) as those who "contributed nothing to me."[288] And when Peter travels to Antioch, the apostle Paul states that:

> I opposed him (Peter) to his face because he stood self-condemned; for until certain people *came from James*, he used to eat with the Gentiles. But after they came, he drew back and kept himself separate for fear of the *circumcision faction*.[289]

It is difficult to believe that the writer of Acts and Paul are recalling the same event. In Acts, Paul appears to defer to the judgment of Jerusalem; to the Galatians he evidences clear disdain for the supposed authority of the mother church. The best that can be said for Peter? Well, he equivocates.

The record of Acts is that, while circumcision was removed as a requirement, Paul was asked to have Gentile believers act by specified Jewish customs regarding foods. However, Paul's epistle to the Galatians does not include this injunction but only a separate supposed request of money for the Jerusalem poor.[290]

The account of Acts also indicates that the emissaries from Jerusalem who accompanied Paul to Antioch were Judas called Barsabbas and Silas, not Peter. How Peter gets to Antioch (as a messenger for James?) to be confronted by Paul is not stated in Acts.

Finally, different reasons appear to be given for the split up of Barnabas and Paul that occurs in Antioch. The writer of Acts indicates that Barnabas wanted to take John Mark on the next missionary journey; Paul did not. To the Galatians, Paul does not identify Mark as a factor in parting company with

---

[288] Galatians 2:6..

[289] Galatians 2:11–12. Paul goes on to note that "even Barnabas was led astray by their hypocrisy."

[290] This may date to an earlier request from church elders to Paul (Saul) and Barnabas, recorded in Acts 11:29–30.

Barnabas; rather, he suggests the split occurs because Barnabas sided with the circumcision faction.

Paul and James have one more in-person encounter at the time of Paul's final visit to Jerusalem before being dispatched to Caesarea and then Rome to hear Paul's appeal. The writer of Acts records that:

> When we arrived in Jerusalem, the brothers welcomed us warmly. The next day Paul went with us to visit James, and all the elders were present.[291]

The Jerusalem church elders remain concerned that Gentiles are not being directed "to circumcise their children or observe the customs." They then ask Paul to go through a rite of purification as a sign to Jewish believers in Jerusalem "that you yourself observe and guard the law."[292]

Somewhat surprisingly though maybe out of interest in self-preservation, Paul complies with this request. However, before the seven days of purification rites are fully completed, Paul is seized in the temple area by Jews from Asia who shout:

> Fellow Israelites, help! This is the man who is teaching everyone everywhere against our people, our law, and this place; more than that, he has actually brought Greeks into the temple and has defiled this holy place.[293]

Paul has challenged the law, is arrested in Jerusalem and eventually sent via Caesarea for trial to Rome. Unknown is whether Paul and James have any subsequent contact after this event.

However, it is noteworthy that James' letter to churches of the dispersion includes a discussion about Torah law before diving into the question of faith versus works. Like Jesus and Paul, James boils the law down to the great commandment as previously announced by brother Jesus. In James' words:

---

[291] Acts 21:17–18.

[292] Excerpted from Acts 21:21–24. While not detailed in Acts, the rituals of seven days of purification and eighth day sacrificial atonement are described at Leviticus 14:8–10.

[293] Acts 21:27–28.

You do well if you really fulfill the royal law according to the Scripture, 'You shall love your neighbor as yourself.' But if you show partiality, you commit sin and are convicted by the law as transgressors. For whoever keeps the whole law but fails in one point has become accountable for all of it.[294]

Salvation via Works. Having set the stage, James' epistle quickly makes up for the mildness of presentation on Torah law to follow with a blistering attack on the notion of salvation via faith alone:

What good is it, my brothers and sisters, if you say you have faith but do not have works? *Can faith save you?* If a brother or sister is naked and lacks daily food, and one of you says to them, 'Go in peace; keep warm and eat your fill,' and yet you do not supply their bodily needs, what is the good of that? *So faith by itself, if it has no works, is dead.*[295]

To make sure the message is not lost, James uses four illustrations to make his point:

- To one who is without clothing and food, there is no value in wishing them well; the value is in offering the person in need clothing and food—meeting their material not just spiritual needs.
- Even demons have faith (or believe) in God—to the point of shuddering in fear; yet obviously this faith by itself is of little benefit.
- The act of Abraham offering his son Isaac on the altar as a sacrifice is seen as "faith brought to completion by the works."[296] It was not enough to trust God in the abstract; Abraham had to actually raise the knife.
- To close out the argument, James reaches back to the example of an Old Testament Gentile and prostitute, Rahab, who also acted at some personal risk by hiding Israeli spies and then helping them escape.[297]

---

[294] James 2:8–10.
[295] James 2:14–17.
[296] James 2:22. This differs from Paul's take that Isaac was a child of the promise (or faith), per Galatians 4:28.
[297] Paul offers the example of Hagar (a slave to the law) as contrasted to that of Sarah

He then wraps up these examples by repeating his main message—jamming his point home one more time:

> For just as the body without the spirit is dead, so faith without works is also dead.[298]

Interestingly, both Paul and James have appealed to Old Testament non-Jewish figures of questioned character. Paul refers to Abraham's wife Sarah as an example of faith and freedom, demonstrating the futility of works alone for concubine Hagar as enslaving. James counters with the example of the prostitute Rahab as a demonstration of works primacy over faith alone.

To James, actions speak louder than words. Belief in God alone does not cut it. Performance is of greater import than intent.

James Emphasis on Practical Justice. Like Luke, James sees justice as pivotal to Christian faith. If there is a difference, it is that Luke emphasizes the broad values of social justice. For James, justice is demonstrated at a more personal, practical, everyday level.

Early on in his letter, James describes how action rather than words serves as an example of the primacy of works, not faith alone, as he states:

> But be doers of the word, and not merely hearers who deceive themselves. For if any are hearers of the word and not doers, they are like those who look at themselves in a mirror; for they look at themselves and, on going away, immediately forget what they were like. But those who look into the perfect law, the law of liberty, and persevere, being not hearers who forget but doers who act—they will be blessed in their doing.[299]

For James, there is no better demonstration of good works than in not exercising partiality day-to-day in every phase of life. Examples given are:

(the free woman and Israel's mother), a counter to James example of Rahab (as demonstrating the significant of works). See Galatians 4:21–27 as compared with James 2:25–26.

[298] Ibid.

[299] James 1:22–25.

- Not showing partiality to wealthy in church over the poor or unkempt.
- Taming the tongue—too easily "set on fire by hell," "a restless evil, full of poison."[300]
- Showing that your "works are done with gentleness born of wisdom" rather than "bitter envy and selfish ambition."[301]
- Avoiding friendship with the world by humbling "yourselves before the Lord…"[302]
- Avoiding judging others and boasting about tomorrow.
- Showing patience even in suffering.
- Confessing sins to one another
- And finally, taking the initiative to bringing back a sinner from wandering which "will save the sinner's soul from death and cover a multitude of sins."[303]

Acceptance of James. After a (brief) period of early post-resurrection leadership by Peter, James somehow becomes the acknowledged leader of this early Christian movement. But he loses out in his mission to keep the Christian movement within the folds of Judaism.

James' mission is sabotaged from three distinctly different directions:

- A headstrong convert in Paul who is equally determined to break the bonds of Judaism by transmitting a new, separate Christian faith and way of life to the rest of the non-Jewish Roman empire.
- Leadership of the Jewish religious aristocracy (the high priest and Sadducees) who intentionally undo James by ordering his execution despite the ensuing objection of other Jewish (and Roman) leaders.
- The obliteration of any subsequent opportunity to revive James' approach to Christianity within Judaism—with the door shut less than a decade later by Roman destruction of Jerusalem.

---

[300] Excerpted from James 3:6–8.
[301] James 3:13–14.
[302] James 4:10.
[303] James 5:20.

Following in James' footsteps, the second bishop of the Jerusalem church has been identified as Simon (or Symeon), the son of Clopas (who was reputed to be Jesus' and James' uncle)—and who also reputedly lived to the age of about 120. Control of the Jerusalem church then passed out of Jesus' family to a Jew named Justus.[304]

After Symeon, the legacy of James fared not much better with the post-Jerusalem church up through the time of Roman emperor Constantine. James' epistle (along with Revelation) was one of the last (and most bitterly contested) books to receive acceptance within the New Testament canon. And extending even beyond Constantine, James' orientation to a Christ-centered Judaism would be further dampened by the 7th century rise of Islam and subsequent 11th century schism dividing western from eastern Christendom.

Any vindication that James may have received through *practices* of the medieval Catholic church (which gravitated toward a theology of salvation through works ranging from participation in crusades to indulgences) was brought back into question by Martin Luther.

If James has finally found a more favorable resting place, it is in the social theology of modern reform Catholicism and mainline Protestantism. James may be the true spiritual father, but credit often is attributed elsewhere—most notably to Luke's gospel of social activism.

James in Summary

James' God wants us as friends to draw near to the divine. Those whom he draws near will be the ones who interact with and show compassion to their neighbor—as God has with us. And James represents a perspective on Jesus that:

- Says doing is more important than believing.
- Identifies personal behaviors of social acceptance and equality as the true test for anyone who purports to be a follower of Jesus.

---

[304] For discussion of family relationships between the families of Mary/Joseph, Clopas/Mary, and Zebedee/Salome, see "All in the Family,"
https://www.jesustheheresy.com/#/all-in-the-family/ (accessed February 28 2024).

- Suggests a path for rapprochement to bridge two millennia of mistrust, animosity and betrayal between Jew and Aryan.[305]

James' pioneering role affects both matters of belief and practice but with substance driving style. The substance is the unambiguous declaration that "faith without works is dead." It is this fundamental belief that then drives the resulting practical application of treating all without favoritism.

Over the last two millennia, James has suffered obscurity, indifference and charges of heresy—as brought by sources extending from the apostle Paul to the centuries later arrival of Martin Luther. Despite lesser apparent status, James may yet have the last word.

Supplement — Post-James Church Leadership

History has not been overly kind to James. During Jesus' life, James was spurned by his own brother (or vice versa). However, with Jesus' resurrection, the animosity between the two was resolved and James would go on to lead the Jerusalem church, respected by Jewish Christians as well as others across much of Jewish society.

Subsequent to James' death, positive feelings of comity between Christ's Jewish followers and other Jews evaporated under the pressures of growing political unrest throughout Judea and Galilee. Christians at Jerusalem evacuated to Pella (in Perea) in about 65 AD—just as the Jewish rebellion against Rome was gathering steam. This served to further alienate Jewish Christians from Judaism.

After the destruction of Jerusalem, it appears that at least some Jewish Christians returned to Jerusalem. However, the damage to the Jerusalem church was done. The murder of James is dated c. 62. The destruction of Jerusalem occurred 8 years later in AD 70. As one theologian has summarized:

---

[305] Josephus, *Antiquities of the Jews,* 20.204–220 describes how the untimely execution of James leads not to rapprochement but to "the beginning of greater calamities" and more widespread civil unrest "under whom the Jews' war with the Romans took its beginning."

The work of James perished with him. The Christian hope now lay in the Dispersion.[306]

Following in James' footsteps, the second bishop of the Jerusalem church has been identified as Simon (or Symeon), the son of Clopas (who was reputed to be Jesus' uncle). Hegesippus (who lived c. 120–180) indicates that Symeon suffered martyrdom by crucifixion at the age of 120 when Trajan was emperor (from 98–117 AD). [307]

Symeon's mother was Mary, noted in John's Gospel as the wife of Clopas. Descendants of Jesus' brother Jude also reportedly lived in the same period as Symeon. After Symeon, control of the Jerusalem church then passed to a Jewish leader named Justus—believed by some to have been a son of James the Just.

After Symeon and Justus, what remained of the Jerusalem-based mother church suffered yet more. As described by the Christian writer Hegesippus in the 2nd century AD:

> But when the sacred band of the apostles had in various ways reached the end of their life, and the generation of those privileged to listen with their own ears to the divine wisdom had passed on, then godless error began to take shape, through the deceit of false teachers, who now that none of the apostles was left threw off the mask and attempted to counter the preaching of the truth by preaching the knowledge falsely so-called.[308]

The ongoing legacy of James fared not much better with the post-Jerusalem church up through the time of Constantine. Some early church patriarchs (including Origen) openly questioned the authenticity of his epistle. James (along with Revelation) was one of the last (and most bitterly contested) books to receive acceptance within the New Testament canon. Even as general consensus around a canon emerged in the 4th century, skepticism has continued

---

[306] W.H.C. Frend, *The Early Church,* Fourth Printing, (Philadelphia: Fortress Press, 1987) 34.
[307] Hegesippus, as cited by Eusebius, *History of the Church, 3.32.*
[308] Ibid. Eusebius at 4.5 also notes that after Justus, there were 12 subsequent bishops of Jerusalem up to the time of the time of the second Jewish revolt and destruction of Jerusalem at the hands of emperor Hadrian (in 135 AD).

up into the Protestant reformation. Martin Luther characterized James letter as "a right strawy epistle" and questioned whether a book of such inferior worth even belonged in the New Testament.[309]

However, as late as the fourth century, Eusebius offers this interesting aside as to a continued following and legacy for James the Just, the brother of Jesus the Christ:

> The throne of James—who was the first to receive from the Savior and His apostles the episcopacy of the Jerusalem church, and was called Christ's brother, as the sacred books show—has been preserved to this day. The Christians there, who in their turn look after it with such loving care, make clear to all the veneration in which saintly men high in the favor of God were regarded in time past and are regarded to this day.[310]

---

[309] Luther also questioned the New Testament canonicity of Hebrews, Jude and Revelation.

[310] Eusebius, *History of the Church,* 7.19.

VII. Peter—Compromised Christianity?

Get thee behind me, Satan.
Matthew 16:23, Mark 8:33, Luke 4:8 (KJV)[311]

With Saint Peter, we get a long look at the life and times of a man perpetually in the eye of the storm. Of Jesus' apostles, Peter's story is most engaging—for at least three reasons:

- *More is written* in the New Testament about Peter than any other of Jesus' original 12 disciples. Peter is also reputedly a primary source of information for Mark's gospel and potential author of two canonical epistles plus perhaps a non-canonical gospel as well.
- Both for Jesus and subsequently for Paul and James, Peter is the *whipping boy*—the person constantly caught in the middle between competing desires to do the right thing and simultaneously to please those with whom he associates.
- Most fundamentally, Peter represents the apostle who attempted to stake out *middle ground* between opposing views of what the way of Christianity was really about. Peter's moderate position found few allies. Christendom has faced the consequences of an ongoing struggle for its soul ever since.

Somewhat surprisingly, this is the longest chapter in this book. But maybe this shouldn't be so surprising. Peter is an enigmatic figure, showing up in

---

[311] In Matthew and Mark, Jesus' comment is directed at Peter. In Luke, the statement is made directly to Satan. The NRSV and other modern versions of Luke 4:8 omit the statement "Get thee behind me, Satan" as it is missing from some early NT manuscripts for Luke.

widely varied contexts throughout much of the New Testament. And we can be left time after time with the question: will the real Peter stand up?

So, get prepared! It's time to consider the man front and center who helped shape a community that has energized followers of Jesus the Christ—both then and now. First, we review Peter's changing roles as lead disciple during Jesus' earthly ministry. We then turn to his possible roles as writer and also what might be considered as contributing author.

Peter As Disciple

Most of what we know about Peter comes not from his own hand, but from what others have to say about him. Of Jesus' 12 apostles, Peter receives far more mention from the gospel writers than any other disciple.

From Bethsaida to Capernaum. John's Gospel states that Simon Peter as well as brother Andrew along with Philip were from the fishing town Bethsaida at the northern edge of the Sea of Galilee.[312] While there is scholarly dispute as to the correct location of Bethsaida (or the possibility of more than one historical location), it appears that during Jesus' ministry Bethsaida was under the jurisdiction of Herod Philip rather than Herod Antipas who was concerned that Jesus might be John the Baptist resurrected.[313]

At some point, Simon Peter relocated to Capernaum, the home town of Zebedee and his sons John and James. This also is the town to which Jesus moves at about the time he starts his earthly ministry and beyond. Luke's gospel clearly identifies "James and John, sons of Zebedee, who were partners with Simon" in the region's flourishing fishing industry. [314]

Call to Discipleship. Jesus' call of Peter to become his disciple is described in two contrasting ways by the available gospel accounts. Matthew describes the call to Peter this way:

---

[312] John 1:44.

[313] Matthew 14:1–10. See also Luke 9:7–10 and Matthew 15:21. Jesus apparently withdrew to Bethsaida to avoid being in the jurisdiction of Antipas. This period of avoidance extended to encompass Jesus traveling to Tyre and Sidon, well outside Herodian and Jewish jurisdiction.

[314] Luke 5:10.

As he (Jesus) walked by the Sea of Galilee, he saw two brothers, Simon, who is called Peter, and Andrew his brother, casting a net into the lake—for they were fishermen. And he said to them, 'Follow me, and I will make you fish for people.' Immediately they left their nets and followed him.[315]

In contrast, John's Gospel indicates that Simon Peter was first introduced to Jesus by his brother Andrew who had initially come to hear John the Baptist:

He (Andrew) first found his brother Simon and said to him, 'We have found the Messiah' (which is translated Anointed). He brought Simon to Jesus, who looked at him and said, 'You are Simon son of John. You are to be called Cephas' (which is translated Peter).[316]

Peter as Lead Disciple. Throughout Jesus' earthly ministry and beyond to the early days of the post-resurrection church, Peter comes across as the foremost of Jesus' disciples—albeit a man whose actions often at time seemed to jump ahead of his thoughts. Peter is the disciple who:

- Is initially brave enough to walk on water until frightened by the storm around him.
- First recognizes and calls Jesus "the Messiah, the son of the living God," but then is rebuked by Jesus who tells Peter to "Get behind me, Satan."[317]
- Tries to rebuke his master when Jesus tells the disciples he must go to Jerusalem to be killed.
- Naively suggests building dwellings for Jesus, Moses and Elijah at the time of transfiguration.
- Asks Jesus how many times one must forgive.

---

[315] Matthew 4:18–20. Almost the same account is noted at Mark 1:16–18. Luke 5:1–11 provides a somewhat different account as Jesus guides Peter to make a large catch of fish, so that Peter "left everything and followed him."

[316] John 1:41–42. Some commentators believe that John records the first encounter; the accounts of the three synoptics record a later encounter.

[317] See Matthew 16;13–23, Mark 8:27–33.

- Complains when telling Jesus that he and the disciples have left everything to follow this Messiah and want to know what they will get in return.
- Goes with John at Jesus' command to go and prepare a Passover room.
- Falls asleep at the Garden of Gethsemane (along with other disciples) as Jesus prays just before being arrested.
- At the Passover meal first refuses to have Jesus wash his feet, then changes his mind and askes Jesus to clean "not my feet only but also my hands and also my head."[318]
- Severs the ear of one of Jesus captors at the time of Jesus' arrest.
- Coming to the house of the high priest, had to be admitted into the courtyard by John who was "known to the high priest."[319]
- Promises never to desert Jesus but then the same evening denies him three times.
- "Wept bitterly" after the cock crowed, realizing his broken promise never to deny his master.[320]
- Swims to shore to meet the resurrected Jesus and is interrogated three times as a test of his love and devotion to "feed my sheep."[321]
- Is then told by Jesus that when "you grow old, you will stretch out your hands, and someone else will fasten a belt around you and take you where you do not wish to go,"[322] a foretelling of Peter's future death (perhaps even crucified upside down).

Peter as Early Christian Spokesman. From the perspective of Luke as probable author, the NT book titled *Acts of the Apostles* is all about the transition of early church leadership from Peter to James to Paul. Peter figures prominently in 11 of the first 15 chapters of Acts, but is not mentioned even once from chapter 16 forward to the conclusion of Acts at chapter 28.

We pick up the account of Peter's continuing leadership role at the beginning of the post-Jesus church, immediately after the ascension of Jesus:

---

[318] John 13:9.
[319] John 18:16.
[320] Matthew 26:75.
[321] John 21:15–17.
[322] John 21:18.

Then they returned to Jerusalem from the mount called Olivet, which is near Jerusalem, a Sabbath day's journey away. When they had entered the city, they went to the room upstairs where they were staying, *Peter,* and John, and James, and Andrew, Philip and Thomas, Bartholomew and Matthew, James son of Alphaeus, and Simon the Zealot, and Judas son of James. All these were constantly devoting themselves to prayer, together with certain women, including Mary the mother of Jesus, as well as his brothers.[323]

As in many similar gospel accounts, Peter is mentioned first in a listing of the disciples. However, note a significant development in the post-resurrection re-emergence of Jesus' brothers. During his earthly ministry, Jesus and his blood kinsmen were often at odds. Now, the family including Jesus' brother James re-enters the scene as key players in early church formation.

Pentecost. Fifty days after the Passover, the event now known as the day of Pentecost arrives. Amid derision and skepticism, Peter launches the post-resurrection Christian movement by speaking to a crowd largely composed of Jews gathered from dispersed lands of the Mediterranean at Jerusalem.

Peter starts from a position of strength—like a rock. He boldly addresses the crowd on behalf of the other 10 apostles, as "Men of Judea..." He immediately refutes the cynical suspicion that the apostles might be drunk, then goes right to the three key themes of his message:

- A hearkening back to a prophecy of the Hebrew Scriptures in which men and women in the last days are to be filled with the Spirit of God.
- A proclamation that anyone who "calls upon the name of the Lord shall be saved."[324]
- Confirmation that this Jesus of Nazareth whom "you crucified and killed" is the long-awaited Messiah and has conquered death by his resurrection.[325]

---

[323] Acts 1:12–14.
[324] Acts 2:21 quoting Joel 2:32.
[325] Acts 2:23.

The writer of Acts records that, upon hearing this message, many in the crowd "were cut to the heart."[326] So, Peter preaches repentance, baptism and the forgiveness of sin. Peter does not stop here, but goes on "with many other arguments." Acts records that the number of Jesus' followers increased by about three thousand persons that same day.

Early fame is rewarded by growing persecution. Peter and John are eventually arrested by the authorities—primarily at the instigation of the Sadducees who are annoyed over any suggestion that "in Jesus there is the resurrection of the dead." The Sadducees recognize the "boldness" of Peter and John, despite the fact that "they were uneducated and ordinary men." After a private consultation, the two are warned not to proselytize any further.[327]

Peter and John answer:

> Whether it is right in God's sight to listen to you rather than to God, you must judge; for we cannot keep from speaking about what we have seen and heard.[328]

This is vintage Peter, repentant from the prior denial—to deny his master no more.

The Incident of Ananias and Sapphira. The bizarre and sobering tale of the *partially generous* couple Ananias and Sapphira features Peter as judge and perhaps also as jury and executioner. The couple have sold property with the proceeds to be given to the early church. But they hold some of the money back and lie about it. It is Peter who accuses Ananias of lying—with Ananias then falling down dead.

Does Peter's role extend further? Is the author of Acts cloaking a human act of judgment and execution within a robe of divine justice? Did Peter go too far?

The author of Acts never says that the deaths were the result of direct divine intervention. Ananias dies after hearing Peter accuse him of lying to God; he simply collapses. Whether this was an act of God or a heart attack brought on by acute anxiety, who knows? Peter has no clearly indicated role in this first death.

---

[326] Excerpts from Acts 2:37, 40.
[327] Excerpts are from Acts 4:2,13, 18.
[328] Acts 4:19–20.

The situation with Sapphira feels different. After hearing her story, Peter essentially tells her she is about to die. At Peter's bequest, the "young men" arrive to carry her out. Whether Peter's role is merely predictive or more overtly prescriptive, again who knows? As the reputed author of Acts, Luke does not directly say. But by not making a definitive statement, the door is left open to interpret Peter as having taken a decidedly more active hand in this second death.

Indeed, Acts reports that "great fear *seized* the whole church" as a result of the incident with this couple.[329] After all, this was the same Peter who John's Gospel describes as cutting off the ear of the high priest's slave—at the time of Jesus' arrest prior to crucifixion.

There is another indication that at least some within the church of the first few centuries harbored suspicions of Peter as having taken a more active hand in the deaths of one or both of these two donors to the first-century church. Interestingly, the story is indicated in the form of a denial or rebuttal to the discussion of Petrine homicide from the fourth century Christian bishop John Chrysostom of Constantinople.

Speaking of Paul's harsh criticism of the Galatians, Chrysostom mentions the Ananias/Sapphira incident with Peter in passing. Chrysostom comments:

"If on this account Paul is to be called a 'reviler,' *Peter may likewise, on account of Ananias and Sapphira, be called a homicide.*"[330]

What is interesting is not Chrysostom's denial of Peter's possible role in a murder, but the fact that he feels compelled to defend the actions of both Paul and Peter. Is it possible that there were concerns among the early Christians of the first four centuries that Peter acted rashly in this matter? We do not know for sure. However, Chrysostom's vehemence appears to have been sparked by issues he wanted to settle once and for all.

Whether the event involving Ananias and Sapphira was interpreted as an overzealous imposition of church discipline leading to the later ascent of James

---

[329] The statement "great fear seized" all who heard occurs twice in the account at Acts 5:5 after the death of Ananias and then again at Acts 5:11 after the death of Sapphira.

[330] John. Chrysostom, *Commentary on the Epistle to the Galatians, Chapter 3, Verse 1,* CCEL website, https://www.ccel.org/ccel/schaff/npnf113.iii.iii.iii.html (accessed February 5, 2024). See the supplement to this chapter for added detail.

is a matter of conjecture. But what is clear is that this event signals *the peak* of Peter's leadership role for followers of the Way.

Leadership Diversification. Following the incident of Ananias and Sapphira, Peter is again arrested together with other apostles by the high priest and Sadducees but with Peter and the apostles declaring "We must obey God rather than any human authority." Due to continued fear of a crowd and sage advice from the esteemed Pharisee Gamaliel, the authorities decide to flog and then release them, essentially as partial mitigation "in the case you may even be found fighting against God!"[331]

After this second arrest and release, the action in Acts begins to shift to a more diverse collection of participants involved in continued spread of the Christian gospel. Due to concern about widows being neglected, seven men are appointed in service (or deacon) roles, reducing the burden on the 12 disciples. As one of these new helpers, a deacon named Stephen is arrested, addresses and accuses the Jewish ruling council, and is subsequently stoned to death.

A young man named Saul makes his first appearance in Acts, coming on the scene at the stoning of Stephen. Saul is the man at whose feet the coats of the witnesses to the stoning are laid. Saul then begins a broader persecution of the church throughout Judea and Samaria. He is described as "ravaging the church," arresting and imprisoning both men and women.[332]

During this time, it is not entirely clear whether Peter, while still a disciple of some repute, remains in charge. The text indicates that Peter and John are "sent" by others at Jerusalem to Samaria.[333] It is increasingly clear that others (such as Philip) also are now stepping forward to help lead the process of church evangelization and discipling.

Philip preaches in Samaria (aided by Peter and John), then is involved in the conversion of the Ethiopian eunuch.

Meanwhile, Saul is blinded and experiences a dramatic conversion on the road to Damascus. Saul eventually tries to join the core group of disciples at Jerusalem but is instead spirited off to Tarsus.

---

[331] Excerpts from Acts 5:29, 39.
[332] Acts 8:3.
[333] Acts 8:14.

Peter reappears on the scene. What follows are two events that set the stage for the decision to take the Christian message beyond a primarily Jewish audience—via Peter as initial but not ultimate messenger.

Peter is involved in the resurrection of a deceased disciple, The story of Dorcas (Tabitha) takes place on the Judean coast—in Joppa—indicating the movement of the Christ message westward from Jerusalem and Galilee. Dorcas is described as a disciple—the only woman to be so described anywhere in the New Testament. Peter is reported as raising her from the dead—an event that "became known throughout Joppa, and many believed in the Lord."[334]

Based on a vision, Peter travels to Caesarea also on the coast to meet with a Roman centurion named Cornielius who is converted as a Gentile to Christianity and receives the gift of the Holy Spirit. The Acts narrative never explicitly states how the centurion responded to Peter's message. Rather, the text notes that even before Peter had finished speaking: "…the Holy Spirit fell upon all who heard the word."[335]

Peter returns to Jerusalem to find unhappiness from other circumcised believers—*the first such direct criticism* leveled at Peter as recorded by Acts. Peter responds with an argument that includes a recounting of his call to Caesarea. His narrative appears to appease the skeptics—at least for the time being:

> When they (the critics) heard this, they were silenced. And they praised God, saying, 'Then God has given even to the Gentiles the repentance that leads to life.'[336]

Later events demonstrate that Peter's victory was temporary and incomplete. He may have won this battle over his authority with the rest of the Jewish church, but Peter would go on to lose the war.

---

[334] Acts 9:42.

[335] Acts 10:44.

[336] Acts 11:18. Prior to this, Stephen had referred to the "covenant of circumcision" as initiated by Abraham, per Acts 7:8. And before Peter could finish his dialogue with Cornelius (together with relatives and close friends), "the circumcised believers who had come with Peter were astounded that the gift of the Holy Spirit had been poured out even on the Gentiles." Per Acts 10:45.

Increased Persecution and Shifting Leadership. Barnabas, the older cousin of John Mark, is dispatched to Antioch to proclaim the message of Jesus Christ to Greeks. He then travels to Saul's home town of Tarsus, returning to Antioch where "the disciples were first called 'Christians.'"[337]

Chapter 12 of Acts takes a darker turn. The action returns to Peter, but the stage has been set. A principal actor is about to retire in favor of a new lead:

> About that time King Herod (Agrippa I) laid violent hands upon some who belonged to the church. He had James, the brother of John, killed with the sword. After he saw that it pleased the Jews, he proceeded to arrest Peter also.[338]

Bound with chains and sleeping between two soldiers, Peter is released by an angel of God. He travels along a lane to the house of Mary, mother of John Mark, and after repeated knocking at the gate, Peter is let in to the relief and joy of the assembled believers. When Peter is finally admitted into the house, his first request is: "Tell this (about the release) *to James* and to the believers."[339]

Jesus' brother James has suddenly appeared—virtually from nowhere—but now in some position of apparent authority. The top priority for Peter with his release from prison was to communicate his current status back to James.

Other historians have noted the change in authority given to Peter. For example, the 20th century writer W.H.C. Frend and author of *The Early Church* observes that when:

> …Peter was released from prison; he was, however, no longer leader of the Christian community.[340]

Meanwhile, Herod Antipas is enraged at Peter's release, ordering the guards to be put to death. Herod was also in a dispute with Tyre and Sidon

---

[337] Acts 11:26.
[338] Acts 12:1–2.
[339] Acts 12:17.
[340] W.H.C. Frend, *The Early Church,* Fourth Printing, (Philadelphia: Fortress Press, 1987), 26.

(likely over need for food in the current famine). So Herod addresses the public with the people shouting back:

> 'The voice of a god, and not of a mortal!' And immediately, because he had not given the glory to God, an angel of the Lord struck him down, and he was eaten by worms and died.[341]

Following the death of Herod, Barnabas and Saul are commissioned at Antioch to preach to Jews and Gentiles the Word of God, reaching further into the Hellenistic Roman empire. This gospel would be proclaimed in each place starting with Jewish synagogues.

John Mark had been traveling with Barnabas and Saul (now going by the name Paul). However, Mark returns to Jerusalem early for reasons not explained. After completing what is known as their first missionary journey through what is now southern Turkey, Barnabas and Paul return to Antioch in Syria.

It was at this point that Paul and Barnabas are confronted by "certain individuals" from Judea who were teaching that:

> Unless you are circumcised according to the custom of Moses, you cannot be saved.[342]

Neither the account of Acts nor that of Galatians specifically identifies who these "certain individuals" might be. Paul does narrow the field a bit in his letter to the Galatians by describing his critics as "certain people (who) came from James."[343] However, it is Peter who bears the brunt of Paul's frontal attack as Paul makes clear to the Galatians just one sentence earlier that "when Cephas came to Antioch, I opposed him to his face, because he stood self-condemned."[344]

Peter's Denouement. Paul and Barnabas are appointed by the congregation at Antioch to discuss this continuing issue with the apostles and elders of the mother church in Jerusalem. It is only upon the subsequent return

---

[341] Acts 12:22–23.

[342] Acts 15:1

[343] Galatians 2:12.

[344] Galatians 2:11.

of Saul (now Paul) to Jerusalem to discuss the issue of Gentile circumcision that we again encounter Peter in Luke's Acts of the Apostles one last time. As recorded by Acts 15:

> The apostles and the elders met together to consider this matter. After there had been much debate, Peter stood up and said to them, 'My brothers, you know that in the early days God made a choice among you, that I should be the one through whom the Gentiles would hear the message of the good news and become believers. And God, who knows the human heart, testified to them by giving them the Holy Spirit, just as he did to us; and in cleansing their hearts by faith he has made no distinction between them and us. Now therefore why are you putting God to the test by placing on the neck of the disciples a yoke that neither our ancestors nor we have been able to bear? On the contrary, we believe that we will be saved through the grace of the Lord Jesus, just as they will.'[345]

Following on this conciliatory introduction, Barnabas and Paul proceed to tell of "all the signs and wonders that God had done through them among the Gentiles."[346] It is at this point that James the brother of Jesus steps in to render the decision of the council:

> Therefore, I have reached the decision that we should not trouble those Gentiles who are turning to God, but we should write to them to abstain only from things polluted by idols and from fornication and from whatever has been strangled and from blood.[347]

The Jerusalem apostles and elders together with "consent of the whole church" agree with this determination. This is memorialized in a letter that is to be delivered by Judas (Barsabbas) and Silas to the church in Antioch.

To summarize, at this first Jerusalem council, Peter begins the discussion and somewhat surprisingly advocates accommodation with Paul. Barnabas and Paul then tell of their corroborating experience; however, it is James who has the last word.

---

[345] Acts 15:6–11.
[346] Acts 15:12.
[347] Acts 15:19–20.

With this one event, the author of the Acts of the Apostles seals Peter's fate. Peter defers to Jesus' brother James for the final decision of the Jerusalem church. And from this point forward, Paul and Barnabas take center stage—with no further mention of Peter through the last thirteen chapters of Acts.

Petrine Authorship Roles

Unlike Paul, most of what we know about Peter is not from his own (reputed) hand, but from what others have to say about him. Of the original twelve apostles, Peter has received far more mention in the New Testament than any other.

Peter plays both direct and indirect roles in formation of the New Testament as well as possibly of non-canonical literature in three respects, as:

- Contributing author to the New Testament Gospels—most specifically the Gospel of Mark.
- Possible direct authorship of one or two Petrine letters—1 & 2 Peter.
- Less likely direct role but possible inspiration for non-canonical literature—notably the now extant and fragmentary Gospel of Peter.

Gospel Formation. From some of the earliest extant documentation, Peter is cited as a source of information for the Gospel of Mark. The early second century church patriarch Papias writes about Mark's reliance on recollections of Peter in writing the Markan gospel. However, Papias also notes that:

> Peter used to *adapt his teachings* to the occasion, without making a systematic arrangement of the Lord's sayings, so that Mark was quite justified in writing down some things just as he remembered them.[348]

In short, both Mark as gospel chronicler and Peter as early leader and often spokesman for the chosen 12 disciples seemingly feel free to exercise personal discretion in shaping the narrative of Mark. Peter acted on the fly, a characteristic noted throughout the New Testament (prompting rebukes from Jesus later from Paul)—likely contributing to his loss of leadership status in the early church.

---

[348] Papias, as quoted by Eusebius, *The History of the Church,* 3.39.

This teaming arrangement of John Mark and Simon Peter to write a gospel represents a bit of doubling down on *fast and loose* recollection—with Peter as narrator and Mark as chronicler. If Mark is the first of the Gospels to be written—the current generally accepted scholarly viewpoint—then this teaming could serve to also affect composition of the other two synoptic Gospels. However, Matthew and/or Luke could have pushed back, for example, with Luke saying right up-front his goal to write an "...orderly account...so that you may know the truth concerning the things about which you have been instructed."[349]

If the Gospel of Matthew was written first—as suggested by Papias and other church patriarchs—or if Luke was written ahead of Matthew (but based on a yet to be found proto-Matthew) suggested as a minority view of scholars, then any damage generated by a fast, loose and cryptic Markan/Petrine gospel might be more circumscribed (or at least fenced in) by the more independent perspectives offered by the other Gospels. In effect, the question of possible Markan priority and sequential links to either or both of the other two synoptic Gospels is an area of scholarship that has been largely overlooked in recent decades but could benefit from manuscript formation reconsideration.

Petrine Epistles. While much of what we know about Peter is from what others have written about him, we also have a body of writing attributed to the man himself. This includes two documents from the New Testament canon— 1 & 2 Peter. However, while Peter's name is on two New Testament epistles. authorship is disputed, especially with 2 Peter. And these epistles are not nearly as well-known as either the New Testament Gospels or the writings of Paul.[350]

Some commentators suggest that 1 Peter was written in the period between about 70 and 90 AD and that 2 Peter was penned between 80–90. In part, this dating reflects waning of the expectation that the first generation of Christians would experience a second coming of their Messiah during their lifetimes.

An alternative, typically more fundamentalist, viewpoint is that 1 Peter was written by 68–69 just before the Roman destruction of Jerusalem. 2 Peter is attributed to the period 65–68. Peter himself is believed to have been executed at Rome c. 64 AD during the reign of Nero.

---

[349] Excerpted from Luke 1:1–4.

[350] Several so-called Catholic epistles are not mentioned by the Muratorian Canon of the 3rd century—James, 1 & 2 Peter, and 2/3 John. Canonicity of 2 Peter also would be questioned by Origen and Eusebius of the 3rd/4th centuries.

Whether Peter wrote one or two New Testament epistles has been disputed since the days of the early church. The strongest case for Peter's authorship is simply that each epistle makes this claim at the outset. Consider 1 Peter's opening salutation:

Peter, an apostle of Jesus Christ.[351]

The second epistle is addressed in similar fashion:

Simeon Peter, a servant and apostle of Jesus Christ.[352]

This second epistle also refers to 1 Peter, with its author stating:

This is now, beloved, the *second letter* I am writing to you…[353]

Countervailing arguments are that: (a) the Greek of 2 Peter is too well written to be that of a Jewish fisherman;[354] (b) the epistles were written after the apostle died (prior to AD 70); (c) early Christian writings may routinely have been ascribed by actual authors to an earlier disciple; and (d) other early church patriarchs questioned the authenticity of these writings. Like 1 Peter, 2 Peter is also viewed by some scholars as a "testament" to a great figure of the past—intended as a sort of last will and testament of a great Christian martyr.

Scholars of all stripes acknowledge that 2 Peter was not as widely recognized as authoritative by the early church.[355] The first statement ascribing possible Petrine authorship of this second epistle is by Origen (185–253), but

---

[351] 1 Peter 1:1–2.

[352] 2 Peter 1:1–2. Other translations including KJV say "Simon Peter."

[353] 2 Peter 3:1.

[354] This argument deserves further research as it appears increasingly likely that resettlement of the Galilee by the Hasmoneans may have involved relocation of better educated and education focused observant Jews from Judea than previously supposed, also if there was special focus in religiously focused communities on religious teaching.

[355] Per Robert Grant, *Formation of the New Testament,* 160: "There is no definite proof that anyone outside Egypt regarded James and 2 Peter as canonical, although their later acceptance suggests that some churches did so regard them."

Origen appears to have some doubts.[356] As late as the fourth century, Eusebius placed it among the accepted books, indicating that most accept this writing as from Peter.[357]

So, now we turn briefly to the substance of these two ostensibly Petrine letters.

1 Peter. The first epistle of Peter is introduced in this fashion:

Peter, an apostle of Jesus Christ, To the exiles of the Dispersion in Pontus, Galatia, Cappadocia, Asia, and Bithynia, who have been chosen and destined by God the Father and sanctified by the Spirit to be obedient to Jesus Christ and to be sprinkled with his blood: May grace and peace be yours in abundance.[358]

The epistle begins with the author introducing himself as "Peter, an apostle of Jesus Christ." As noted, there is no ready scholarly consensus as to whether Peter really authored this book. Those favoring Petrine authorship cite growing attestation to Peter's writings by church patriarchs of the first to third centuries.[359]

Perhaps the most significant teaching of 1 Peter is the message of conforming to authority—whether earthly or heavenly. To Peter, this submittal may occur in ways that seem quaintly antiquated and overly submissive by modern standards.

In one of the most well-known (and currently controversial) excerpts from this letter, Peter suggests that the hierarchy of the social and governmental order is not to be altered by the message of Jesus Christ. Rather, Peter suggests that:

---

[356] Origen suggested that 2 Peter was among writings that "lacked early and continuous attestation, were probably not written by apostles or their disciples, and perhaps were not easily reconcilable with accepted writings." Per Robert Grant, 172.

[357] However, the 4th century church historian Eusebius expressed personal doubts as to the authenticity of 2 Peter.

[358] I Peter 1:1–2.

[359] Early church leaders noted as referring to 1 Peter begin with I Clement (c. AD 95) and include Polycarp, the author of the Gospel of Truth, Irenaeus, Tertullian, Clement of Alexandria and Origen. By the fourth century, church historian Eusebius could write that this epistle was universally accepted.

For the Lord's sake, *accept the authority of every human institution,* whether of the emperor as supreme, or of governors, as sent by him to punish those who do wrong and to praise those who do right. For it is *God's will* that by doing right you should silence the ignorance of the foolish. As servants of God, live as free people, yet do not use your freedom as a pretext for evil. Honor everyone. Love the family of believers. Fear God. Honor the emperor.[360]

In this single passage, Peter distills the concept of submission into an even more precise formula for adherence to secular authority than anything espoused by Paul.[361] In the space of a few short paragraphs, Peter goes on to preach submission of all citizens to the emperor, slaves to masters, wives to husbands, and the young to elders.

These words do not rest well with hearers of the third millennium. Like Paul, they place Peter in the role of protecting the authority of the existing power structure—first century and beyond.

But this is more than just a defense of the status quo. Peter makes it clear that submission is warranted even when it is to authorities *who are in the wrong.* There is a payoff for submittal, though it is neither necessarily tangible nor immediate. In Peter's view:

…it is better to suffer for doing good, if suffering should be God's will, than to suffer for doing evil.[362]

And for Peter, the premise of submittal goes back to a view of the Christian's role as an alien in a strange world:

Beloved, I urge you *as aliens and exiles* to abstain from the desires of the flesh that wage war against the soul. Conduct yourselves honorably, so

---

[360] The full passage is found at I Peter 2:13–17.

[361] Paul expounds on the question of submission to governing authorities in Romans 13:1–7, and on the relationships of slaves to masters and wives to husbands at Colossians 3:18–4:1.

[362] 1 Peter 3:17.

that, though they malign you as evildoers, they may see your honorable deeds and glorify God when he comes to judge.[363]

Peter also includes a curious passage which has long engendered controversy as to its meaning. Peter writes:

> For Christ also suffered for sins once for all, the righteous for the unrighteous, in order to bring you to God. He was put to death in the flesh, but made alive in the spirit, in which also he went and made a proclamation to the spirits in prison, who in former times did not obey, when God waited patiently in the days of Noah, during the building of the ark, in which a few, that is, eight people, were saved through water.[364]

From the text, this event appears to have occurred between the time of Jesus death by crucifixion and his resurrection three days later. The question is whether Jesus was offering dead sinners a second chance toward salvation or whether his preaching was solely for the purpose of confirming their continuing condemnation.

2 Peter. While canonicity of this work has been extensively debated starting with the early church, the message of 2 Peter can be viewed as continuing the Petrine tradition, albeit with a different theme than that of the first epistle.

Here the main message is one of rejecting the liberalization of Christianity—removing the movement from its earliest moral foundations. 2 Peter also picks up on and further develops a theme begun in 1 Peter—the eschatology for the second coming of Jesus Christ.

At the conclusion of the epistle, Peter even reaches out to his sometimes nemesis, the self-proclaimed apostle Paul. Peter offers words of conciliation despite some obvious remaining tension:

> So also our beloved brother Paul wrote to you according to the *wisdom given him,* speaking of this as he does in all his letters. There are some things in *them hard to understand,* which the ignorant and unstable twist to their own destruction, as they do the other Scriptures. You therefore,

---

[363] 1 Peter 2:11–12.
[364] 1 Peter 3:18–20.

beloved, since you are forewarned, beware that you are not carried away with the error of the lawless and lose your own stability.[365]

Peter describes Paul's writings as containing "wisdom," with the status of Scripture. However, he can't resist a bit of a dig, noting that some of Paul's writing can be critiqued as "hard to understand."

As in his first epistle, Peter clearly preaches a message of judgment. As with the first epistle, again it is not entirely clear in 2 Peter whether the author believes that some will perish eternally or whether salvation is eventually and potentially in store even for the godless.

On the one hand, Peter clearly indicates that "destruction of the godless" occurs as a result of judgment. On the other hand, Peter's Lord again is a God of mercy, one who "is patient with you, not wanting any to perish, but all to come to repentance."[366]

Non-Canonical Gospel of Peter. We can also now move beyond the New Testament canon to a fragmentary gospel narrative discovered by French archaeologists in an Upper Egyptian monk's grave in 1886. The fragments available contain portions of a passion story, an epiphany, the account of an empty tomb and the beginnings of what appears to be a resurrection story.

Though fragmentary, this reputed gospel takes us places no other purported gospel account goes—except Mark. For example, both Mark and Peter appear to end with women leaving the tomb after the resurrection of Jesus in fear (despite the angelic assurance). End of story.

The most fascinating new information provided by this Petrine non-canonical manuscript is of an apparent split in the Jewish leadership over the wisdom of having crucified Jesus. This split in Jewish leadership over how to handle Christianity occurs at least one more time—a generation later—with the death of Jesus' brother, James (as recorded by Josephus).

If reliable, this non-canonical account also reinforces the notion of a strong effort to reconcile Judaism and Christianity—both pre- and post-Easter—a message carried by the widely respected James until his untimely death. And a message subsequently obliterated with the Roman destruction of Jerusalem at 70 AD.

---

[365] 2 Peter 3:15–17.
[366] Excerpted from 2 Peter 3:7–9.

Also noted is that this non-canonical and fragmentary Gospel of Peter also claims Petrine authorship, though at the end rather than the beginning of the currently recovered fragment, as follows:

> But I, Simon Peter, and Andrew, my brother, took our fishing nets and went away to the sea. And with us was Levi, the son of Alphaeus, whom the Lord…[367]

Not surprisingly, authorship of the more recently discovered non-canonical Gospel of Peter is also disputed. A determination of authorship is, of course, problematic since the earliest extant text is only fragmentary and dates to only the 8th or 9th century.

However, the 1972 discovery of a separate manuscript known as Oxyrhynchus Papyrus 2949 introduced two added tiny fragments, one of which yields a yet different twist on the request by Joseph of Arimathea to Pontius Pilate for the body of Jesus. Unlike the canonical Gospels, the Petrine gospel also presents a different order of events that, interestingly, is consistent with the papyrus fragments.

Both fragments suggest that Joseph of Arimathea requested burial rights for Jesus from Pilate *before rather than after* his execution. In this non-canonical Gospel of Peter, Joseph also is presented as "a friend of Pilate and the Lord."[368]

Whether or not Peter actually wrote one or more of these canonical and non-canonical works is undoubtedly a subject for ongoing research and debate. But even if authorship by Peter cannot be clearly established, the two canonical epistles coupled with this non-canonical text can be viewed as expressing what has long been understood to represent a Petrine viewpoint.

Compromised Christianity

Peter is a simple man who lived amid complex and continually changing circumstances. So, it is no simple matter to cut to the core of his legacy on behalf of the Christian movement. Rather, there is a progression in Peter's changing apostolic role that is worth watching as it unfolds.

---

[367] Gospel of Peter 14:3. The remainder of the manuscript has not been recovered.
[368] Gospel of Peter 2:1.

Peter as Foil for Jesus. A close reading of the four Gospels clearly indicates that Peter is an important role player—best supporting actor to the lead played by Jesus.

This is no match of equals. Rather, Peter repeatedly serves as a bumbling contrast to the message and actions of Jesus as protagonist. In a nutshell, the foibles of Peter serve to put Peter in his place time and again, as described by all of the four gospel writers.

Mark on Peter. There is no better place to view Peter as the straight man or fall guy for the antics of Jesus than from the vantage point of Mark's gospel. This reflects Peter's growing humility with advancing age as he recounts the narrative of Jesus' ministry combined with Mark's love of the quick quip.

For Jesus, the opportunity to use Peter as a foil is demonstrated perhaps most clearly as the master begins to teach "quite openly" of the coming rejection and suffering he would endure as the Son of Man. Both Matthew and Mark write that Peter takes Jesus aside and begin to rebuke him. Jesus responds abruptly:

> ...turning and looking at his disciples, he rebuked Peter and said, 'Get behind me, Satan! For you are setting your mind not on divine things but on human things.'[369]

A second example of Peter getting caught with *foot in mouth* occurs shortly thereafter with an incident involving Peter together with the two other most intimate of Jesus' disciples.

> Six days later, Jesus took with him Peter and James and John, and led them up a high mountain apart, by themselves. And he was transfigured before them, and his clothes became dazzling white, such as no one on earth could bleach them. And there appeared to them Elijah with Moses, who were talking with Jesus. Then Peter said to Jesus, "Rabbi, it is good for us to be here; let us make three dwellings, one for you, one for Moses, and one for Elijah." *He did not know what to say,* for they were terrified. Then a cloud overshadowed them, and from the cloud there came a voice, "This is my

---

[369] Mark 8:33.

Son, the Beloved; listen to him!" Suddenly when they looked around, they saw no one with them anymore, but only Jesus.[370]

Here, Peter is like the person at a party trying to break the ice with conversation, but with no ability to control what comes out of his mouth. At this event of the transfiguration, Peter's opener is embarrassing, but provides the opportunity for a heavenly response. The real meaning of the occasion—authentication of this Son of Man as deserving of divine attention—is clearly signified.

And so it goes. Mark's gospel tends to portray Peter in the harshest light. But while the touch is lighter in the other three Gospels, Peter's role is much the same—whether it is Peter announcing his grandiose plan for Jesus, Elijah and Moses at the transfiguration or denying his leader when Jesus is arrested and brought to the residence of the high priest.

Matthew on Peter. Mark's gospel includes virtually no parables. In contrast, both Matthew and Luke make extensive use of parables. And in these parables, Peter's inquisitiveness often elicits a sharp response. For example, at the conclusion of one parable, it is Peter who asks, "Explain this parable to us."[16] Jesus' curt rejoinder as recorded by Matthew: "Are you *also* still without understanding?"[371]

Luke on Peter. Most of what Luke has to say about Peter has already been said by Matthew and/or Mark. However, there are some noteworthy exceptions. Part of a story common to all three synoptics but with Petrine involvement unique to Luke's gospel account is that of the woman suffering 12 years of hemorrhages, who touches the fringe of Jesus' garment. Jesus senses the touch and asks: 'Who touched me?'

No one around Jesus confesses to the touching but instead in Luke's version Peter jumps in as if to rebuke Jesus: "Master, the crowds surround you and press in on you." But Jesus said, "Someone touched me; for I noticed that power had gone out from me." At this, the woman confesses; and Luke's Jesus responds kindly: "Daughter, your faith has made you well; go in peace."[372]

---

[370] As recorded Mark 9:2–8. Luke 9:28–36 also records this event similarly noting that Peter "was not knowing what he said." Matthew 17:1–7 also records the event but omits the reference to Peter not knowing what to say.

[371] Matthew 15:11–16.

[372] Excerpted from Luke 8:43–48.

Among the synoptics, Luke's gospel is also unique in that Peter plays a prominent post-resurrection role (consistent with the introduction to the Acts of the Apostles). As in Matthew and Mark, the women are first on the scene:

> Now it was Mary Magdalene, Joanna, Mary the mother of James, and the other women with them who told this to the apostles. ¹¹ But these words seemed to them an idle tale, and they did not believe them. But *Peter got up and ran* to the tomb; stooping and looking in, he saw the linen cloths by themselves; then he went home, amazed at what had happened.[373]

Once more, Luke gives Peter a better treatment. Alone among the male disciples, Peter is the only one (as recorded by Luke) to view an empty tomb and *go home* knowing something remarkable has happened.

John on Peter. If anyone should be able to offer insights into the character of Peter, it would be John the apostle. Like Peter and James, John was part of the apostolic inner circle—purportedly having the closest relationship with Jesus. Peter and John also are fellow fishermen; both hail from Capernaum.

In fact, the gospel attributed to John offers a unique perspective on Peter (as it does with many other aspects of Jesus' earthly ministry). Like the synoptics, John's Peter is brash and inquisitive. John adds another element—a Peter who though close to Jesus is not as close as another of the disciples, notably John himself.

In his accounting of the Passover supper, John's Gospel differs from the synoptics in a couple of noteworthy ways. Most readily apparent is the foot washing routine, recorded only by John.

When Jesus gets to Peter, Peter refuses to let Jesus perform this servant's function. But once he understands Jesus' admonition that "Unless I wash you, you have no share with me." Peter immediately shifts gears from forward to reverse.[374] He is now ready to go all the way, asking Jesus to bathe not only his feet but hands and head as well.

Second, John's account of the last supper also introduces the disciple "whom Jesus loved" sitting (or reclining) next to Jesus. Rather than being able to ask Jesus himself who the betrayer is (as it was noisy at the table), Peter motions this other disciple (ostensibly John) who then is the one to ask Jesus who the traitor might be. No one else (other than John) must have heard the

---

[373] Luke 24:10–12.

question, because no one else seemed to understand the significance of Jesus dipping bread with Judas.

Later on in this Passover evening, after Jesus and disciples had traveled down the Kidron Valley to the Garden of Gethsemane, an added event recorded only by John comes at the time of Jesus' arrest:

> Then *Simon Peter, who had a sword*, drew it, struck the high priest's slave, and cut off his right ear. The slave's name was Malchus. ¹¹ Jesus said to Peter, "Put your sword back into its sheath. Am I not to drink the cup that the Father has given me?"[374]

This is the only action recorded in the Gospels wherein a follower of Jesus resorts to physical violence. And John is the only one of the gospel writers to also record that the sword-wielder is none other than Peter.

This little Johannine tidbit is followed by another apparently first-hand Petrine account—that of Peter's denial of Jesus—offering details provided only by John. In John's account, another disciple (besides Peter) goes into the courtyard of the high priest (presumably John himself). As John's Gospel attests, this disciple actually was known to the high priest and was the one who was able to gain admittance for Peter.

John records that Peter and others were standing around a charcoal fire started by slaves and police in the courtyard at a time of late winter/early spring to warm themselves. It was around this warming fire that Peter three times in succession denied being a disciple of Jesus.

John's account also is noteworthy in that the last questioner of Peter is a "one of the slaves of the high priest, a relative of the man whose ear Peter had cut off." [375] Another reason for Peter to be intimidated.

The final event recounted only in John's Gospel also features Peter prominently, but Peter is once again upstaged by the disciple "whom Jesus loved." The resurrected Jesus has appeared to his disciples at the Sea of Galilee, where Jesus is fixing breakfast. In response to Peter's thrice repeated denial in Jerusalem, Jesus asks three times of Peter: "Do you love me?" Jesus' resulting and repeated admonition is: "Feed my sheep."[376]

---

[374] John 18:10–11.
[375] John 18:26.
[376] As recounted by John 21:15–18.

Then Peter is subject to one last stark warning by the master—in response to what may have been a final impertinent question from Peter (as John closes out his gospel):

> Peter turned and saw the disciple whom Jesus loved following them; he was the one who had reclined next to Jesus at the supper and had said, "Lord, who is it that is going to betray you?" When Peter saw him, he said to Jesus, *"Lord, what about him?"* Jesus said to him, "If it is my will that he remain until I come, what is that to you? Follow me!" So the rumor spread in the community that this disciple (i.e., John) would not die. Yet Jesus did not say to him that he would not die, but, "If it is my will that he remain until I come, what is that to you?"[377]

Post-Resurrection Church on Peter. Experiences of the post-Easter and post-resurrection Peter are recorded primarily by the Acts of the Apostles. From the vantage point of its author, Acts is all about the transition of early church leadership from Peter to James to Paul. Starting with a mission aimed toward a largely Jewish church in Palestine, the emphasis shifts decisively to non-Jewish converts located throughout the reaches of the Roman empire—most evidently so after the Council of Jerusalem.

The NT book of Acts comprises 28 chapters. Peter figures prominently in 11 of the first 15 chapters, but is not mentioned once from chapter 16 forward. Jesus' stepbrother James transitions from being a skeptic of his brother in the Gospels to a follower post-resurrection and would emerge as pre-eminent even to Peter in authority over the nascent church.

Peter becomes a central figure in the incident involving prevarication and subsequent death of Ananias and Sapphira. The incident with donor couple also appears to represent the peak of Peter's authority and responsibility with the Jerusalem church. What follows is greater diversification of church authority—evidenced by the conversions and emerging roles of Stephen, Philip, Barnabas, and Saul (renamed Paul).

James and Paul on Peter. After being released from his second imprisonment, Peter's #1 priority was to communicate his release to James who has suddenly appeared as primary leader of the church. Peter takes on the

---

[377] John 21:20–23.

role of emissary, leaving Jerusalem to encounter and reach accommodation with prospective Gentile converts.

The Council of Jerusalem is set to settle the matter of what Jewish-driven customs should be imposed on Gentile believers. The effective result is that Paul and Barnabas would be free to lead the mission(s) to the Jewish diaspora and Gentile world of the Mediterranean—although it is not clear as to whether Paul actually implemented the conditions agreed to at Jerusalem.

Throughout this transition, we can gain little added information on James' relationship with Peter—including whether and how their respective roles and responsibilities might have been determined. The author of Acts appears content to gloss over the details of why and how this transition occurred.

As Peter lost out to James as leading the mother church, he also suffered harsh criticism from Paul with regard to authority for conversion of Gentiles throughout the Roman empire. Paul feels no compunction about taking on Peter head-to-head, as most clearly evidenced by his letter to the Galatians:

> *But when Cephas (Peter) came to Antioch, I opposed him to his face, because he stood self-condemned...*[378]

Peter had previously endured criticism from members of the Jerusalem church for catering to non-Jews. Now Paul criticizes him for apparently reverting back to the company of those who espoused the Jewish rite of circumcision. Peter must think: I can't win.

Meanwhile, James solidifies his hold as leader of the Jerusalem mothership—becoming a subject of increasing respect among God-fearing Jews and a political figure of importance to Rome. His death at the hands of a portion of the Sanhedrin becomes a spark that ultimately leads to the Jewish rebellion against Rome starting in the Galilee, followed by destruction of Jerusalem and the temple in 70 AD.

For Peter, the remarkable thing is that he took his loss of position and authority to both James and Paul with grace and humility. A remarkable achievement for a guy who got his start as a rugged fisherman known for thoughtless action and bluster.

---

[378] Galatians 2:11.

Acceptance of Peter the Disciple, Writer and Missionary. As a concluding observation, it remains important to distinguish between views of Peter as a disciple and author. As a disciple, Peter is accorded due prominence during the period of Jesus' ministry, in the early post-Easter church, and subsequent to his reputed death as a martyr—crucified in Rome (between 64 and 68 AD), very likely upside down. A shrine was even erected over his reputed place of burial by about 160.

Acknowledgment of the prominence that Peter receives as disciple is somewhat counterbalanced by the type of role Peter also plays—as foil for Jesus and as outmaneuvered by Paul and James in the first-century church. The division created early on is reported, for example, by Paul who observes "quarrels" between those who say 'I belong to Paul,' or 'I belong to Apollos,' or 'I belong to Cephas,' or 'I belong to Christ.'[379]

As a writer or contributing author, Peter's role and significance also receives mixed reviews. The two canonical Gospels attributed to Peter have been challenged for a variety of reasons both early on and down through the centuries.

Peter's ostensible role as contributor to Mark's gospel also may be considered as a bit of a mixed blessing. Teaming with Mark makes for a fast-paced and lively narrative but without the teaching for which the other Gospels are recognized.

Peter would yield to correction by his master, trading brashness for humility as his Chrisian experience matured. And Peter would inevitably yield to Paul's intellectual vigor, but even then could not resist a little dig of his own, noting that despite Paul's wisdom, there are "some things in them (Paul's letters) hard to understand."[380]

Like Paul, Peter appears to have extended his role well beyond that of the Jerusalem mother church. The 4th century church historian Eusebius of Caesarea would record that:

---

[379] 1 Corinthians 1:12.

[380] 2 Peter 3:16. Peter would go on to say that the difficulty understanding Paul's writings can be used by "the ignorant and unstable twist to their own destruction, as they do the other scriptures."

Peter seems to have preached in Pontus, Galatia and Bithynia, Cappadocia and Asia, to the Jews of the dispersion. Finally he came to Rome where he was crucified, head downward at his own request.[381]

Church tradition also is that Peter was the first Bishop of Rome. His death occurred during the persecutions of Nero about AD 64–65, roughly 2–3 years after the execution of James in Jerusalem.

Compromised Christianity? Whether in business, politics or religion, the toughest place to be is in the middle. This is the place for those with fluid rather than fixed positions—often more focused more on maintaining interpersonal relationships than purity of ideological purpose. So, it seems to have been for Peter, Christ's disciple.

A man of bluster followed by after the fact reflection. Easily swayed by those around him, especially those more committed to their position regardless of the cost. Was Peter too easily compromised? And if so, what are the implications for Christian faith and practice as evolved over the last two millennia?

Would Christendom have been better served if it had more rigorously followed the example of Paul for whom faith trumped all else including works? Or better off if the message of James was the priority—recognizing that "faith without works is dead"?

If Peter were stronger in conveying and sticking with his convictions—even in the radical middle—could he have forced a more explicitly defined resolution of God's purpose for the people of the original covenant to Abraham's descendants with those Greeks of the new covenant? Could models of conflict resolution been framed in ways that would provide greater unity of purpose between those of all faiths while leaving liberty to lesser (or greater) matters of personal conscience before God?

Conversely, if Peter had not been so overly quick to judge and execute, could he have held back rather than severing the ear of an arresting officer or the lives of lying congregants. As James has written:

> My brothers and sisters, if anyone among you wanders from the truth and is brought back by another, you should know that whoever brings back a

---

[381] Eusebius, 3.1.

sinner from wandering will save the sinner's soul from death and will cover a multitude of sins.[382]

Ultimately, the question of fight versus flight rests on the shoulders of the savior. He's the one who says that he came to bring not peace but conflict. How does the master address conflict? That's a question that will rest until Chapter 12. For now, we rest on the foibles and heart of Simon Peter of Bethsaida.

Peter in Summary

We come to the end of our consideration of a man called Peter—the disciple about whom more has been written in the New Testament than any other. At the end of this journey, two questions remain:

- How and why was this heir apparent to the ministry of Christ, this recognized leader of the fledgling church at Pentecost, so easily shoved aside by James and Paul?
- What is the ongoing relevance (if any) of Peter's life, his writings, his example, to this current generation?

As the first leader of the early church, Peter proves to be out of step primarily on matters of both style and substance. Substantively, he has difficulty holding to any specific position though the epistles attributed to him emphasize submission to authority whether earthly or heavenly. However, it is his style of often rash and erratic behavior that puts him outside the mainstream of our other Christian pioneers.

Peter's reputation for acting before thinking—an asset at Pentecost—became a liability as the early church required stronger and more consistent leadership. The unusual deaths of Ananias and Sapphira may have been *nails in the coffin* for Peter's leadership. And compared to Paul, James (and John), Peter was no intellectual giant. Rather, he was a man who wore his heart on his sleeve.

Simon Peter could act out of well-intentioned ferocity before thinking. This penchant may have been reinforced by his conception of the divine. From

---

[382] James 5:19–20.

a front row seat during Jesus' ministry, the best Peter can do is to describe a God of strong and unbending personality—a stern but loving Father.

Peter had a problem with articulating and then holding to a position. Vacillation over the issue of Gentile circumcision undoubtedly lost friends on both sides of the aisle. His heart may have been in the right place, but he could never articulate the case for a moderate position clearly enough to hold his own in the heated debates of the early church.

Yet more so than any of the other disciples (except possibly John), Peter received the unparalleled opportunity both to define and to experience the Godhead—through the crucible of personal interaction. He paid a price—serving as foil to the agendas of James, Paul and ultimately his savior.

Over time, Peter has fared substantially better in the annals of church history than his early counterpart in leadership, James the brother of Jesus. This is despite Peter's loss of official church leadership to James and transfer of missionary mantle to Paul.

Maybe this is because so many of us see something of ourselves in Peter. A man with a heart of gold, but for whom courage evaporates at the critical hour. A person who can be bold and impetuous, yet who ultimately compromises for sake of keeping everyone happy.

Both in life and death, Peter exemplifies personal struggles that many followers of the way have also experienced over the last two millennia. Sadly, his message of conciliation is not the message that carries the day. Rather, Christianity has been led by dogmatics—heirs to the actions of a more rash Peter combined with the narrower (albeit conflicting) theologies of Paul and James.

Supplement—John Chrysostom on Ananias and Sapphira

A noteworthy reference to the possibility of Petrine homicide in the case of Ananias and Sapphira arises in the form of a rebuttal to the suggestion of same from John Chrysostom, bishop of Constantinople, written about 395 AD. This reference to the conniving couple occurs as Chrysostom is writing about the vehemence of the apostle Paul's message to the Galatian church.

Peter's Role. In the middle of his commentary on the Galatians, John Chrysostom gives passing reference to Peter's role in the affair with Ananias and Sapphira, to wit:

Let not his (Paul's) calling them "foolish" surprise you; for it is not a transgression of Christ's command not to call one's brother a fool, but rather a strict observance of it. For it is not said simply, "Whosoever shall say to his brother, Thou fool," (Mat. v: 22) but, whosoever shall do so, "without a cause."[383] And who more fittingly than they could so be called, who after so great events, adhered to past things, as if nothing else had ever happened? If on this account Paul is to be called a "reviler," *Peter may likewise, on account of Ananias and Sapphira, be called a homicide;* but as it would be wildness to do so in that case, much more in this. Moreover it is to be considered, that this vehemence is not used at the beginning, but after these evidences and proofs, which, rather than Paul himself, might now be held to administer the rebuke. For after he had shown that they rejected the faith, and made the death of Christ to be without a purpose, he introduces his reproof, which, even as it is, is *less severe than they merited.*[384] *(italics* added*)*

Chrysostom undoubtedly is a dense read. The question is: why would a respected theologian raise the supposedly unlikely counterfactual of Petrine complicity in possible murder(s) three or four centuries after the event? The only reasonable answer is that there must have been rumors floating around Christendom about Peter's behavior not just briefly, but conceivably over several centuries.

Example of Paul. In effect, John Chrysostom is saying that those who would condemn Paul for his calling the Galatians foolish might just as well call Peter a murderer of Sapphira (and possibly of Ananias as well). And to Chrysostom, both allegations are ridiculous. In fact, he concludes by observing that Paul's chastisement of the Galatians is "less severe than they merited."

Significance for Chrysostom. What is interesting is not the denial by Chrysostom, but the fact that he feels forced to defend the actions of both Paul

---

[383] Chrysostom is quoting Jesus from Matthew 5:22.
[384] John. Chrysostom, *Commentary on the Epistle to the Galatians, Chapter 3, Verse 1,* CCEL website, https://www.ccel.org/ccel/schaff/npnf113.iii.iii.iii.html (accessed February 5, 2024. What added punishment in addition to earthly death Ananias and Sapphira may have merited Chrysostom does not directly state.

and Peter—centuries after their deaths. Is it possible that there were concerns among the Christians of the early church that Peter acted rashly in this matter?

We do not know for sure. However, Chrysostom's vehemence appears to have been sparked by issues he wanted to settle once and for all. Furthermore, this bishop left a legacy of condemning the material excesses of the church. In fact, John Chrysostom was an ascetic who, as one historian has noted, was:

> ...severely critical of the economic circumstances of the times. He pilloried the rich for their blindness to the needs of the poor. He argued that private property was introduced only as a consequence of Adam's sin. He criticized vanity in dress and the "double standard" of sexual morality as between husbands and wives. His preaching was not only edifying but on frequent occasion prophetic and blunt even to the point of indiscretion.[385]

Chrysostom's Agendas. Interestingly, John Chrysostom was no friend of Judaism. Preaching in Antioch in the later part of the fourth century, he targeted many of his sermons against Judaizers who wanted to adopt or maintain Jewish practices with Christianity. For example, when Jews began new excavations on the Temple, explosions were touched off from gaseous deposits beneath. Chrysostom identified the earlier destruction of the Temple and subsequent Jewish failure to rebuild as clear evidence of the divinity of Christ.

Chrysostom also made the mistake of defending the teachings of another ascetic, the great third century theologian Origen—both of whom came to advocate subordinationism (or the concept of Jesus as a second God). Consequently, Chrysostom would himself be deposed by a church synod. The ruling was upheld by the imperial court as the empress Eudoxia had been enraged at John Chrysostom's criticism of her greed and injustice.

After a brief reinstatement, Chrysostom again brought the royal court to task, comparing the empress to both the Biblical pariahs Jezebel and Herodias. This time, he was exiled to Armenia.[386] His banishment led to riots in the capital including burning of the cathedral built by prior Emperor Constantius—

---

[385] Williston Walker, et al, *A History of the Christian Church,* 4th Edition, 160–161.
[386] John Chrysostom subsequently died in 407 AD enroute to a yet more distant exile.

leading to subsequent construction of the Hagia Sophia on the same site by future emperor Theodosius.

If John Chrysostom felt no compunction about criticizing the imperial court for its material excesses, he certainly had no doubt about the divine nature of an earlier judgment against Ananias and Sapphira. As Peter had acted as an agent of divine justice, so John Chrysostom would act by the imputed divine authority of his office to take on the empress of the Roman empire.

VIII. Thomas—Mystery and Wisdom

Give to the emperor what belongs to the emperor,
give God what belongs to God,
and give me what is mine.
Jesus, as quoted in the Gospel of Thomas 100:2 (SV)

In 1945, a copy of a lost "gospel" known as the Gospel of Thomas was discovered together with a large collection of ancient texts now known as the Nag Hammadi Library. The prologue to the gospel reads:

These are the secret sayings that the living Jesus spoke and Didymus Judas Thomas recorded.

With 114 seemingly disjointed sayings, there is no attempt by this so-called gospel to compose a narrative. This gospel named after Thomas was written in Coptic, the common language of Egypt during the period of the early church.

References to such a document were known reaching back to earlier antiquity. Three Greek fragments of this gospel known as the Papyrus Oxyrhynchus had been discovered around the turn of the 20th century. Though "lost" for more than a millennium, the Gospel of Thomas had been characterized as heretical by at least some early orthodox church patriarchs.

Rediscovery of the Thomas manuscripts ignited new controversies about the New Testament between Biblical scholars. However, even today, Thomas remains little known outside the ecclesiastic and academic realms.

For followers of the historic Jesus and students of the New Testament, the Gospel of Thomas is important for at least three reasons:

- This non-canonical gospel likely appears to have been composed contemporaneously with the four Gospels that are now part of the New Testament; the discovered manuscript actually predates any known

complete and authenticated manuscript of Matthew, Mark, Luke or John.
- Thomas offers both independent corroboration as well as challenges to conventional views about the teachings of Jesus.
- Thomas is also decidedly counter-cultural—as a type of non-traditional wisdom literature and proto-Gnostic teaching.

It is tempting to dismiss non-canonical works such as Thomas (and the Gospel of Mary) as outside the bounds of scriptural authority. These and other so-called non-canonical Gospels lack the provenance that accompanies the majority of the accepted New Testament texts.

Their inclusion in this discussion is neither to endorse nor disparage their authenticity or relevance to Christian faith and practice. However, due to their reputed (partial) manuscript age, the often controversial natures of their protagonists, and (most importantly) the way in which they supplement or fill out scriptural accounts, they are included here as deserving a hearing—to rise or fall on their own merits.

In its simplest form, the purported heresy of the Thomas gospel is that while Jesus introduces the kingdom of God, this kingdom is available to only a few who are called to unravel the mystery. The outcome is attainment to a wisdom that reaches beyond conventional spiritual or material thinking.

Background of Thomas

About the background of Thomas as a disciple and his writings relatively little is known. Interpretation is as yet unfolding. With this so-called gospel, part of the problem is that the most intact version is written in Coptic, a language that few modern scholars have mastered.[387]

Gospel Dating. Writings that have been attributed to Thomas include not only the Gospel of Thomas. Also attributed to Thomas are documents known as the Book of Thomas, the Acts of Thomas and the Infancy Gospel of Thomas. While these additional works are covered briefly, the primary (though not

---

[387] There are differences noted between the intact Coptic Gospel of Thomas and what is acknowledged as previously discovered three Greek fragments of the Papyrus Oxyrhynchus—including different orderings of the sayings of Thomas.

exclusive) focus of this discussion is placed on the much celebrated Gospel of Thomas.

Scholars who have evaluated the Gospel of Thomas text place its date of composition in the period 70–100 AD. This is roughly the same time frame given by non-fundamentalist scholars for the New Testament's canonical Gospels.

For some scholars, Thomas represents a collection of sayings that may even predate the Gospels of the canon. At the very least, the sayings of Thomas appear to come from a time before Matthew, Mark, Luke and John had achieved general, universal acceptance among early Christian churches.

To at least one noted Thomas scholar and enthusiast, the case can be made for an even earlier date:

> The evidence for a mid-first century date for Thomas is considerable, although not conclusive. Thomas had access to very early oral and, perhaps, written sayings traditions which were independent of and, occasionally, superior to traditions in the synoptics. This would probably not have been possible much later than the year ~AD 90. Are there any sayings of Jesus in second-century writings which are considered superior to their parallels in the synoptics? Even John and the Pastorals, the Didache, and the Letters of Clement and Ignatius seem to have no sayings superior to their synoptic parallels (of Matthew, Mark and Luke).
>
> Thomas contains a substantial number of the same kinds of sayings—parables, wisdom sayings, and proverbs—that are in the collections in the synoptic Gospels and in Q.[388] Clearly, Thomas originated in a milieu and at a time where Christians wanted to preserve that kind of material. Collections of that kind of material are certainly not characteristic of second-century Christian texts.[389]

Another document known as the *Infancy Gospel of Thomas* is a different matter. It belongs to a genre of literature offering what generally might be construed as a highly fanciful legend concerning Jesus' youth.

---

[388] "Q" is a hypothetical but unproven fifth New Testament gospel of sayings that may have preceded and served as source material for Matthew and/or Luke.

[389] From Stevan L. Davies, *The Gospel of Thomas and Christian Wisdom*, (New York: Seabury Press, 1983) 16.

The first infancy gospel in extant form is a Syriac manuscript dating to the sixth century. However, this document was known by as early as the second century. Irenaeus, bishop of Lyon, wrote in his work *Against Heresies* of spurious tales that include an incident from Thomas' infancy gospel. As early as this time, such Gospels were considered to represent a heresy associated with groups of Gnostic Christians. This heresy was to be shown as contrary to views of the orthodox church leadership.

A separate *Book of Thomas* was totally unknown and discovered with the Gospel of Thomas at Nag Hammadi. The *Acts of Thomas* is an apparently Gnostic historical romance focused on the travels of Thomas to India.

Authorship. As noted, the opening prologue sets the stage for the *Gospel of Thomas,* stating:

These are the secret sayings that the living Jesus spoke and Didymus Judas Thomas recorded.[390]

This introductory statement fits within a formula familiar to readers of the New Testament canon. Either Thomas composed the document or his followers attribute this collection to him.[391] Thomas was particularly popular in Syria, where he may have had the status of patron saint.

Similarly, the *Infancy Gospel of Thomas* opens with the words:

I, Thomas, the Israelite, am reporting to you, all my non-Jewish brothers and sisters, to make known the extraordinary childhood deeds of our Lord Jesus Christ—what he did after his birth in my region. This is how it all started.[392]

---

[390] *Gospel of Thomas, prologue.* Unless otherwise indicated, quotations from this gospel are from Robert J. Miller (editor), *The Complete Gospels: Annotate Scholars Version (SV), (*San Francisco: Polebridge Press/Harper, 1994).

[391] An early church patriarch, Cyril, claimed that the Gospel of Thomas was written by a Syrian disciple (also named Thomas) of the gnostic Mani.

[392] Infancy Gospel of Thomas, 1 (SV). Quotations from this gospel are per *The Complete Gospels,* noted above.

Given what may be the more fanciful nature of the Infancy Gospel, our review focuses primarily on: (a) what is known of Thomas from the current New Testament canon; and (b) what is known from the Gospel of Thomas.

Rediscovering Thomas. Before its rediscovery in 1945, there were no known complete manuscripts of the Gospel of Thomas. This was one of those non-canonical writings referenced by the church patriarchs, but with specific contents unknown for centuries.

The story of the gospel's rediscovery reads as good as most murder mysteries. Essentially, this manuscript and what is known as the entire Nag Hammadi Library were discovered by two men plotting a murder. While digging at an earthen mound for fertilizer, they struck a clay pot. Inside were 13 leather bound books or codices. See the supplement to this chapter for added detail.

The Tradition of Thomas. Identified in the fourth NT gospel as Thomas Didymus (the Twin), the tradition of Thomas is one of skepticism and mystery—whether considered from canonical or non-canonical sources.

Three of Jesus' twelve disciples are known for their *skepticism* toward the authenticity of Jesus' mission. Judas is an obvious choice; his disillusion led to the betrayal of Jesus. Peter fits the mold but for a different reason: most notably he betrays Jesus' trust through three denials as Jesus goes to trial.

And then there is the apostle somewhat derisively known down through the last two millennia as "doubting Thomas." This is the disciple who would not believe that Jesus had returned from the dead until he could feel his flesh—the nail holes in his hand and the spear hole in his side.

Thomas also may be considered as an apostle of *mystery.* To this disciple is attributed a writing of Gnostic orientation—indicating that Christ is to be approached and experienced through special knowledge rather than a revealed text or even centuries old tradition. The sense of mystery is deepened by the claim that Thomas the disciple ministered after Jesus' resurrection in the orient, perhaps traveling as far east as the Indian subcontinent.

But back to the New Testament accounts. With the three NT synoptic gospels, Thomas the disciple gets short shrift.

In each gospel, he is mentioned only once—as part of the naming of all twelve disciples.[393] Thomas plays a substantially more prominent role in

---

[393] Matthew mentions Thomas seventh in his listing; Mark and Luke put Thomas in eighth position. The difference in order is that Mark and Luke list Matthew ahead of

John's Gospel. He is mentioned in seven verses representing four different events—all pivotal to John's portrayal of Jesus' ministry.

John first introduces Thomas at the death and resurrection of Lazarus. In making the decision to travel to Bethany, Jesus first informs his disciples: "Lazarus is dead. For your sake I am glad I was not there, so that you may believe. But let us go to him."[394]

Thomas who John notes "was called the Twin" suggests to his fellow disciples, "Let us also go, that we may die with him."[395] Whether this was suggested out of fear, cynicism, or an attempt at gallows humor is not clear from the New Testament text. In any event, Thomas appears to have been well aware of the risk that Jesus' planned return to Judea could pose not just for his master but for all the disciples.

Thomas next makes his presence known when Jesus' is attempting to unveil the mystery of heaven to his disciples. At the beginning of a lengthy soliloquy, Jesus declares:

> Do not let your hearts be troubled. Believe in God, believe also in me. In my Father's house there are many dwelling-places. If it were not so, would I have told you that I go to prepare a place for you? And if I go and prepare a place for you, I will come again and will take you to myself, so that where I am, there you may be also. And you know the way to the place where I am going.[396]

Thomas interjects:

Lord, *we do not know* where you are going. How can we know the way?[397]

Jesus responds directly to Thomas with this widely quoted affirmation:

Thomas, Matthew mentions his own name just after Thomas. The labeling of Thomas as "the Twin" is of uncertain meaning, although various possibilities have been theorized.

[394] John 11:14–15.
[395] John 11:16.
[396] John 14:1–4.
[397] John 14:5.

I am the way, and the truth, and the life. No one comes to the Father except through me. If you know me, you will know my Father also. From now on you do know him and have seen him.[398]

While some might point to Jesus' encounter with Nicodemus as the seminal event in John's Gospel, a strong case could be made for Jesus direct pronouncement that he (and only he) offers the correct route to Father God. For Thomas, both the question and the affirmation are pivotal—even as we shall see when considering contents of the Thomas gospel in more detail.

Thomas' reputation for skepticism is now firmly established, Thomas' next appearance in the Gospel of John comes belatedly, after the resurrection of Jesus. For reasons not mentioned, Thomas is not present when Jesus first reappears to his disciples.

However, this is the pivotal event, the one that secures this disciple's reputation for all time as "doubting Thomas." As John tells it:

But Thomas (who was called the Twin), one of the twelve, was not with them when Jesus came. So the other disciples told him, "We have seen the Lord." But he said to them, "Unless I see the mark of the nails in his hands, and put my finger in the mark of the nails and my hand in his side, *I will not believe*."

A week later his disciples were again in the house, and Thomas was with them. Although the doors were shut, Jesus came and stood among them and said, "Peace be with you." Then he said to Thomas, "Put your finger here and see my hands. Reach out your hand and put it in my side. Do not doubt but believe." Thomas answered him, "*My Lord and my God!*" Jesus said to him, "Have you believed because you have seen me? Blessed are those who have not seen and yet have come to believe."[399]

As if to be sure that Thomas does not forget, Jesus makes his presence known one more time—this time in a familiar setting beside the Sea of Galilee. Seven disciples are present as John tells it. These are:

---

[398] John 14:6–7.
[399] John 20:24–29.

> Simon Peter, Thomas called the Twin, Nathanael of Cana in Galilee, the sons of Zebedee, and two others of his disciples.[400]

In this account, Thomas gets second billing—just behind Peter.

The name of Thomas surfaces one more time in the canonical New Testament book of Acts, as the disciples return from the Mount of Olives to Jerusalem—recounted this way:

> When they had entered the city, they went to the room upstairs where they were staying, Peter, and John, and James, and Andrew, Philip *and Thomas*, Bartholomew and Matthew, James son of Alphaeus, and Simon the Zealot, and Judas son of James. All these were constantly devoting themselves to prayer, together with certain women, including Mary the mother of Jesus, as well as his brothers.[401]

A couple of items are of note in this brief account. First, Thomas has improved his position in this updated listing of the now eleven disciples. He is identified sixth, an improvement of two positions assuming that the same author (i.e., Luke) penned both the Gospel of Luke and Acts. Second, at the outset to his story of the early church, the author of Acts also immediately introduces a few others alongside the apostles, namely certain (unnamed) women plus a portion of Jesus' family including his mother and brothers. This represents a major turn-around for Jesus family—from skepticism during the period of Jesus' Galilean ministry to renewed familial and spiritual alliance post-resurrection.

Non-Canonical Tradition. Confusion over Thomas' name has persisted through the centuries.

According to church historian Eusebius, his real name was Judas.[402] This may have been a mere confusion with Thaddeus, who is also mentioned in the extract. But it may also be that Thomas was a surname.

Out of this name has also grown one tradition that Thomas had a twin-sister, Lydia. Another tradition has it that Thomas was a twin-brother of Jesus

---

[400] John 21:2.
[401] Acts 1:13–14.
[402] Eusebius 1:13.

which is consistent with his identification with Judas.[403] Yet others suggest that Thomas never existed as a real person but only as the representation of a concept or message not found elsewhere in early Christian literature.

The first-century Christian patriarch Papias identifies Thomas as one of several disciples and elders who "taught the truth."[404] Papias places Thomas in the company of Peter, Andrew, Philip, James, John and Matthew as well as someone named Ariston and the Presbyter John.

Thomas is said to have been born most likely in the Galilee, possibly a fishing village named Pansada on or near the Sea of Galilee.[405] Early traditions, as believed in the fourth century (for example, by Eusebius), represent him as preaching in Parthia or Persia, and as finally buried at Edessa (in southeast Turkey). Later traditions place him as far east as India. For example, the Mar Thomas church in India traces its origins to Thomas.

The martyrdom of Thomas, whether in Persia or India, is said to have been occasioned by a lance. The date of Thomas' martyrdom is commemorated by the Latin Church on December 21, by the Greek church on October 6, and by the Indians on July 1.[406]

Orthodoxy and Heterodoxy

The writers of the New Testament introduce us to *doubting Thomas*—clearly a disciple who marches (or perhaps meditates) to the beat of a different drummer. The gospel of the canon portrays Thomas as a skeptic and an empiricist—he has to see to believe.

The non-canonical Gospel of Thomas—rediscovered only in this last century in the sands of Egypt—carries the inquiring mind a step further. We are carried into the world of the Jesus of mystery and wisdom—some would say to Gnosticism.

---

[403] A non-canonical *Acts of the Holy Apostle Thomas* includes a comment attributed to Jesus saying: "I am not Judas who is also Thomas, I am his brother." https://www.newadvent.org/fathers/0823.htm (accessed Feb. 24. 2024).

[404] As quoted by Eusebius, *History of the Church*, 3.39.

[405] Pansada is identified by *Orthodox Wiki*, "Apostle Thomas," https://orthodoxwiki.org/Apostle_Thomas (accessed February 22, 2024). However, there is little other evidence of a 1st century Galilean place by that name.

[406] *Smith's Bible Dictionary,* "Thomas," https://biblehub.com/topical/t/thomas.htm (accessed Feb. 22, 2024).

The gospel writer John draws us up to the threshold of this mystery of the word with the revelation of a personalized divinity. Thomas crosses the threshold—yielding tantalizing, sometimes disconcerting glimpses of the mysteries of God's earthly and heavenly domain.

The Jesus of the Thomas Gospel offers a unique spin to many of the parables found in the New Testament Gospels. His Jesus clearly preaches a gospel of the here and now.

And the Jesus of Thomas gives often conflicting advice. The portrait of a conflicted Jesus clearly emerges from this long-buried, non-canonical work often considered by orthodox Christians as heresy. In the canonical New Testament, the conflicts are still also present; they just have to be coaxed out more gently.

The three canonical synoptics all record Jesus responding to the question of whether and how to pay taxes to the emperor, with the canonical Jesus saying:

Give to Caesar the things that are Caesar's and to God the things that are God's.[407]

Thomas' Jesus is the only one to say:

Give the emperor what belongs to the emperor, give God what belongs to God, *and give me what is mine*.[408]

The Jesus of Thomas wants his share; In this non-canonical work, Jesus also appears to distinguish himself—his own identity—as separate from that of God the Father.

And, this is the Thomas of the bizarre who, for example, ends his non-canonical gospel's list of sayings with Jesus telling Peter about how he will transform Mary:

---

[407] Mark 12:17. Very similar statements are noted at Matthew 22:21 and Luke 20:25.
[408] Thomas 100:2.

Look, I will guide her to make her male, so that she too may become a living spirit resembling you males. For every female who becomes male will enter the domain of heaven.[409]

Varied interpretations can be drawn from this cryptic remark. Is this intended as a put-down reflecting a lesser acceptance into God's kingdom for women than for males? Could this be even be interpreted (in today's parlance) as a basis for transgender identity?

Is Thomas arguing not so much for a literal physical transformation as for a different (more male) spiritual orientation and attitude? Or is Thomas simply having fun (perhaps like Mark) with reshaping the narrative, in this case, putting' Jesus response into a more mystical or Gnostic framework?

Similar questions can be asked of numerous other sayings in the Gospel of Thomas. In effect, the best interpretation is often inconclusive—left to be shaped by perspectives of the reader as much as those of the original author(s).

Mystery and Wisdom. In the Gospel of Thomas, we are introduced to the mysteries and wisdom of Jesus in at least three remarkable ways:

- **A different twist on parables**—new interpretations that may be similar to but often with a spin oddly different from that presented by the synoptic Gospels of the New Testament.
- **Emphasis on the kingdom of God as being in the here and now**—not somewhere else or at some unspecified time in the future but approachable only by those who take time to penetrate the mysteries of the divine in the here and now.
- **Presentation of a conflicted Jesus**—a teacher who often contradicts himself.

A Different Twist on Parables. Of all the non-canonical Gospels uncovered as of this dawn of the third millennium, only the Gospel of Thomas follows in the parabolic tradition of two New Testament synoptics—Matthew and Luke.[410]

---

[409] Thomas 114.

[410] In addition to the four gospels of the New Testament canon, at least a dozen other non-canonical works labelled as gospels have been identified. In addition, there are a variety of fragmentary gospel-like documents, as well as what might be termed orphan

Out of 114 chapters containing separate sayings, at least 13 involve use of the distinctive parable format.

The first is Thomas 8 which opens very much in the style of a synoptic parable: "The human one *is like* a wise fisherman…" This wise fisherman discovers a large fish. And then the Thomas writer records, "Jesus threw all the little fish back into the sea, and easily chose the large fish."[411]

Thomas is in effect suggesting that Jesus is only interested in "large fish" or important persons. This runs counter to contrasting accounts of the New Testament suggesting that the "last shall be first."

Thomas' interpretation also runs counter to Matthew's recounting of the same (or similar parable). In Matthew, the fisherman distinguishes between "good" and "bad" fish, not necessarily "large" and "little."

Of the 13 parables contained in Thomas, all but two are also found in one or more of the synoptic Gospels. It is noted that four are paralleled only by Matthew and one is found only in Luke. Over one-half (7 of 13) parables found in Thomas start with: "The Father's imperial rule (or kingdom)…"

A few of the Thomas parables closely parallel those found in the canonical New Testament. An example is the parable of the sower found in Thomas as well as with all three synoptics. Other comparables include the parables of the mustard seed, the weeds, the merchant who buys the pearl, the yeast and bread, and the hidden treasure. All of these parables including that of the sower are also found in Matthew 13.

While similar to Matthew, Thomas offers at least a couple of novel interpretations. In Thomas, the merchant who buys the pearl is described simply as "prudent" while it is Matthew who makes it clear that the pearl is "priceless"—potentially going well beyond prudent.

Matthew's version of the parable of the hidden treasure emphasizes the subsequent decision of the discoverer to bury the treasure and then buy the field. Thomas suggests that the first owner did not know of the treasure, but upon death leaves the field to the son who makes the discovery. The action of the son is that he "began to lend money at interest to whomever he wished."[412]

---

sayings and stories. As per *The Complete Gospels,* Robert J. Miller, Editor.

[411] Thomas 8:1–3. The synoptic parallel is found in Matthew 13:47–50, the parable of the net, which reads that "when it (the net) was full, they drew it ashore, sat down, and put the good into baskets but threw out the bad."

[412] Thomas 109.

This reveals a potential level of financial interest by Jesus reaching beyond anything suggested in the canonical New Testament.

A couple of parables found in Thomas closely parallel the parable of the wedding banquet and tenants found in Matthew 21 and 22. Then there is the parable of the lost sheep, also told in Matthew 18.

However, in Thomas' version, upon discovering the sheep, Jesus is blunt, ostensibly saying to the lost sheep: "*I love you more* than the ninety-nine."[413]

There also is the parable of the rich fool, the only one of the New Testament parallels found only in Luke but not Matthew. Thomas simply describes the rich fool's conceit and death as the result. Luke's version of the parable includes a more explicit statement about the moral of the story, with God speaking to make it clear that this is "the way it is with those who save up for themselves, but aren't rich where God is concerned."[414]

Then there are two parables recounted in Thomas but not found in the New Testament at all. One is a parable concerning little children. It goes like this:

They (the disciples) are like little children living in a field that is not theirs. When the owners of the field come, they will say, "Give us back our field." They take off their clothes in front of them in order to give it back to them, and they return their field to them.[415]

This parable seems odd for at least two reasons. First, the owners are taking away a field from little children, a theme seemingly at variance with canonical picture of a Jesus who says that it is children who populate the kingdom of God. Second, there is the somewhat obscure if not bizarre response of the children taking off their clothes.[416]

---

[413] Thomas 107. The version of Matthew 18:12–14 offers slightly different and less intimate wording, indicating that the shepherd "rejoices over it more than the ninety-nine…"

[414] Luke 12:21 (SV).

[415] Thomas 21:2–4. This parable is given in response to a question from Mary, who asks: "What are your disciples like?"

[416] Editors of *The Complete Gospels* (in a footnote to Thomas 21:4) suggest three possible alternatives to this "obscure" passage based on clues from later literature: a) removal of clothing may be to show sexual indifference, the conquering of desire through asceticism; b) this may refer to the baptismal ritual common in the early

The second parable found in Thomas but not in the New Testament is that of a murder or execution:

> The Father's imperial rule is *like a person who wanted to kill someone powerful.* While still at home, he drew his sword and thrust it into the wall to find out whether his hand would go in. Then he killed the powerful one.[417]

This seems to make the interesting point of *practice makes perfect,* albeit with a definitely morbid illustration. It is another example of Thomas' willingness to either recount or fabricate parables that are beyond the bounds of what are recounted by the synoptic gospel writers.

In some of the other sayings compiled in Thomas, Jesus does not employ the device of parable but will use a commonplace example to illustrate his point. This approach is exemplified by the saying wherein Jesus is quoted to observe:

> A grapevine has been planted apart from the Father. Since it is not strong, it will be pulled up by its root and will perish.[418]

Kingdom of God is Here and Now. The three synoptic Gospels all refer on numerous occasions to the "kingdom of God" or, as termed in the Scholars Version (SV as used herein), the father's "domain" or "imperial rule." With the synoptics, one is never quite sure of when or where this kingdom or this imperial rule is to appear.

With Thomas, the answer is quite simple. The kingdom is here and it is here now. Although the kingdom is not necessarily readily apparent, it is nonetheless everywhere.

---

church where initiates were baptized in the nude; or c) to the Platonic and Gnostic notion that the soul sheds the body as "clothing" upon death before ascending to the heavenly realm.

[417] Thomas 98. Editors suggest that the parable suggests a home of mud brick, the walls of which could be used as a surface on which to practice sword thrusts.

[418] Thomas 40.

This is made clear in the second to last saying of the Thomas gospel, with the disciples asking Jesus: "When will the <Father's> imperial rule come?" Jesus replies:

> It will not come by watching for it. It will not be said, 'Look, here!' or 'Look, there!' Rather, the Father's imperial rule is spread out upon the earth, and *people don't see it*.[419]

Thomas provides 16 other references to the kingdom or imperial rule. Note that many of these references are introduced through the device of simile. The kingdom generally is described not in terms of the future but the here and now. In most cases (but three), the operative verb lies in the present rather than the future tense. With the following examples, key concepts are *italicized* for effect. Chapter and verse references are noted as applicable:

> The <Father's> imperial rule *is inside you and outside you.* When you know yourselves, then you will be known, and you will understand that you are children of the living Father. (Thomas 3:3–4)

> The disciples to Jesus: "Tell us what Heaven's imperial rule is like." Jesus: "It's like *a mustard seed.*" (20:1–2)

> Jesus sees babies nursing: "These nursing babies are like those who enter the <Father's> domain."
> The disciples: "Then how shall we enter the <Father's> domain as babies?"

> Jesus: "When you make the two into one, and when you make the inner like the outer and the outer like the inner, and the upper like the lower, and when you make male and female into a single one, so that the male will not be female nor the female be female, when you make eyes in place of an eye, a hand in place of a hand, a foot in place of a foot, an image in place of an image, *then you will enter* [the <father's> domain]." (22:1–7)

---

[419] Thomas 113.

"Congratulations to those who are alone and chosen, for you will find the <Father's> domain. For you have *come from it*, and you will return there again." (49)

"Congratulations to *the poor,* for to you belongs Heaven's domain." (54)

"The Father's imperial rule is like a person who had *[good] seed.*" (57)

"The Father's imperial rule is like a merchant who had a supply of merchandise and then *found a pearl.*" (76)

"Whoever is *near me* is near the fire, and whoever is far from me is far from the <Father's> domain." (82)

"The Father's imperial rule is like [a] woman who took a *little leaven*, [hid] it in dough and made it into two large loaves of bread." (96)

"The [Father's] imperial rule is like a woman who was carrying a [jar] full of meal. While she was walking along [a] distant road, the handle of the jar broke and the meal *spilled behind her* [along] the road. She didn't know it; she hadn't noticed a problem. When she reached her house, she put the jar down and discovered that it was empty." (97)

"The Father's imperial rule is like a person who *wanted to kill* someone powerful. While still at home, he drew his sword and thrust it into the wall to find out whether his hand would go in. Then he killed the powerful one." (98)

To the disciples notifying Jesus of the presence of his mother and brothers: "Those *who do what my Father wants* are my brothers and my mother. They are the ones who will enter my Father's domain." (99:2)

"The <Father's> imperial rule is like *a shepherd* who had a hundred sheep. One of them, the largest, went astray. He left the ninety-nine and looked for the one until he found it. After he had toiled, he said to the sheep, 'I love you more than the ninety-nine.'" (107)

"The <Father's> imperial rule is like a person who had a *treasure hi*dden in his field but did not know it. And [when] he died he left it to his [son]. The son [did] not know <about it either>. He took over the field and sold it. The buyer went plowing, [discovered] the treasure, and began to lend money at interest to whomever he wished." (109)

From his disciples: "When will the Father's imperial rule come?" Jesus: "It will not come by watching for it. It will not be said, 'Look, here!' or

'Look there!' Rather, the Father's imperial rule is spread out upon the earth, and people don't see it." (113)

"For every *female who makes herself male* will enter the domain of Heaven." (114)

So consider this range of features of the imperial domain as described by Thomas. It is both inside and outside you. It is like a mustard seed, nursing babies, a good seed, a pearl, a fire, a woman who makes bread, a woman who spills meal from a jar, one who wants to kill, a shepherd, a treasure. It's also like those eligible to enter who include those alone and chosen, the poor, those who do the Father's will.

Many of these kingdom metaphors also are found in the canonical New Testament. Examples are those of the mustard seed, the good seed, the pearl, the leaven, the shepherd, and the treasure. These all relate to seemingly insignificant actions or undervalued assets that take on greater importance than had been initially accorded.

Jesus' blessing to the poor as recorded by Thomas is consistent with Luke's gospel, but not Matthew's. The admonition that the kingdom's brother- and sister-hood is limited to those who do what the Father wants is a very explicit and sobering warning among otherwise obtuse comparisons with the kingdom.

The observation that the kingdom is right here but people don't see it also parallels a message embedded in Luke's gospel. And there are definitive statements about the kingdom—about God's domain—that are found only in Thomas. These represent even more radical departures from conventional wisdom about who is eligible to experience this kingdom.

Thomas suggests that entering the father's domain depends on achieving impossible contradictions—making the two into one, the inner like the outer (and vice versa), male and female into one. The kingdom also appears open to those who are "alone and chosen" and to "every female who makes herself male."

Thomas suggests that being near Jesus is like being near fire, like a woman who unwittingly loses flour from a jar, and even like the person who wants to murder someone powerful.

Finally, some of Thomas' sayings exhibit parallels with the canonical Gospels, albeit with a different slant. For example, Luke's Jesus says the kingdom is "among you."[420] The Jesus of Thomas is more elliptical—the imperial rule is inside and outside you.

The Lord of the synoptics says that one must be as a child to enter the kingdom. Thomas takes the comparison one step further. One needn't be a child, but could be even a nursing baby.

Canonical Exclusion

It is not difficult to understand why the orthodox church felt uncomfortable with Thomas and the associated specter of Gnosticism. The established church positioned itself as the arbiter of Biblical interpretation and atonement—particularly starting with and then following the Roman emperor Constantine. In contrast, Thomas suggested that each individual may have a different interpretation and spiritual experience—and that is just plain okay.

The Question of Gnosticism. Since the discovery of the complete Coptic text of Thomas in 1945, the general view has been that Thomas expresses Gnostic or proto-Gnostic views. At the simplest level, Gnostics believed that the world is evil, essentially a mistake in the divine order.

In general, Gnostics can be said to denote a form of Christianity involving those who choose a life of asceticism.[421] These are followers of the Christ who often regard abstention from food and drink as indicative of and necessary for

---

[420] Luke 17:21.

[421] Exceptions may be the followers of Simon Magus and Mani who were less likely to view Jesus as the bearer of hidden wisdom.

spiritual excellence, and who may demand sexual continence as a principal requirement of Christian practice.[422]

As described by the editor of the Scholars Version (SV), the Gospel of Thomas provides insight into:

> ...an early Christian community taking its first steps in the direction of Gnosticism, its counter-cultural wisdom a blossom of the anti-cosmic Gnostic orientation that would reach its full flowering among Christians only in the second century. Thomas shares with Gnosticism a basic concern for personal identity within a world that was widely perceived as brutal and mean.[423]

It is against this flowering of Gnosticism that established church authorities ultimately prevailed—aided and abetted by the political aspirations of the 4th century emperor Constantine. However, we are ahead of the game. This is the subject for a subsequent chapter.

In the meantime, if there is doubt about Thomas' intent, consider this shortest of Thomas statements attributed to Jesus: "*Be passerby*."[424] This has been interpreted by some as a call to take up the itinerant life of a follower of the way; by others it is seen as a Gnostic calling to pass through this world and life without becoming attached.

Or consider Jesus' statement:

> Whoever has come to know the world has discovered a carcass, and whoever has discovered a carcass, of that person the world is not worthy.[425]

In other words, be careful not to discover the world. And another on the unveiling of the mysteries of wisdom. The Jesus of Thomas says:

---

[422] Clement of Alexandria suggested a more simplistic definition of gnostic as someone who penetrates deeper into the mysteries of truth than the average believer.
[423] *The Complete Gospels: Annotated Scholars Version,* 304.
[424] Thomas 42.
[425] Thomas 56. See also Thomas 80.

I disclose my mysteries to those [who are worthy] of [my] mysteries. Do not let your left hand know what your right hand is doing.[426]

God's heavenly domain is a secret, unveiled only to those who reject the world and are chosen to penetrate through to the light. And finally, Jesus the Zen philosopher:

I am the light that is over all things. I am all: from me all came forth, and to me all attained. *Split a piece of wood; I am there.* Lift up the stone, and you will find me there.[427]

This view of Thomas as a forerunner of full-blown Gnosticism is not universally accepted. To some, the arguments presented represent circular logic—as indicated by the following statement from a Thomas follower:

When authors who claim that Thomas is Gnostic explain what they mean by Gnostic (and this they rarely do), they tend to admit that Thomas has almost no Gnostic characteristics. The conclusion that Thomas is Gnostic is based upon the premise that Thomas is Gnostic. It was found among a collection of documents, many of them Gnostic, and so it is argued Thomas must be Gnostic.[428]

Acceptance of Thomas. Due to the recent 20th century appearance of a complete Thomas manuscript, not much is known about early Church acceptance of this work. However, an awareness of this gospel has been around since the days of the early church.

The Greek fragments of Thomas were discovered about one-half century before the more complete and better known Coptic version, just before the turn of the 20th century—in the debris of an ancient trash-heap of Oxyrhynchus, a Roman-era city in upper Egypt.[429] Prior to this, there was an awareness of this writing, but it was thought to have been lost forever.

---

[426] Thomas 62.

[427] Thomas 77.

[428] Stevan Davies, *The Gospel of Thomas and Christian Wisdom* (New York: Seabury Press, 1963), 23.

[429] The handwriting in the earliest Greek fragments can be dated to the late second or early third century. There are some differences between the Greek and Coptic

Scholars have been aware of the existence of the Gospel of Thomas since the origins of Christianity, but no (known) copies have survived any of the puritanical purges of earlier times. The work is mentioned by the early orthodox church fathers, and (not surprisingly) almost always in a negative context. [430]

The early third century Christian writer Hippolytus mentions a 'Gospel of Thomas' that is used by the Naassene Gnostics and quotes this saying from the Thomas gospel:

> Jesus said, "The person old in days won't hesitate to ask a little child seven days old about the place of life, and that person will live; for many of the first will be last, and they will become a single one."[431]

The Valentinians who also followed in the Gnostic tradition used at least one saying of Jesus which is found in the *Gospel of Thomas*. As early as the second century, a follower of Valentinus named Marcus regarded the Thomas gospel as canonical.[432] [433]

During this same time period (about 233), Origen mentions the Gospel of Thomas as part of a list of heterodox Gospels. The general consensus since has been that Origen "explicitly rejected the apocryphal Gospels of Thomas…"

Not quite a century later, Eusebius of Caesarea cites several "Gospels" including that of Thomas as "published by heretics under the name of the apostles." He goes on to state that the "ideas and implications of their contents are so irreconcilable with true orthodoxy that they stand revealed as the forgeries of heretics…they must be thrown out as impious and beyond the pale."[434]

---

manuscripts. For example, the Coptic version claims the writer as Didymus (the Twin) Judas Thomas; the Greek refers to him simply as Judas Thomas. As noted in *The Complete Gospels,* 324.

[430] Much of this material is excerpted from Stevan Davies, *the Gnostic Society Library*, http://gnosis.org/naghamm/gosthom-davies.html (accessed February 7, 2024).

[431] Thomas 4.

[432] Lavinia Cohn-Sherbock, *Who's Who in Christianity (London: Routledge, 1998), 196.*

[433] Robert Grant, *Formation of the New Testament, 170.*

[434] Eusebius, 3.25.

And yet another century later, the historian Philip of Side (c. 430), referring back to Eusebius, says:

> ...most of the elders had completely rejected the so-called Gospel of Thomas as well as the *Gospel of the Hebrews* and that of Peter, saying that these were the work of heretics.[435]

However, there is some evidence that the 3rd century theologian Origen may have equivocated as in his *Commentary on the Gospel of Matthew*.[436] In this commentary, Origen focuses on a cryptic note from Matthew's gospel at a time of Jesus' transition from teaching disciples about mysteries of the kingdom to reach back out to a broader audience. Matthew writes:

> When Jesus had *finished* saying these things (to his disciples), he left Galilee and went to the region of Judea beyond the Jordan. Large crowds followed him, and he cured them there.[437]

What had Jesus finished? He had been teaching his disciples about who is greatest in the kingdom, avoiding temptation to sin, going after those lost in sin, church discipline, and forgiveness vs. unforgiveness. Unveiling to his disciples mysteries of the kingdom, Jesus has accomplished what he set out to do with his disciples. In a contemporary review of Origen's commentary, it is noted that:

> Origen points out that nowhere in Scripture is this phrase used about Moses or any of the prophets, while it is suitable for the definitive revelation proclaimed by Jesus. An interpreter could therefore explain the phrase as indicating that only Jesus had truly fulfilled his words.[438]

---

[435] The Gospel of the Hebrews is generally believed to be a version of Matthew (minus the nativity) used by the Ebionites—with the Jerusalem Christians headed by lineal descendants of the apostles. Ebionites were considered heretics for stressing Jewish roots in a church movement increasingly dominated by Gentiles.

[436] Origen, *Commentary on Mathew,* 14,14.

[437] Matthew 19:1–2.

[438] Matteo Grosso, "A New Link between Origen and the Gospel of Thomas: Commentary on Matthew 14,14," *Vigiliae Christianae* 65 (2011), 250.

For Origen, may there have been a remembrance of a similar *logion,* oracle or Word of God drawn on by Jesus? For example, a saying as from the *Gospel of Thomas* where Jesus is reputed to have said:

I *disclose* my mysteries to those [who are worthy] of [my] mysteries.[439]

So what has happened? Jesus has disclosed mysteries of the kingdom to a group of disciples he views as worthy—despite human frailties. Is there a link between how Origen comments on Jesus' action to Origen's potential recollection of a saying from the non-canonical Gospel of Thomas? Maybe so, as this current day reviewer concludes that:

…while recalling the one who delivered the divine mysteries to the worthies, Origen was referring to the same saying attested (in Thomas), where that very act is attributed to Jesus himself. Of course, this does not mean that Origen drew that expression directly from a copy of the *Gospel of Thomas* that he had in front of him, nor even that he purposely quoted from that writing. Nevertheless, it is sufficiently clear that, independently of the source from which he drew it, a remembrance of that saying surfaced in the flow of his (Origen's) argument.[440]

Is Origen consciously or otherwise equivocating on the potential albeit perhaps more circumscribed value of the Gospel of Thomas? If as may also be the case based on preliminary evidence, the 4th to 5th century theologian Jerome were to similarly equivocate, that would leave only Eusebius as a primary and steadfast patriarchal opponent to inclusion of the Thomas sayings. And it would allow for reconsideration of what Stevan Davies has suggested, that the pejorative view toward the Thomas account should transition to a more balanced and evidenced refreshed perspective as to this unique gospel's contribution to Christian faith and practice.

As one last aside, it is interesting that the Thomas gospel shares one noteworthy similarity with the Gospel of Mark. Both appear to take a somewhat creative if not playful approach to the writings composed in their names. The question ahead would then be: can the creative juices of a Thomas yet conform to an authentic Christian message—as has been the case with Mark?

---

[439] Thomas 62:1.
[440] Grosso, *Vigiliae Christianae,* 256.

In short, as an editors' note to *The Complete Gospels* regarding Thomas concisely concludes:

There is still much work to be done before this text is fully understood.[441]

The Wrap on Thomas. The writers of the New Testament introduce us to *doubting Thomas*—clearly a disciple who marches (or perhaps meditates) to the beat of a different drummer. The gospel of the canon portrays Thomas as a skeptic and an empiricist—he has to see to believe.

The non-canonical Gospel of Thomas—rediscovered only in this last century in the sands of Egypt—carries the inquiring mind a step further. We are carried into the realm of one Jesus—a God-man of mystery and wisdom.

Whether considered in his role as disciple and/or as possible author of the gospel named for him, Thomas has come across as being outside the mainstream of Christian orthodoxy. His heresy is primarily one of belief rather than practice—rooted in skepticism whether as disciple and/or in free form license as gospel author.

The existence of a skeptical Thomas both in the canon and in non-canonical literature demonstrates the importance of the skeptic to Christian faith and practice down through the centuries to today. Christ's acceptance of Thomas offers a message of comfort to doubting Thomases both then and now.

The gospel writer John has drawn us up to the threshold of this mystery of the word with the revelation of a personalized divinity. Thomas crosses the threshold—yielding tantalizing, sometimes disconcerting, even heretical glimpses of the mysteries of God's earthly and heavenly domain.

The Jesus of Thomas offers a unique spin on many of the parables found in the New Testament Gospels. Like Mark, this Jesus of Thomas clearly preaches a gospel of the here and now, also of immediate action in experiencing the kingdom of God on earth as a foretaste of what may be to come. The portrait of a conflicted Jesus also emerges from this long-buried, non-canonical very Thomasine work—whether heretical or not.

In the canonical New Testament, the conflicts are also present; they just have to be coaxed out more gently. Thomas' Jesus is the only one to say:

---

[441] *The Complete Gospels*, 304.

> Give the emperor what belongs to the emperor, give God what belongs to God, and *give me what is mine*.[442]

The Jesus of Thomas wants his share; he is also portrayed by Thomas as distinguishing himself from God the Father. And this is the Thomas of the bizarre, who ends his list of sayings with Jesus telling Peter about how he will transform Mary:

> Look, I will guide her to make her male, so that she too may become a living spirit resembling you males. For every female who becomes male will enter the kingdom of heaven.[443]

In retrospect, it is not difficult to understand why the orthodox church felt uncomfortable with Thomas and the associated specter of unbridled Gnosticism. The established universal (or Catholic) church positioned itself as the arbiter of Biblical interpretation and atonement—particularly after Constantine. In contrast, Thomas suggested that each individual may have a different interpretation and spiritual experience—and that may yet be ok.

We have had less than a century to rediscover the Jesus of Thomas. It may take some time and a willingness to drop prejudices over loaded terms like Gnosticism and mystery cults to experience the Jesus that Thomas labored—through a series of seemingly disjointed sayings—to unveil.

To summarize, the benefit of Thomas and his purported gospel is to take Christian faith beyond what is readily observable to that which may be otherwise unknown, confusing or downright incomprehensible. The downside also seems fairly clear—a gospel that may be too incomprehensible to be useful or just plain wrong.

Which brings us full circle back to the start—to the first saying of Jesus in Thomas that:

> Whoever discovers the interpretation of these sayings will not taste death.[444]

---

[442] Thomas 100.
[443] Thomas 114.
[444] Thomas 1.

And the second:

Those who seek should not stop seeking until they find, When they find, they will be disturbed.

When they are disturbed, they will marvel, and will rule over all. [445]

As we hurtle into this new millennium, there are yet a few that bother to seek. Some have begun to find. And as with today's specter of artificial intelligence (AI) or possibly even alternate universes, the ensuing disturbance has yet to fully unfold.

Supplement — Recovering the Gospel of Thomas

Before its rediscovery in 1945, there were no known complete manuscripts of the Gospel of Thomas. This was a non-canonical writing referenced by church patriarchs, but with contents unknown for centuries.

The tale of the gospel's rediscovery reads as good as most murder mysteries. This gospel and what is known as the entire Nag Hammadi Library were discovered by two brothers plotting a murder. While digging at a mound for fertilizer, they struck a clay pot. Inside were 13 leather bound books or codices.

Taking the books home, their mother found these papers useful as kindling for her stove. At least three of the codices were likely burned by the mother of the two brothers.

About a month after the find of the jar, the two brothers and other siblings found a man who had murdered their own father half a year earlier. The father of the two brothers had been working as a night watchman and was killed by an intruder on a field he was watching. Exacting their revenge, they made the

---

[445] Thomas 2:1–2. A more contemporary version of Thomas' saying might be that of the now deceased American composer and conductor Leonard Bernstein who stated: "A work of art does not answer questions, it provokes them; and its essential meaning is in the tension between the contradictory answers." Per Leonard Bernstein, *the Infinite Variety of Music* (Amadeus Press, 2007), 141.

attack at night and "...hacked off his limbs bit by bit, ripped out his heart, and devoured it among them, as the ultimate act of blood revenge."[446]

During the subsequent murder investigation, one of the brothers decided to distribute the books to others for safe keeping. A Coptic priest and his brother were instrumental to recognize the potential value of the books, In effect, the library was 'discovered' by others who recognized their antiquity. The first portion of the library to be translated made its way into the hands of none other than the well-known psychologist Carl Jung.

Today, the Nag Hammadi Library is back together again, conserved in the Coptic Museum.[447]

---

[446] James E. Robinson, *The Nag Hammadi Library in English,* rev. ed. (San Francisco: Harper Collins, 1990), 23.
[447] Robinson, 25.

IX. Mary—Life and Resurrection

Do not hold on to me, because I have not yet ascended to the Father.
But go to my brothers and say to them,
'I am ascending to my Father and your Father,
to my God and your God.'
Jesus to Mary Magdalene, as recorded in John 20:17

Mary Magdalene has long been controversial both within the church and in the broader cultural arena. To some, a source of embarrassment. To others, a symbol of repentance, forgiveness and hope.

To yet others, a model of devotion and intimacy. And perhaps for all, a lesson in suppressed history.

This is the story of how one Mary—the Magdalene—became *the bridge* between the dead and the resurrected Christ, keeping the flame of emerging Christian faith alive during its earliest and darkest hour.

The Mary Account

First a bit of background. We start with the inevitable confusion that has surrounded all of the Marys who appear in the New Testament. This is followed by an abbreviated account of the historical Mary, then also the consideration of writings attributed to this one Mary—the Magdalene.

Six New Testament Marys. There are at least six persons who go by the name of Mary that can be identified in the New Testament:

- Mary the mother of Jesus—also very likely the mother (and/or stepmother) to James, Jude, Joseph, Simon and unnamed sisters to Jesus.
- Mary the sister of Martha and Lazarus—with a home at Bethany.
- Mary the Magdalene—*our subject*

- Mary the wife of Clopas (or Alpheus)—first mentioned on the day of the crucifixion standing by the cross and, later, sitting desolate at the tomb with Mary Magdalene.
- Mary, mother of John Mark—reputed author of the Gospel of Mark.
- Paul's Unidentified Mary—noted at the conclusion to his epistle to the Romans with the message: "Greet Mary, who has worked very hard among you."[448]

Our interest is with the Mary ready to embrace Jesus—the one to meet her "Rabbouni" after his resurrection from the tomb.

The Magdalene

Different explanations have been given of this name; but the most natural is that she came from the town of Magdala on the southwest coast of the Sea of Galilee. After Jesus cast seven demons from her, she became one of His followers.

According to the Talmud (the collection of Rabbinic writings that make up the basis of religious authority for traditional Judaism), the export-oriented and fishing-based city of Magdala had a reputation for prostitution—a factor that justly or unjustly has contributed to taint Mary's reputation over the last two millennia.

Available New Testament accounts do not describe this Mary's illness in any greater detail. This information, coupled with the observation that Luke first mentions Mary Magdalene immediately following his account of the sinful woman leads some to the conclusion that the two women are one and the same.

John's Gospel does not name the woman accused of adultery; however, this person also has been widely assumed for centuries to be none other than the Magdalene.

A Romantic Connection? Over the centuries, Mary Magdalene has also been linked romantically with Jesus. The non-canonical Gospel of Philip is the most direct:

---

[448] Romans 16:6.

As for the Wisdom who is called "the barren," she is the mother of the angels. And the companion of the [...] Mary Magdalene. [...] loved her more than all the disciples, and used to kiss her often on her [...]. The rest of the disciples [...]. They said to him, "Why do you love her more than all of us?" The Savior answered and said to them, "Why do I not love you like her? When a blind man and one who sees are both together in darkness, they are no different from one another. When the light comes, then he who sees will see the light, and he who is blind will remain in darkness."[449]

Some have speculated that Mary Magdalene and Jesus were married and had children. For example, one recent writer goes so far as to suggest that Magdalene died in AD 63, at age 60 in what is now southern France.[450]

In the book *Rabbi Jesus: An Intimate Biography,* author Bruce Chilton suggests a plausible social context for Jesus' relationship with Mary:

Jesus' itinerant life precluded marriage and raising children. Loyalty to the Torah precluded adultery. But adultery was defined in Judaism as taking the wife of another, which, like seducing a maiden (who might become another's wife), is clearly forbidden. But sexual contact with an unmarried woman who was not a virgin, particularly a sinner or a formerly demon-possessed person, did not fall under the definition of adultery or seduction. There is no evidence that Jesus did or did not enjoy sexual contact during his life, but seven-demoned Miriam (i.e., Mary) remains the most likely candidate if he did so, because she is the only woman, apart from his mother, with whom he had persistent contact. Indeed, her status made her the kind of woman Jesus' mother might once have hoped her *mamzer* son would marry.[451]

---

[449] Wesley W. Isenberg, trans., "The Gospel of Philip," *The Nag Hammadi Library in English,* James E Robinson, ed. (San Francisco: Harper Collins, 1990 Revised ed,) 148.

[450] Laurence Gardner, *Bloodline of the Holy Grail* (New York: Barnes & Noble Books, 1997) 113.

[451] Bruce Chilton, *Rabbi Jesus: An Intimate Biography* (New York: Doubleday, 2000), 145. Mamzer is a Yiddish slang word for "bastard," a person born as the result of forbidden sexual relationships in Hebrew culture.

Gospel Accounts. Beyond the speculation, it is instructive to consider how the Magdalene is portrayed in the New Testament Gospels. The only definitive mention of Mary Magdalene prior to the reported crucifixion and resurrection of Jesus occurs in Luke's gospel, which goes like this:

> Soon afterward he (Jesus) went on through cities and villages, proclaiming and bringing the good news of the kingdom of God. The twelve were with him, as well as some women who had been *cured of evil spirits and infirmities*: Mary, called Magdalene, from whom seven demons had gone out, and Joanna, the wife of Herod's steward Chuza, and Susanna, and many others, *who provided for them out of their resources.*[452]

As Luke describes it, Mary and the other key women followers of Jesus appear to have two characteristics in common. They have experienced healing from Jesus and, in turn, appear to be women of substantial resources to provide for Jesus and his disciples. Later and at the site of the crucifixion, Mark's gospel puts it this way:

> There were also women looking on from a distance; among them were Mary Magdalene, and Mary the mother of James the younger and of Joses, and Salome. These used to follow him and provided for him when he was in Galilee; and there were many other women who had come up with him to Jerusalem.[453]

The women specifically named by Mark are different from those mentioned by Luke except for Mary Magdalene. But these appear to play similar roles of being not only followers, but ones who also "provided for" or "ministered" to Jesus. These passages clearly indicate three items worth noting:

- Along with other women, Mary Magdalene had been cured of some form of spirit possession (or similar infirmity).

---

[452] Luke 8:1–3.
[453] Mark 15:40–41.

- The other women mentioned (and possibly the Magdalene) were individuals of some resources (or wealth), who apparently helped to fund the travels not only of Jesus but for the twelve disciples as well.
- The roles of the Magdalene and other women extended beyond providing material resources to include a more encompassing service of ministering to Jesus—essentially a form of ongoing discipleship.

So there we have it, most all the events in the canonical New Testament that directly relate to Mary Magdalene—at least prior to Jesus' crucifixion and resurrection. But not quite, because there are two other matters often attributed to the Magdalene to be covered—in summary fashion:

- Mary Magdalene has been associated with the "woman in the city who was a sinner" who washed Jesus' feet, but there is no definitive New Testament basis for this Mary being the one who did this.[454]
- The Magdalene also is often associated with the woman whom Jesus saved from stoning after she had been taken in adultery, again an association with no supporting evidence.[455]

Crucifixion. The next time that we definitely encounter Mary Magdalene is at the crucifixion. As the first appearance reported by Matthew of the Magdalene; the gospel writer provides this account:

> Many women were also there, looking on from a distance; they had followed Jesus from Galilee and had provided for him. Among them were Mary Magdalene, and Mary the mother of James and Joseph, and the mother of the sons of Zebedee.[456]

For Matthew, this apparently is a woman who needs little to no introduction. And in this account, the Magdalene even takes precedence over another Mary at the crucifixion—either the mother of Jesus or the mother of

---

[454] Luke 7:37. Though Luke does not identify the sinful woman, he first introduces Mary Magdalene just after this account at Luke 8:2.

[455] John 8:1–11. This passage is not included in some of the earliest extant manuscripts of the New Testament.

[456] Matthew 27:55–56.

the sons of Alphaeus (Clopas). Beyond the crucifixion, Mary Magdalene also was present at the gravesite as Jesus was placed in the tomb that had been previously prepared for the future burial of Joseph of Arimathea:

> So Joseph took the body and wrapped it in a clean linen cloth and laid it in his own new tomb, which he had hewn in the rock. He then rolled a great stone to the door of the tomb and went away. Mary Magdalene and the other Mary were there, sitting opposite the tomb. [457]

Resurrection. We now turn to the events of resurrection morning. Here the accounts, while similar, diverge in the details. Matthew starts it this way:

> After the Sabbath, as the first day of the week was dawning, Mary Magdalene and the other Mary went to see the tomb.[458]

Matthew then recounts how the two women see an angel who tells them not to be afraid, that Jesus is risen, and that they should go tell the disciples. Both leave the tomb "quickly with fear and great joy."[459]

Mark's gospel offers a nearly identical story, with two notable variations. First, Mark appears to identify the two Marys and also Salome as visiting the tomb on Sunday morning. Second, and of greater interest, Mark does not refer to the sense of "great joy" recorded by Matthew. Rather this second gospel states:

> So they went out and fled from the tomb, for terror and amazement had seized them; and they said nothing to anyone, for they were afraid.[460]

---

[457] Matthew 27:59–61. Mark 15:40–47 provides a similar account, although Mark also identifies Salome as an observer at the crucifixion. Mark describes these as women who "used to follow him and provided for him when he was in Galilee; and there were many other women who had come up with him to Jerusalem." Luke does not identify the women by name but at 23:55–56 states: "The women who had come with him from Galilee followed, and they saw the tomb and how his body was laid. Then they returned, and prepared spices and ointments."

[458] Matthew 28:1.

[459] Matthew 28:8.

[460] Mark 16:8.

And here Mark's gospel ends—at least the earliest known manuscripts. Later manuscripts of Mark's gospel add one of two variations. The first and shorter end of the gospel narrative variations ends this way:

[[And all that had been commanded them they told briefly to those around Peter. And afterward Jesus himself sent out through them, from east to west, the sacred and imperishable proclamation of eternal salvation.]][461]

The second and more conventional longer ending of Mark starts this way:

Now after he rose early on the first day of the week, *he appeared first to Mary Magdalene*, from whom he had cast out seven demons. She went out and told those who had been with him, while they were mourning and weeping. But when they heard that he was alive and had been seen by her, *they would not believe it*.[462]

With either ending, Mary Magdalene figures prominently as a pivotal *closer* to Mark's gospel. She seals the deal. The question posed by the alternative endings is whether she left in fear and amazement *or* with joy and confidence.

Luke's gospel provides an account that is similar to the longer, more conventional ending to the Gospel of Mark. However, Luke adds a follow-up sequence—with Peter also going to the tomb following the earlier arrival of the women:

Then they remembered his words, and returning from the tomb, they told all this to the eleven and to all the rest. Now it was Mary Magdalene, Joanna, Mary the mother of James, and the other women with them who told this to the apostles. But these words seemed to them *an idle tale*, and they did not believe them. But Peter got up and ran to the tomb; stooping and looking in, he saw the linen cloths by themselves; then he went home, amazed at what had happened.[463]

---

[461] Mark 16:8 (shorter ending). This ending of Mark is believed to have been added no earlier than the 4th century.
[462] Mark 16:9–11.
[463] Luke 24:8–12. Unclear is whether "home" refers to temporary lodging in Jerusalem

Finally we get to John's Gospel, which makes Mary of Magdalene the clear star of the resurrection narrative. Not only does she get there first (in this account unaccompanied), she also is the first to meet and greet the risen Jesus:

> Early on the first day of the week, while it was still dark, Mary Magdalene came to the tomb and saw that the stone had been removed from the tomb...[464]

Peter and the other disciple (i.e. John) then go to the tomb with John arriving first. But John's gospel makes clear that the men *"did not understand the scripture, that he must rise from the dead."*[465] The action now returns to the Magdalene:

> But Mary stood weeping outside the tomb. As she wept, she bent over to look into the tomb; and she saw two angels in white, sitting where the body of Jesus had been lying, one at the head and the other at the feet. They said to her, "Woman, why are you weeping?" She said to them, "They have *taken away my Lord*, and I do not know where they have laid him." When she had said this, she turned around and saw Jesus standing there, but she did not know that it was Jesus. Jesus said to her, "Woman, why are you weeping? Whom are you looking for?"
> Supposing him to be the gardener, she said to him, "Sir, if you have carried him away, tell me where you have laid him, and I will take him away." Jesus said to her, "Mary!" She turned and said to him in Hebrew, "*Rabbouni!*" (which means teacher). Jesus said to her, "*Do not hold on to me*, because I have not yet ascended to the Father. *But go to my brothers and say* to them, 'I am ascending to my Father and your Father, to my God and your God.'" Mary Magdalene went and announced to the disciples, "I have seen the Lord"; and she told them that he had said these things to her.[466]

---

or eventual return to Galilee.

[464] Similar to Luke, John's account then tells of Peter and the "other disciple" also going and witnessing the empty tomb. They leave and return to their homes.

[465] John 20:9.

[466] John 20:1–18.

To summarize, the New Testament Gospels leave us with a portrait of a woman who clearly was a long-time follower of Jesus after her healing by the Savior. She was a doer, evidenced by initiative to attend to the grave of her master at the earliest opportunity after death and then after the intervening Sabbath.

If we had just the three synoptic Gospels of Matthew, Mark and Luke, that might be the end of the story. But John's Gospel opens a new dimension—a story that clearly portrays a more intimate, closer connection between the rabbi and the Magdalene. A closeness evidenced by the imminence of her reaching out to embrace a newly resurrected Savior—stopped only by the request of Jesus not to be touched.

The Magdalene's Gospel

For this Christian pioneer, we look both to canonical and non-canonical accounts. The New Testament canon is important as a baseline for information—in effect a bit of a teaser. But this is not necessarily the whole story. For when it comes to the role of women in the life and times of Jesus and of the early church, there may well be more than what found its way into the canon of orthodoxy.

At least, three non-canonical works are of importance in presenting a decidedly unorthodox view of women's roles in the development of 1st century Christianity. One is the Gospel of Mary; the other two are known as the *Dialogue of the Savior* and the *Gospel of Philip*. All three are considered as part of the Coptic Gnostic Library—containing three Berlin or Akhmim Codex documents including the Gospel of Mary discovered in Akhmim, Egypt in 1896. This predates the discover of the more extensive documents of the Nag Hammadi Library uncovered in 1945.

For this ensuing discussion, we focus on the narrative as provided by the New Testament Gospels coupled with the non-canonical Gospel of Mary and as further supplemented by the other two non-canonical Gospels—the Dialogue of the Savior and the Gospel of Philip.

Did Mary Magdalene Write The Gospel Ascribed to Her? The answer: Who knows? No New Testament documentation is attributed to a woman, much less Mary Magdalene. However, one non-canonical document is attributed and in fact is widely known for its in-depth portrayal of the Magdalene. For centuries, this gospel has remained virtually unknown.

The Gospel of Mary re-surfaced in 1896, when Papyrus Berolinensis 8502 (Akhmim Codex) was acquired in Cairo by Dr. Rheinhardt. This Coptic manuscript dates to the 5th century but, unfortunately, was not published until 1955. This now extant Mary manuscript is fragmentary, missing its first six pages and another four pages toward the middle of the codex.

All told, there are only three fragmentary manuscripts that have been recovered in recent years. Two are 3rd century Greek fragments in addition to the longer 5th century Coptic translation. While date and the place of initial composition are unknown, some argue that the Gospel of Mary could have been written in the late first or early second centuries in Syria or Egypt. The papyrus dates to the third century. There also are Patristic references to a *Gospel of Mary* as early as the third century.

Authorship of the Gospel of Mary also is uncertain. There is no explicit claim made that Mary Magdalene is the author of this gospel, although she figures as the subject of much of the discussion with Jesus and with the disciples.

The Two Other Non-Canonical Works. Two other documents which reference Mary Magdalene are included with the later Nag Hammadi discovery. The *Dialogue of the Savior* was composed as a conversation between the *Lord* and several disciples including Mary.

As is the case with the Gospel of Mary, there is no author clearly identified. The Dialogue was composed as a collection of sayings similar to that of the Gospel of Thomas. Mary is identified as the source of at least a quarter of 41 currently known sayings. The Dialogue was originally written in Greek, but now survives only in one fragmentary Coptic manuscript from Nag Hammadi. The manuscript is believed to have been written around 150 AD.

The *Gospel of Philip* contains both sayings of and stories about Jesus, from a Gnostic (Valentinian) perspective. The account is not altogether coherent but often rambling and disjointed. The available Coptic text is believed to be a translation of a Greek text written perhaps as late as the second half of the third century.

The Gospel of Philip is named for this disciple, perhaps because this is the only apostle named. However, actual authorship is uncertain. This non-canonical work has received attention largely because of its suggestion of a potential romantic relationship between Jesus and Mary the Magdalene (as considered in more detail later in this chapter).

Life and Resurrection

John's Gospel quotes Jesus as saying: "I am the resurrection and the life." Herein lies the pioneering path and potentially the heresy of Mary the Magdalene. This also possibly serves as a reason for the prolonged disappearance of Mary's account of Jesus and his disciples. In effect, Mary's heresy is two-fold:

- As witness and advocate of the resurrection.
- As holding together a group of men ready to abandon the church in its earliest hours.

A New Testament Feminist Perspective. Is there a war of the sexes at work in the early church, even earlier in the midst of Jesus? Consider the evidence which is increasingly well documented—beginning back at Easter morning. Even the gospel writers can't hide the undertones of gender tension at play.

Start with Luke's account of the resurrection: The women (including Mary Magdalene) arrive at the tomb, see two angels, and then return to tell the eleven of what they have seen. Luke's gospel records the negative reaction of the disciples: "But these words seemed to them an idle tale, and they did not believe them." So Peter has to run off to the tomb on his own, and comes back, as Luke says, "amazed at what had happened."[467]

The disciples gave little credibility to the women's account; Peter is incredulous when he finds that the women have not hallucinated, dreamed, or fabricated, but have perceived the situation correctly.

The two alternative accounts of Mark's gospel are the most telling: The earliest available manuscripts end Mark's gospel with women who have:

> ...fled from the tomb, for terror and amazement had seized them and they said nothing to anyone, for they were afraid.[468]

For Mark, this is the end of story and hardly a flattering view of the women at the tomb.

---

[467] Excerpted from Luke 24:11–12.
[468] Mark 16:8 (the last verse the gospel in as recorded in the earliest extant manuscripts).

Introduce Matthew's version: Matthew recounts how the two women see an angel who tells them not to be afraid, that Jesus is risen, and that they should go tell the disciples. They leave the tomb "quickly with fear and great joy."[469]

Back to Mark: The second and more conventional ending of Mark puts a more conventional spin on the event (more similar to that of Luke's gospel):

> Now after he rose early on the first day of the week, he appeared first to Mary Magdalene, from whom he had cast out seven demons. She went out and told those who had been with him, while they were mourning and weeping. But when they heard that he was alive and had been seen by her, they would not believe it.[470]

In this account, which appears in virtually all conventional bibles from the King James forward, Mary is vindicated. In fact, this longer version of Mark's gospel indicates that once Jesus finally appears to the eleven:

> …he upbraided them for their lack of faith and stubbornness, because they had not believed those who saw him after he had risen.[471]

It is also useful to consider John: For the writer of John's Gospel, the women's credibility with male disciples comes across as less of an issue. Like Luke, John indicates that Mary arrives first, goes and tells Peter who comes back with the beloved disciple.

Mary lingers at the tomb site, where she then has her encounter with the gardener, actually Jesus, who asks Mary to:

> …go to my brothers and say to them, 'I am ascending to my Father and your Father, to my God and your God.' Mary Magdalene went and announced to the disciples, "I have seen the Lord"; and *she told them that he had said these things to her.*[472]

---

[469] Matthew 28:8.

[470] Mark 16:9–11.

[471] Mark 16:14. Mark also indicates that after appearing to Mary, Jesus had appeared "in another two of them as they were walking into the country," and then to the 11 disciples.

[472] John 20:17–18.

Jesus has used Mary as his envoy, taking a message back to the other (male) disciples. While these disciples are not cited as being openly contemptuous of the message of Mary, they still don't seem to get it without Mary.

The precise chronology of what happens going forward to the time of Jesus ascension is somewhat difficult to reconcile based on the four gospel accounts. Key events appear to include Mary and the other women relaying Jesus' message to the disciples (whether in greater or lesser detail), Jesus' appearance that same day to two travelers to Emmaus, and then most likely on Easter evening to the disciples, at some point a return by the disciples (and perhaps the women) to the Galilee, and then return to near Bethany (likely the Mount of Olives) for ascension to heaven.[473]

Beyond the New Testament. If the tension between the apostolic men and women of the Jesus movement is muted in the canonical New Testament, it flares into the open with several non-canonical works (all from the Coptic Gnostic Library discoveries of the late 1800s and mid-1900s).

Start with the most famous of the Nag Hammadi works, the Gospel of Thomas. In the very last of 114 sayings, Thomas makes this tension explicitly clear:

Simon Peter said to them, "Make Mary leave us, for *females don't deserve life*." Jesus said, "Look, I will guide her to make her male, so that she too may become a living spirit resembling you males. For every *female who makes herself male* will enter the domain of Heaven."[474]

Not only is the tension palpable, but the Jesus of Thomas appears to at least partially side with the women—albeit in a form that suggests continued submission of woman to man. A similarly anti-feminist viewpoint is attributed to Jesus in a separate work from the Nag Hammadi Library, the *Dialogue of the Savior:*

---

[473] The person Cleopas (Clopas, variation Alphaeus) encountered by Jesus on the road to Emmaus (per Luke 24:13–32) is very likely a brother of Jesus' step-father Joseph. Clopas was married to the "other Mary" who would therefore be sister-in-law of Mary the mother of Jesus.

[474] Thomas 114.

Judas said: "Why then, in truth, do (the living) die and (the dead) live?" The Lord said, "Whatever is from the truth does not die; whatever is from woman dies."[475]

In the very next saying, Mary has what may be considered as a possible [albeit fragmentary] rejoinder:

Mary said, "Tell me, Lord, why have I come to this place—to gain or to lose?"

The Lord said, "(You have come) to reveal the greatness of the revealer."

Mary said to him, "Lord is there a place that [...] or lack the truth?"

The Lord said, "The place where I am not."

Mary said, "Lord, you are fearful and marvelous, and [.] those who do not know you."[476]

Back to the Resurrection. It takes the non-canonical Gospel of Mary to offer a more cohesive counterpoint to male-centric Christianity. For this, we travel back to the resurrection—this time as told by Mary's so-called Gospel.

Mary's account begins mildly enough. Upon issuing a commandment to "preach the good news of the domain" (much as is recorded in the four Gospels), Jesus leaves the disciples who "were distressed and wept greatly."[477] It is at this point that Mary takes command:

Then Mary stood up. She greeted them all and addressed her brothers: "Do not weep and be distressed nor let your hearts by irresolute. For his grace will be with you all and will shelter you. Rather we should praise his greatness, for he has joined us together and made us true beings." When Mary said these things, *she turned their minds* [to]ward the good, and they began to ask about the wor[d]s of the Savi[or].[478]

Following this, Peter is reported as saying to Mary:

---

[475] Dialogue of the Savior, 23:1–2 (SV).

[476] Dialogue 24:1–5.

[477] Gospel of Mary 5:1.

[478] Gospel of Mary 5:4–10. All references to this gospel are from the Scholar's Version (SV) with *the Complete Gospels,* Robert J. Miller, ed. (San Francisco: Polebridge Press/Harper, 1994).

"Sister, we know that the Savior loved you more than any other woman. Tell us the words of the Savior that you know, *but which we haven't heard.*" Mary responded, then proceeds to "rep[ort] to you as much as I remember that you don't know."[479]

After speaking of the secrets of what she terms the seven Powers of Wrath, Mary falls silent. At this point, gender resurfaces as a pivotal remaining issue:

> Andrew said: 'Brothers, what is your opinion of what was just said? I for one don't believe that the Savior said these things, because these opinions seem to be so different from his thought.'
> After reflecting on these matters, Peter said, 'Has the Savior spoken secretly to a woman and not openly so that we would all hear? *Surely he did not wish to indicate that she is more worthy than we are?*'
> Then Mary wept and said to Peter, 'Peter, my brother, what are you imagining about this? Do you think that I've made all this up secretly by myself or that I am telling lies about the Savior?'[480]
> Levi (aka Matthew) said to Peter, 'Peter, *you have a constant inclination to anger* and you are always ready to give way to it. And even now you are doing exactly that by questioning the woman as if you're her adversary. *If the Savior considered her to be worthy, who are you to disregard her?* For he knew her completely and loved her devotedly.'
> 'Instead, we should be ashamed and, once we clothe ourselves with perfect humanity, we should do what we were commanded. *We should announce the good news as the Savior ordered,* and not be laying down any rules or making laws.'
>
> After he said these things, Levi left and began to announce the good news.[481]

The Gospel of Mary (at least with the fragments currently available) ends here. Clearly, this non-canonical (if not heretical) gospel provides the most open assessment of the tension between the sexes that surfaced early in the

---

[479] Mary 6:1–3.
[480] Mary 5:1–10.
[481] Mary 10:1–14.

history of the Christian movement. For women, the message of this gospel is one of hope; Mary prevails over the objections of other prominent male disciples.

What do we make of this? It certainly appears that the New Testament accounts demonstrate reluctance of the men to accept the women as credible witnesses. Three different Nag Hammadi documents suggest that the issue may extend beyond a question of credibility to include outright resentment of Mary's special relationship with Jesus.

This may be more than just a difference in perspective. It apparently leads to a confrontation between the men and an embryonic women's movement led by Mary—essentially a tussle for early direction of the Christian movement.

Making A Difference. Coming from a non-canonical source (via the Gospel of Mary), it is easier for some to discount Mary's critical contribution. But don't we get the same message from the NT canon—all four Gospels? Just more veiled?

In Matthew, the angels tell the two Marys to "go quickly and tell his disciples."[482] Mark's version: "But go, tell his disciples and Peter that he is going ahead of you to Galilee…"[483] Luke's message from two men in dazzling clothes: "He is not here but he is risen."[484] John has Jesus telling Mary: "But go to my brothers and say to them, 'I am ascending, to my God and your God.'"[485]

From Life to Resurrection. Is the Mary story simply about a first-century version of women's liberation? It would be easy (and tempting) to stop here.

If we continue to dig, is there more? Or are we merely grasping at straws—at a vapor positioned just beyond our senses? The evidence available is often fragmentary, often ambiguous. Yet, there is yet more to capture.

We begin back with the New Testament gospel accounts of Mary Magdalene on Easter morning. While their accounts differ, all four gospel writers place Mary as either the first or with the first who approach the tomb:

---

[482] Matthew 28:7.
[483] Mark 16:7.
[484] Luke 24:5.
[485] John 20:17.

- The three synoptic writers identify Mary as with those 2–3+ women who first encounter an angelic presence at the tomb; the Gospel of John gives Mary the first audience (alone) with the risen Christ.
- In Matthew, the women are enjoined by the risen Jesus to go tell the disciples; in Mark, it is a "young man, dressed in a white robe" who gives this instruction. In Luke, the women go to the disciples (without mention of any prior direction) and in John's account Mary is instructed by Jesus to go to "my brothers."
- In Luke, the account of the women is not believed by the disciples; in Matthew and Mark (longer version), the disciples express doubt (even after other sightings). And in John, Peter and the beloved disciple are described as though they did "not understand" that Jesus would rise from the dead—despite having just witnessed an empty tomb. Thomas is identified as another apostolic doubter.

An Interesting Situation. Mary (and perhaps other women) are the first to visit the empty tomb and to experience the risen Jesus. The male disciples doubt the veracity of their accounts. Some apostles express doubts even after witnessing the empty tomb or hearing accounts of resurrection from others.

The question arises: is the first acknowledgement of resurrection by Mary coincidental, a fluke? Or is there something more significant? Is the initial acknowledgement by Mary instrumental to achieving broader recognition among other followers of this incomprehensible resurrection back to life? In short, would the Easter story have been possible without Mary?

Before answering, return again to the non-canonical Gospel of Mary. The gospel records Jesus commissioning the disciples to "preach the good news of the domain," then indicates that: "After he said these things, he left them."[486]

This gospel records that the disciples "were distressed and wept greatly." It is Mary who then "stood up" and addressed the disciples. She finishes, having "turned their minds toward the good, and they began to ask about the words of the Savior."[487] Here Mary plays a pivotal role not only with the Easter resurrection, but also as a path forward to the post-resurrection ascension.

---

[486] Mary 4:8,11.
[487] Excerpted from Mary 5:4–10.

One more clue, this time back to the canonical account, in Acts. After the ascension of Jesus, the disciples return to the upper room in the city. Not only the disciples, but also present are *"certain women,* including Mary the mother of Jesus, as well as his brothers."[488] The presence of the Magdalene is not clearly stated but implied as a key certain woman and participant in other recent events.

The Magdalene together with the other Marys mediate and deliver the message of a risen savior to skeptical male disciples. But this is a challenging message—especially coming from women in first-century Palestine. It's bad news for the messenger, as Mary is relegated to whispered rumors, even the risk of being dismissed and subsequent obscurity.

Fortunately, the message is revived and appropriated—by the apostle Paul. And what was heresy before could go *mainstream* as Christianity became liberated from the perceived straight-jacket of Judaism and repackaged as more appealing to a more diverse Gentile audience.

Could Christianity have survived without this radical message of resurrection? Unlikely. Even 20 centuries later, it has been written:

> And yet the confidence that God raises life from the dust of death, for all the various ways it is presented in the New Testament and later theology, is the *genetic chain* informing and sustaining the entire organism of Christianity.[489]

From whence do these good genes arise? None other than the life, the message and persistence of a woman and women named Mary.

Reconciling Radical Feminist and Life/Resurrection Messages. At the end of the day, one nagging question remains: how to reconcile Mary the radical feminist with Mary the mediator of life and resurrection. Are these *flip sides* of the same coin? Or different coins altogether?

One possible path toward reconciliation is that of necessity. Mary is emboldened—taking command—because the male apostles remain confused and weak even following Jesus' reported resurrection and then his ascension. A darker version of this path could portray Mary as opportunistic—taking

---

[488] Acts 1:14.
[489] Bruce Chilton, *Rabbi Jesus*, 288.

advantage of her intimacy with Jesus and access to information not otherwise available to others.

An alternative path is one of special understanding and insight not available to or discerned by her male colleagues. In this view, Mary emerges as a radical leader simply because she possesses an understanding of Jesus that has yet to penetrate the consciousness of the other apostles.

As Peter reportedly asks Mary: "Tell us the words of the Savior that you know, but which we haven't heard." Mary explains by saying: "I saw the Lord in a vision and I said to him…"[490] This clearly suggests not only that Mary received special insight while Jesus was physically present but also the possibility of some ongoing form of dialogue or visioning even post-ascension.

Yes, this is from a non-canonical source (the Gospel of Mary), making it easier from some to discount. But don't we get the same message from the canon—all four Gospels?

Here, at the post-resurrection starting point of the Christian church, Mary *is in command* of pivotal information available to none of the other disciples. She is commissioned to bring a message to those who are skeptical, fearful, confused. She is asked to take charge—bringing the disciples and, by them, others to understanding.

Mary Magdalene in Summary

This is the end of a tale—of events rapidly unfolding at a pivotal juncture in the history of the Christian faith. With Mary the Magdalene, there is that devoted patience to linger at the tomb when others who are more impatient depart.

If the Gospel of Thomas is disconcerting with its introduction to mystery and wisdom, the non-canonical so-called *Gospel of Mary* takes us yet another step—further into the uncharted waters of an historic Jesus transitioning to modern Christendom.

Mary's unorthodox approach to Christian belief and practice comes across as being a matter primarily of style rather than substance. Reflected by her personal connection to the Savior, she was able to step beyond the bounds of traditional norms for women to exert leadership in getting something done—

---

[490] Mary 6:2, 7:2.

at a moment when the post-resurrection movement was confused, even on the verge of collapse.

It was to the Magdalene that a newly resurrected Jesus first appeared, as recorded by John's Gospel saying:

> *Do not hold on to me*, because I have not yet ascended to the Father. But *go to my brothers* and say to them, 'I am ascending to my Father and your Father, to my God and your God.'[491]

The non-canonical Gospel of Mary picks up the rest of the story—the parts not told within but seemingly consistent with the account of the canonized New Testament. The rest of the story is that of Mary who exhorted the disciples not to be distressed, one who "turned their minds to the good."

Rather than presenting two discordant views of Jesus resurrection and mission going forward, the combination of the canonical and non-canonical accounts may be considered as pieces of a jigsaw puzzle. Not discordant but complementary—making it more readily possible to fully understand the big picture.

Mary Magdalene understands because she first inquires—incessantly. Whether or not written by her, the gospel named for her reveals a Lord who tells the rest of the story. Even as a vision of Jesus complimenting Mary for her pivotal contribution. As he says:

> Congratulations to *you for not wavering* at seeing me. For where the mind is, there is the treasure.[492]

From both NT and non-canonical sources, the weight of the combined evidence now available is clear. Without the Magdalene to carry the message of resurrection, there might well have been no Christian church.

This is a message based on the experiences of a woman who achieved the confidence of her Rabbouni both before and after resurrection. Experiences too intimate, too exclusive to be duplicated by others—except vicariously. Yet this is the Mary who almost single-handedly animates the Christian church to faith

---

[491] John 20:17.
[492] Mary 7:3–4.

in the goodness of the present and confidence of ongoing life beyond the human realm.

Supplement — Life in Magdala

While not directly stated in the New Testament but as implied by her name, Mary Magdalene is generally believed to be from the city of Magdala situated on the Sea of Galilee.

The city is known by its Aramaic name as Magdala (meaning the "tower"), in Hebrew as Migdal or more fully as Migdal Saba'ayya ("tower of the fish"), and in Greek as Taricheae (meaning "fish factories").

Leading up to and through the time of Jesus earthly sojourn, Magdala has experienced three primary phases of development—from the 2nd to 1st century BC with resettlement of the Galilee by the Hasmoneans, then from the 1st to 3rd century AD in the Roman period at the height of its prosperity, and later the Byzantine period of the 6th to 7th century with pilgrimage and then declining population and subsequent transition to Islamic control. With a rectilinear street grid, Magdala would become an early example of Greek or "Hellenistic-style urban planning in Jewish Galilee."[493]

Prior to relocation of the Galilean capital of Herod Antipas from Sepphoris in the Galilean highlands (near Nazareth) to the shores of Galilee as Tiberias (in about 19–20 AD), Magdala was the only urban center on the western shores of the lake. And as implied by its name, Magdala served as a dominant center of fishing and fish processing in the Galilee. Its salted fish and fish sauce were viewed as delicacies throughout the Roman empire and as a major source of export from Jewish Palestine. The city also benefited by its location of crossroads of the main trade routes of the Galilee.

Harbor activities were situated on or near the lake with much of the residential and cultural development further inland. Both observant Jewish and pagan Greco-Roman influences are evident. Magdala had its own synagogue, the only one of the pre-70 period in the Galilee discovered and excavated to date.

---

[493] Richard Bauckham and Stefano De Luca, "Magdala As We Now Know It, Early Christianity,6 (2015), p. 96. Much of this discussion is drawn from research involving these authors and other archaeologists in recent years.

Magdala also was associated with mikveh ritual baths—potentially the only ones in the Galilee. At the same time, the city also bore clear evidence of pagan Greco-Roman influence especially in the harbor area—including a quadriporticus (square courtyard with colonnades used for recreational exercise) and the only identified public baths in Jewish Palestine (other than near the palaces of Jericho). While Magdala included a palestra (in conjunction with the courtyard) and a hippodrome (as for chariot and horse racing), there is no evidence of a theater or nymphaeum (i.e., fountain house).

Residential areas included a mix of homes representing a cross-section of local elites, working people and itinerants. While less sumptuous than homes of the affluent in Jerusalem, Magdalen flourishes included upper end homes, for example, with mosaic floors.

With the first Jewish revolt of AD 66–70, the person who would become the Jewish historian—Josephus—was named as governor of the Galilee and made Magdala his headquarters for the Jewish rebellion against Rome. Under the command of the future Roman emperor Titus, the city was conquered as the result of a naval battle on the lake—despite a fleet of 230 small (primarily fishing) boats commandeered by Josephus to oppose the better equipped Romans.[494]

Natural events also shaped and undid Magdala. The 1st century AD coincided with a time of substantial rainfall with the highest water levels in the history of the Sea of Galilee. The city would be essentially destroyed by earthquake in 363 AD.

This brief survey indicates that like Sepphoris and Tiberias, Magdala was a relatively cosmopolitan Galilean community that accommodated a mixture of Jewish and Greco-Roman influences—likely more so than other smaller Jewish villages throughout the rest of the Galilee. Local populations, particularly involving the local elites, were able to adapt to aspects of Hellenistic culture, as with baths viewed as not directly idolatrous and allowing for conformity with Jewish purity rules.

---

[494] Josephus The Wars of the Jews, trans. Whiston, Book 2, 21.635.

X. Constantine—Monolithic Christianity

By this sign you will conquer.
Dream of Emperor Constantine, 313 AD

In 313 AD, the Roman co-emperor Constantine was battling Maxentius for clear title as emperor of the western Roman empire. Maxentius brought his troops out from Rome to confront Constantine at the Milvian Bridge across the Tiber River.[495]

On the eve of the battle, Constantine dreamed. Via this vision, he saw the initialed symbols of the name of Christ with the words: "By this sign you will conquer."[496] With this omen, Constantine had the Chi-Rho monogram painted on the shields of his soldiers. On April 30, Maxentius lost the ensuing battle and his life; Constantine entered Rome victorious.

During the ensuing reign of Constantine, Christianity emerged from the shadows as a way of life and faith for a marginalized minority to become the new Roman state religion. What proved to be of even greater significance was the formulation of a credal position at the Council of Nicaea that in 325 AD articulated what beliefs and practices would be within versus outside the bounds of orthodox (or Catholic) Christianity.

Key hallmarks of this uneven transition extending from the first to fourth centuries AD can be defined as a three-step process:[497]

---

[495] Also known as Mulvian Bridge.
[496] Williston Walker, et al, *A History of the Christian Church,* 4th ed. (New York: Charles Scribner's Sons, 1985) 125. Chi Rho are the first two letters of the Greek "Christos" or Christ. Much discussion is drawn from this source.
[497] This discussion also draws from E. Glenn Hinson, *The Early Church: Origins to the Dawn of the Middle Ages* (Nashville, Abingdon Press: 1996).

- Pre-Nicene emergence of diverse Christian movements extending from the time of initial post-resurrectgion evangelization as recorded by the book of Acts up to the point in 313 AD when Christianity began the transition from being a persecuted religion to the religion of the state.
- The church-wide Council of Nicaea in 325 which for the first time solidified how orthodox Christian belief was to be defined and practiced empire-wide.
- A post-Nicene period lasting through the end of the 4th century of continuing controversy up to the point of coalescing around a refined Nicene approach to orthodoxy in belief and practice.

Pre-Nicene Christianity

Constantine's stroke of genius—wedding church and state—was not entirely of his own doing. The seeds had been planted over a period of more than two centuries leading up to his reign. Constantine recognized and was adroit enough to reap the harvest.

In this context, it is useful to briefly consider the roles of key leaders within the early Christian movement—those who followed those who actually knew Jesus—extending from the period of the latter half of the 1st century to early in the 4th century.

Post Apostolic Christianity. This covers a time period extending from the Roman destruction of Jerusalem in 70 AD. The leader of the Jerusalem church, James the brother of Jesus, was put to death in about 62 AD. The death of the apostle Paul likely occurred pre-64 and Peter also by 64. The years immediately following the fall of Jerusalem are what one writer has described as "among the most obscure in the life of the primitive Church."[498]

An early reported conflict with Roman authority appears to have been occasioned by the conflagration of Rome in 64 AD. This occurred during the imperial reign of Nero who found scapegoats described by Roman historian Tacitus as "those whom the populace called Christians, who were detested because of their shameful deeds."[499]

---

[498] W.H.C. Frend, *The Early Church,* Fourth Printing, (Philadelphia: Fortress Press, 1987) 35.
[499] Tacitus, *Annals* 15:44.

In the aftermath of the fire, Christians were arrested, tried and put to death—often as part of public entertainment spectacles.

By the beginning of the second century and despite periodic persecution, a hierarchical ecclesiastical structure had begun to take shape with designation of bishops and deacons associated with centers of Christian worship. The interest in maintaining an authentic Christian heritage was considerable, as reflected in the letter of second century Ignatius commending the church congregants at Ephesus "who have always been of the same mind with the apostles through the power of Jesus Christ."[500]

Roman persecutions of Christians during this period tended to be sporadic and brief but intense. Early persecutions occurred under the reigns of emperors Nero, Domitian and Trajan. Nonetheless, by about 100 AD, there were Christian groups in Asia Minor, Syria, Macedonia, Greece and the city of Rome. By 130, there was a clear Christian presence in Egypt.

Apologists and Gnostics. From about 130–180 AD, the emerging doctrines of the early mainstream church are derived from the teachings of early writers known as the Apologists. As perhaps the best known of the early apologists, Justin Martyr made extensive use of the idea of a divine Logos as the first born, the spirit and the power from God. His theology represented an initiative to open dialogue between Greco-Roman philosophy and Christianity. These were the beginnings of what might be considered as a more scientific theology.

At the same time as defenders of the Christian faith were stepping forward, a new counter-movement was taking shape. This alternative to early orthodox Christianity consisted of relatively diverse ideas but with commonalities often labeled under the umbrella term of Gnosticism. The term is derived from the Greek word *gnostikos,* meaning "one who knows," in turn based on a word for "knowledge," *gnosis.*

To the Gnostics, knowledge was not derived from ordinary sources; it came from divine revelation. Secret knowledge came only to a select number of people. For Christian Gnostics, Jesus Christ was the main source of revelation.

Gnosticism served to help force the creation of orthodox, written Christian doctrine. The church's first doctrinal teachings crystallized in response to this sect that was seen as separating Jesus from his humanity.

---

[500] Ignatius, *Ephesians* 11.2.

Logos vs. Monarchian Theology. After a long period of Roman tolerance toward Christians, a less congenial administration took hold under the reign of emperor Marcus Aurelius (161–180). Apologists argued the truth of monotheism, claiming that only Christian worship of a single God was valid. However, this teaching was soon ensnared in a trap from which recovery proved elusive. Was Christianity a teaching of one, two or three god-like figures?

Toward the close of the second century, Logos theology was formulated as an orthodox response by Christian theologians such as Justin Martyr, Irenaeus, Tertullian and other apologists—specifically to distinguish between God the Father and the Son. For Justin, the "Son of God" was "another God" who existed alongside the "sole unbegotten," or Father. By creating a "second God," the Logos theology appeared to critics as inconsistent with the principle of monotheism, except by further subordinating the son to the Father.

The reaction to the Logos theology was Monarchianism, an attempt to restore a purer form of monotheism. In its initial form, Monarchians asserted that "Christ was a mere man" who was adopted into divinity by his resurrection.[501] A variation of this was modalism, positing that Father, Son and Holy Spirit referred not to different persons but to different ways (or modes) by which the one God interreacts with creation.

Imperial Persecution and Christian Reaction. From 249–259, two imperial persecutions jolted what had become an increasingly comfortable world for Christians throughout the Roman Empire. The first persecution under emperor Decius was relatively brief, lasting from December 249 to late 250. Christians could get off the hook by sacrificing to the gods of Rome.

The aftermath created a new dilemma for churches—whether and how to readmit those who had lapsed or recanted, particularly members of the clergy. A second persecution ensued in 258 under emperor Valerian.

The final so-called Great Persecution of Christians was launched on February 23, 303 in Nicomedia (of Asia Minor) during the 19th year of rule by the Emperor Diocletian. Christian Scriptures were to be surrendered and burned, churches to be dismantled, and no further worship meetings held.

In 304, Roman governmental authority effectively passed from Diocletian to Galerius and the level of imperially sanctioned intimidation increased.

---

[501] This was the viewpoint of Theodotus, a tanner from Byzantium, ca. 190, for which he was excommunicated.

Diocletian had begun to train a young Constantine (son of Constantius Caesar of the West). In 306, Constantine traveled to Britain and arrived just in time to be on hand when his father died on July 25.

That same day, the Roman army in Britain proclaimed Constantine as Augustus. The events of that day and Constantine's subsequent rise to power mark what one historian describes as:

> ...a lust for power, a strong element of cruelty, a capacity for quick thinking and acting, and a religious sense which allowed him (Constantine) to attribute his success to the intervention of higher powers.[502]

In 311, emperor Galerius became ill (possibly with cancer of the bowels). In an act of moderation, he issued an edict of amnesty, stating that "Christians may exist again, and may establish their meeting houses, yet so that they do nothing contrary to good order."[503]

Official Roman sanction to persecute Christians came to an end in 313 when Constantine and Licinius issued the Edict of Milan establishing freedom of religion.

Donatism. The end of governmentally sanctioned persecution was not accompanied by any substantial improved internal harmony within the church itself. A new schism took root in North Africa—a direct result of the Diocletian persecution. The question was how those who had recanted their faith in the face of the Diocletian persecution were to be treated now that the persecution was over.

A bishop of Carthage named Donatus came to be regarded as chief spokesman of the movement that also appropriated his name. Donatists insisted that those who had apostatized or recanted during the Diocletian persecution should not administer the Christian sacraments.

Eventually, the resolution would involve the direct intervention of this new emperor—Constantine. The first ecclesiastical tribunal convened through imperial authority occurred on September 30, 313, at the coastal home of

---

[502] Frend, *The Early Church,* 120.

[503] Lactaintius, *On the Death of the Persecutors,* recounting "The Toleration Edict of Galerius 30 April 311," as recorded by J. Stevenson, ed., *A New Eusebius* (New York: The Macmillan Company: 1957) 256. References noted for *A New Eusebius* are by document number rather than page number.

Constantine's wife Fausta. Donatus was condemned for disturbing established disciplinary procedures, specifically via the unauthorized act of rebaptizing (lapsed) clergy and creating schism within the church.

After some vacillation, severe restrictions were placed on the African church, including orders for confiscating church property of the Donatists and exile of Donatist leaders. The African church resisted the imperial edict.

On May 5, 321, that the emperor reversed his prior decision and offered the Donatists toleration. Constantine had been worn down (as would occur again in the future). His attention also was diverting to a new and even more serious religious controversy arising elsewhere from the east—that of an Alexandrian presbyter named Arius.

Arianism. This is the most famous of the controversies of the early church and was the cause of Constantine's decision to call the legendary Council of Nicaea. The roots of the movement can be traced to an Egyptian Bishop named Meletus imprisoned through 304–05 under Diocletian. Like Donatus, Meletus favored a rigorous policy toward re-admittance of clergy who had lapsed (or recanted their Christian beliefs) during the persecution of Diocletian.

Around 318, a church presbyter from Alexandria named Arius began to expound the view that the Logos is a creature called into being by God "out of the non-existent," meaning there was a time when the Logos did not exist.[504] Since there cannot be two gods in a monotheistic religion, it follows that the Son is a creature. As a created being, the Logos could change and was capable of either virtue or vice.

In correspondence, Arius reputedly had written that Jesus "is not equal, no, not one in essence with Him (God)."[505] This was in opposition to the Monarchian view that there was no distinction of entities between Father and Son.

The views of Arius were well aligned with those of the esteemed theologian Origen (of the prior century) but became increasingly opposed by

---

[504] Sozomen, "Arius and His Heresy," as recounted by *A New Eusebius,* 291.

[505] Athanasius, "Extracts from the *Thalia of Arius,"* Heresy," as recounted by *A New Eusebius,* op cit., 296. Except for three complete letters, the *Thalia* is the primary theological work of Arius, of which no extant copies remain. The extracts noted are incomplete and out of order as recounted by Athanasius, the chief Nicene opponent of Arius. Unlike the Nicene Creed, the views of Arius can be viewed as was more consistent with the Jewish Shema.

Alexander, pope of Alexandria. In 318–319, Alexander convened a council of 100 bishops; Arius was condemned and exiled.

As sole emperor, Constantine once again turned to matters of religion and found this dispute simmering between Arius and Alexander. He initially attempted to get the competing sides to mediate, suggesting that the issue being debated was "unprofitable."

Nicaea

With mediation proving to be just as unprofitable, Constantine called a universal council of the church at Nicaea, situated about 30 miles from the emperor's capital at Nicomedia. An estimated 250–300 bishops and staff attended, mostly from the east but with some representation from the west.

Homoiousios, Homoousios and Homoios. The central question debated by those attending the Nicene Council was the relationship of Jesus the Son to God the Father. A number of alternatives (as expressed in the *Greek*) were possible, each with its own adherents:

- *Anomoios*—the (extreme) viewpoint taken that the Son is "unlike" the Father.
- *Homoios*—the more generic viewpoint that the Son is "like" the Father, a term more consistent with New Testament writings, but not viewed as specific enough by some participants in the debate. As a possible compromise position, this term nonetheless was ultimately rejected at Nicaea.
- *Homoiousios*—another moderate viewpoint that the Son is "of like essence" with the Father.
- *Homoousios*—which proved to be the prevailing Nicene formulation that the Son is consubstantial or "of the same essence" as the Father.

Convened on May 20, 325, the council had about evenly split minorities initially supportive of and opposed to Arius; the majority were positioned somewhere in the middle. The bishop Eusebius of Caesarea (also church historian) offered a baptismal creed from his church for consideration.

However, the creedal statement proposed by Eusebius reflected a moderate view—avoiding a direct endorsement of any of the more extreme alternative terms as to the substance of Jesus. This compromise was not strong enough for those opposed to Arius and, more significantly, was not acceptable to Emperor Constantine.

In a subsequent letter to his church at Caesarea, Eusebius writes that:

> On this faith being publicly put forward by us, no room for contradiction appeared; but our pious emperor, before anyone else, testified that it was most orthodox. He confessed, moreover, that such were his own sentiments; and he advised all present to agree to it, and to subscribe to its articles and to assent to them, with the *insertion of the single word consubstantial...(emphasis* mine).[506]

The Nicene Formulation. So, a more specific statement including incorporation of the term "consubstantial" was inserted into the creed as adopted together with anathemas to condemn the propositions advanced by the Arians. In other words, Jesus the Son was to be considered as being of the same essence rather than being of either similar or dissimilar essence vis-à-vis God the Father.

As reported by Eusebius, this first of the official orthodox church creeds was adopted as follows:

> We believe in one God, the Father, Almighty, Maker of all things visible and invisible:
> And in One Lord Jesus Christ, the Son of God, begotten of the Father, Only-begotten, that is, *from the substance of the Father*; God from God, Light from Light, Very God from Very God, begotten not made, Consubstantial with the Father, by Whom all things were made, both things in heaven and things in earth; Who for us men and for our salvation came down and was incarnate, was made man, suffered, and rose again the third day, ascended into heaven, and is coming to judge the living and dead.
> And in the Holy Ghost.
> And those who say 'There was when he was not,' and 'Before he was begotten he was not,' and 'Before His generation He was not,' and 'He came to be from nothing,' or those that pretend that the Son of God is 'Of

---

[506] "Letter of Eusebius of Caesarea to His Church on the Creed of Nicaea" in *A New Eusebius,* 301.

other hypostasis or substance,' or 'created,' or 'alterable,' or 'mutable,' the Catholic and Apostolic church *anathematizes*.[507] (*emphasis* mine)

Arian Defeat and Aftermath. Despite their protests—including the observation that the formulation "of the same essence" was not to be found in any of the New Testament writings—the Arian supporters lost. The Nicene Council ended by condemning the person and views of Arius, authorizing his excommunication and degradation from the presbyterate. Emperor Constantine sent Arius and three others into exile.

Subsequent to the council, the emperor made known his views of this dissenter:

While more than three hundred bishops remarkable for their moderation and shrewdness were unanimous in their confirmation of one and the same faith, which is in accurate conformity to the truth expressed in the laws of God, Arius alone, beguiled by the *subtlety of the devil,* was discovered to be the sole disseminator of this mischief, with unhallowed purposes, first among you, and afterward among others also.[508]

In separate correspondence, the emperor also stated his purpose for having called the council:

My sole desire was to effect universal concord, and in particular to refute and dispose of this question which began through the madness of Arius the Alexandrian…[509]

In case anyone was not catching the full imperial thrust, Constantine gets more explicit:

---

[507] "Letter of Eusebius of Caesarea to His Church on the Creed of Nicaea" in *A New Eusebius,* 301.

[508] From a letter of the emperor Constantine to the Church of the Alexandrians, c. 325, from *A New Eusebius,* 303. Constantine's letter appears to ignore the fact that two bishops Secundus of Ptolemais and Theonas of Marmarica had also held to anti-Nicene views.

[509] "The Conduct and Exile of Eusebius of Nicomedia" in *The New Eusebius,* 304.

"So I decided to take action against these ungrateful individuals: I ordered them to be arrested and banished to the most distant region possible."[510]

The strength of the emperor's disdain for those *he viewed as heretics* also is revealed by the following imperial edict:

VICTOR CONSTANTINUS, MAXIMUS AUGUSTUS, to the heretics. Understand now, by this present statute, ye Novatians, Valentinians, Marcionites, Paulians, ye who are called Cataphrygians, and *all ye who devise and support heresies* by means of your private assemblies, with what a tissue of falsehood and vanity, with what destructive and venomous errors, your doctrines are inseparably interwoven; so that through you the healthy soul is stricken with disease, and the living becomes the prey of everlasting death. Ye haters and enemies of truth and life, in league with destruction! All your counsels are opposed to the truth, but familiar with deeds of baseness; full of absurdities and fictions: and by these ye frame falsehoods, oppress the innocent, and withhold the light from them that believe.[511]

So, here we have it. The wedding of church and state. And the silencing of dissenting voices pursuant to the apostolic, Catholic authority of a single monolithic church—emerging to rule with full force of imperial law for over a millennium.

In addition to dealing with Arianism, the council, for the first time, passed canons to define a formal church structure above the local level. This ecclesiastical order was to be modeled on provincial divisions of the civil government. In this way, the authority of local churches also was constrained.

Special status was confirmed for Rome, Alexandria, and Antioch (in Syria). And the council established a dating system for Easter using the Roman rather than Jewish calendar.

---

[510] Ibid., 304.
[511] Eusebius, "Edict Against the Heretics," *Life of Constantine,* 3:64–65. https://en.wikisource.org/wiki/Edict_Against_the_Heretics, (accessed February 8, 2024).

Post-Nicaea

The years leading up to the council were marked by the dramatic conversion of a Roman emperor and entire empire from reverence to the pantheon of Roman gods to the monotheistic and previously suppressed beliefs of Christians. The years following the Council of Nicaea would be marked by strife within the emperor's own household, interest in finding and restoring places in the holy land where Jesus had ministered, and by the ensuing flip-flops of the emperor and his successors to repeatedly challenged creedal confessions.

The anti-Arian side of the controversy found a new champion in an individual who has become known as a great defender of orthodox faith. Athanasius became the Bishop of Alexandria. From 325 to the ascension of Julian as emperor in 360, Athanasius worked vigorously to enforce the creed of Nicaea—supported by the majority of Western bishops plus those in Egypt.

The viewpoint of Athanasius was undergirded by support directly from the emperor who wrote to the church of Alexandria:

"For that which he has commended itself to the judgment of three hundred bishops cannot be other than the judgment of God."[512]

Three months after Nicaea, Constantine found that Eusebius of Nicomedia and Theognis, Bishop of Nicaea, still held to Arian views. They were exiled to Gaul and a new election of bishops was ordered. At one point, the emperor wrote to denounce Eusebius and issue a personal warning about high treason.

In subsequent writing, Constantine went beyond individual sanctions, placing whole congregations viewed as being outside of the Catholic faith at risk:

And in order that this remedy may be applied with effectual power, we have commanded, as before said, that you be *positively deprived* of every gathering point for your superstitious meetings, I mean all the houses of prayer, if such be worthy of the name, which belong to heretics, and that

---

[512] Socrates, *Historia Ecclesiastica,* 1.9. Socrates was a 5th century Greek church historian. A similar statement is made with "Constantine's View of the Work of the Council of Nicaea," *A New Eusebius,* 372.

these be made over without delay to the *Catholic church*; that any other places be confiscated to the public service, and no facility whatever be left for any future gathering; in order that from this day forward none of your unlawful assemblies may presume to appear in any public or private place. Let this edict be made public.[513]

And later, the imperial punishment for lesser religious infractions became more severe. In an edict issued eight years after the Council of Nicaea, Emperor Constantine stipulated:

This therefore I decree, that if any one shall be detected in concealing a book compiled by Arius, and shall not instantly bring it forward and burn it, the penalty for this offense *shall be death*; for immediately after conviction the criminal shall suffer capital punishment. May God preserve you![514]

Flip-Flops Ahead. However, the emperor was aging and would flip-flop in his never-ending effort to secure ecclesiastical unity. The Arians had a renewed chance. Constantine was reportedly desirous of restoring Arius. But on the day before his full restoration in 336, Arius died (possibly by poison). The next year, on May 22, 337, Constantine died after receiving baptismal rites at the hands of Eusebius of Nicomedia.

It was to be almost 35 years from the council at Nicaea before a resurgent Arian theology would formally prevail at the Council of Nice on New Years Day, 360 AD. But within just three years, Arianism was again discredited. By the beginning of the fifth century, orthodox Trinitarian views had fully prevailed—up to this present era of the 21st century.

Nicaea Reconvened. In 327, Constantine reconvened the Council of Nicaea. Arius was readmitted to communion. Eusebius of Nicomedia and Theognis were restored to their sees (or seats of authority).

---

[513] Eusebius, Life of Constantine (Philip Schaff and Henry Wace, trans.), *Book III, Chapter LXV: The Heretics are Deprived of their Meeting Places.*
https://www.tertullian.org/fathers2/NPNF2–01/Npnf2–01–29.htm#P7817_3230830 (accessed February 8, 2024).

[514] "Constantine's Proscription of the Works of Porphyry and Arius," *A New Eusebius,* 313.

But the debate continued. Led by the ever-energetic Athanasius, anti-Arians refused to recognize Arius and supporting bishops. In turn, they became victims of their own medicine and were condemned at a council in Constantinople and themselves exiled. In some ways, this swing of Constantine back to the Arian position is explained by the emperor's preference for those willing to compromise (i.e., Arians) versus those who would not (i.e., Nicaeans led by Athanasius).[515]

But then Arius overreacted. In 332 or 333, he protested directly to the emperor, emphasizing his support in Libya. Constantine responded with a severe letter condemning Arius. The emperor then ordered the works of Arius burned; anyone who would not surrender their copy was to be executed.

Arius was invited to defend himself, which he did at a gathering of bishops two years later at Jerusalem (following an early meeting at Tyre to condemn Athanasius). The synod of Jerusalem in September 335 cleared Arius and notified Athanasius of this action, together with Constantine's approval.

Continuing to press for a united Christian church, Constantine convened a another council at Caesarea in 334.

Athanasius refused to attend because he feared an attempt by the two Eusebiuses to get Arius again reinstated. Athanasius did attend a council at Tyre a year later (under threat of deposition against any no-shows). Seeing that he was outvoted, Athanasius and his Egyptian delegation withdrew, wherein the council condemned Athanasius in absentia and accepted a new orthodox confession of faith from Arius.

Athanasius appealed directly to the emperor but was exiled (the first of five times) after Constantine learned that Athanasius had threatened to prevent shipment of grain from Alexandria—breadbasket of the empire.[516] Despite imperial directive, Egyptian bishops still refused communion with Arius.

---

[515] Constantine continued to vacillate. In 332, Meletians accused Athanasius of murdering the bishop Meletus (producing a severed hand as evidence). Athanasius then produced the supposed victim, infuriating the emperor against the Meletians. About the same time, Arius petitioned "to be received back" to the Alexandrian church but was denounced by the emperor in violent terms.

[516] Athanasius would serve out much of his exile in Trier, in what is now part of Germany.

The emperor recalled Arius to Constantinople, ordering Bishop Alexander to serve Arius communion. The day before the event, Arius dropped dead—again thwarting imperial hopes for ecclesiastical reconciliation.

Household Turmoil. It is not readily possible to fully disentangle the Constantine the ruler from Constantine the converted Christian and Constantine the husband and father.

The year following the Council of Nicaea, Constantine precipitated a household tragedy of his own making. In 326, the emperor executed his son Crispus and then wife Fausta, under what more than one chronicler has described as "mysterious circumstances." [517]

Based on the information available, it appears that Constantine's second wife Fausta accused Crispus of raping or having an affair with her and plotting to overthrow Constantine. In angry response, Constantine had his son killed.[518]

Later, it was discovered that Fausta had been lying. So then Constantine had his wife murdered in her bath. What appears most likely was that Fausta was locked in and the temperature of the water gradually raised so that she either suffocated due to the heat and steam, in effect boiled alive.

In part, Fausta likely engaged in this treachery in order to make way for her sons—Constantine II, Constantius II and Constans—as ultimate heirs to their father's dynasty. Later, the emperor would come to regret his conduct, considering that he had acted too hastily.

---

[517] This is the case, for example, with J. Stevenson, *A New Eusebius,* editorial note at p. 337. Crispus had been living at Trier with his grandmother Helena, mother of Constantine. Crispus lived from 303 until 326 AD; he served as Caesar from 317 until 326. Crispus was the eldest son of Constantine and his first wife, Minervina. He was Consul three times and governor of Gaul from the year 320. Crispus also was recognized as an able and popular military commander, winning victories against German barbarians.

[518] Constantine's first wife Minerva and mother of Crispus was actually the emperor's concubine. "Second" wife Flavia Maxima Fausta was the daughter of the previous emperor Maximianus. In 307 AD, at about age seventeen, she was married to Constantine the Great in order to seal his alliance with the regime of her father and her brother, Maxentius in Rome. Other reasons, in addition to or as a replacement to the notion of an affair, have also been advanced for Crispus and his sudden loss of imperial favor—notably the idea that Fausta worked to make Constantine envious of Crispus to clear the way for her sons' future accession to the throne.

Holy Land Veneration. A major force in the emperor's household—particularly after Fausta's death—was the emperor's mother, Helena. She personally took an interest in the deteriorated state of the holy city, Jerusalem, and led the first effort to identify, protect and rebuild the city's sacred sites. Emperor and mother built new churches to commemorate Jesus' birth in Bethlehem, burial and resurrection in Jerusalem, and ascension from the Mount of Olives.[519]

Later Years. his later years, Constantine turned ever more toward theology coupled with the building of a new imperial capital at Constantinople (now Istanbul, Turkey). Constantine became a builder, in part as a political strategy. The new Roman imperial capital of Constantinople was established in 330 at the junction of Europe and Asia—and as a planned Christian city.

The Nicene Council had established a special privileged status for the Bishop of Jerusalem. Through his mother's efforts, Constantine uncovered what were believed to be the site(s) of the crucifixion, burial, and resurrection of Jesus in Jerusalem, and built on it the initial portions of the Church of the Holy Sepulcher.

Constantine erected a Church of the Apostles in Constantinople, with his own coffin prepared and surrounded by six disciples on each side (or twelve total). In this way, the author Eusebius notes that "he now consecrated the church to the apostles, believing that this tribute to their memory would be of no small advantage to his own soul."[520]

Particularly in the east, Constantine turned more attention to tearing down the remaining vestiges of paganism—all but the imperial cult. From about 330 on, pagan temple treasures—gold, silver, bronze, art—were removed to enrich Christian churches or the new capital. Temples were demolished, particularly those that offended Christians with rites of sacred prostitution.

Constantine became ill shortly after Easter 337. He traveled to a nearby spa with thermal hot springs. He then traveled to Nicomedia. He had hoped to be baptized at the Jordan River in Palestine but this was no longer possible. Instead, he was baptized at his deathbed by Eusebius of Nicomedia, the bishop he had once sent into exile for his support of Arian theology.

---

[519] Helena is buried in Trier, Germany. She is reputed to have brought from Jerusalem the Robe of Christ and a nail from the true cross together with relics from St. Mattias, the apostle selected to replace Judas Iscariot.

[520] Eusebius, "The Last Days of Constantine," *The New Eusebius,* 319.

Constantine died at Pentecost. He hoped to be considered as the 13th apostle. The Christian emperor was buried in Constantinople's Church of the Apostles; but the Roman Senate deified him. Upon his death, new coinage was struck for the realm. As was described by the other Eusebius (the historian):

> On one side appeared the figure of our blessed prince, with the head closely veiled: the reverse exhibited him sitting as a charioteer, drawn by four horses, with a hand stretched downward from above to receive him up to heaven.[521]

In Their Father's Footsteps. Following Constantine's death, the empire was divided between the emperor's three surviving sons—all of Fausta. All three sons followed their father's Christian beliefs, stepped up his attacks on paganism and continued to intervene at will in affairs of the church.

As the oldest son of Fausta and Constantine, Constantine II ruled the western empire including Britain, Spain and Gaul. As the youngest, Constans reigned in the rest of the west as far east as Thrace.

Constantius II ruled the east. In 342, Constantine II charged Constans with flouting his authority, invaded Italy and was killed, leaving two-thirds of the empire in the hands of the youngest.

Then in 350, a German officer named Magnentius overthrew Constans but was himself defeated by Constantius II in 351—reuniting the empire under a single Augustus. As western rulers, Constantine II and Constans had leaned toward the Nicaeans but the eastern Constantius II was more of Arian persuasion.

In 341, bishops at Antioch reaffirmed the Nicene credal formula but deposed the chief defender of Nicaea, Athanasius. Prior to his death, Constans had prevailed upon Constantius to reinstate Athanasius after his second exile—consistent with results of the Council of Sardica in 342/343.

With no brother around, Constantius convened the Council of Milan in 355—to force the bishops to choose between their own exile and the condemnation of Athanasius.[522] The bishops resisted, causing the emperor to

---

[521] Ibid, 396.

[522] Other synods including those at Sirmium (341, 357, 358), Arles (353), Antioch (358) Acyra (358), Constantinople (360) and Alexandria (362) also favored the Arian position. Arianism may have reached its peak at Sirmium (located in modern day

appeal for Arian support and to further declare: "My will is the canon."[523] And in 356, Constantius ordered the closing of temples and cessation of sacrifices under penalty of death.

Toward a Fully Christian State. Upon the death of Constantius in 361, Julian ascended to the throne.[524] As a nephew of Constantine the Great, Julian's reign was marked by the last official resurgence of paganism across the empire. Julian ordered reopening of pagan temples and sacrifices. He also authored treatises against Christian theology including his more important work *Adversus Christianos.*

Julian's reign lasted but two years. Killed in battle, his generals elected Jovian in 363 as the new emperor. Jovian reinstated a policy of religious toleration, continued by his successor Valentinian from 364–379.

Gratian began joint rule with Valentinian in 367. He generally continued a policy of religious non-interference, albeit authorizing confiscation of Donatist property in North Africa in 376 and banning of certain Christian sects.

Theodosius was invited to share rule with Gratian in 379. This is the emperor who completed the process of transforming the empire into a fully Christian state. As a Spaniard, Theodosius was Nicene by inclination and practice. Consequently, Arian bishops were replaced with adherents to the Nicene Creed.[525]

Nicaea Confirmed. After the death of Constantius, the theological debate between the Nicaeans and Arians continued, albeit with increased complexity. However, there were efforts to reconcile these viewpoints. Some who favored the Nicene formulation of *homoousios* were nonetheless put off because this definition obscured the distinctiveness of the persons of the Trinity.[526]

For Athanasius, Father, Son and Spirit essentially represented *one being* living in a threefold form, much as one person might be a father, son and brother at the same time. In his lifetime and beyond, Athanasius had become known as the chief defender of the outcome of the Nicene Council.

Serbia), with denials of the true divinity of the Son, Jesus.

[523] As quoted by E. Glenn Hinson, *The Early Church: Origins to the Dawn of the Middle Ages* (Nashville, Abingdon Press, 1996), 209.

[524] Julian (the Apostate) was the nephew of Constantine I (the Great).

[525] Despite imperial opposition, Arianism continued as the preference for converted Gauls, Vandals, Lombards and Burgundians over the next couple of centuries.

[526] Much of this discussion is adapted from Hinson, *The Early Church,* 236–239.

As one of the Cappadocians, Basil of Neocaesarea tried out a further compromise—by way of analogy. For Basil, the three entities could be described as three like or equal beings sharing a common nature, much as different persons share in the common nature of humanity.

As an ardent Nicene, Theodosius I convened the second ecumenical Council of Constantinople in 381. An estimated 150 Nicene and 36 Arian bishops—all from the east—attended. The earlier Nicene Creed had been lost and was reformulated as we know it today—with *homoousios* as the centerpiece. Arians and other "heretics" were condemned.

The die was cast. The Western (Roman Catholic) church would stay with Athanasius; the Eastern (Orthodox) would prove to follow the route of the Cappadocians who sought reconciliation between Nicene and Arian theology. In effect, the legacy of Constantine's Nicene formulation would live on—now enforced by increasingly centralized ecclesiastical authority.

Lasting Results

It is now time to consider Constantine's pioneering and lasting contributions to Christianity vis-a-vis his heresy—monolithic Christianity. As ruler of the Roman empire, Constantine was able to do what no Christian before—not even the apostle Paul—could dare to achieve. In one fell swoop, Christians went from being the oppressed minority to the triumphant majority.

The transition was sudden, unexpected, and bred consequences that reverberate up to today—the early years of the third millennium.

In 325 AD, the Roman emperor Constantine took the step that forever changed Christianity; he convened the first universal council of the church at Nicaea in Asia Minor. The council was convened to resolve a theological controversy over the nature of God and Christ. The results of the conference involving 200 to perhaps more than 300 bishops were at least threefold:

- The adoption of a universal statement of Christian faith known today as the Nicene Creed—declaring Father and Son to be consubstantial (of the same essence).
- The marriage of church and state—essentially placing ecclesiastical under secular imperial authority—a situation to remain in force throughout much of the Mediterranean and Europe for over a millennium.

- Suppressing diverse expression of Christian belief and expression—including the practice of anathematizing and excommunicating leaders who would not adopt the newly established doctrine of the emperor and church at Rome.

By coming out from the shadows, Christianity lost its informality, its spontaneity, its diversity and colorful eclecticism. The Christianity of Constantine was forever solidified as hierarchical. After all, if an organization built on rigorous hierarchy could propel Roman military and imperial might for a millennium, then why not the church?

If there is a positive side to Constantine's conversion and subsequent church leadership, it is that Christianity would serve to survive impending collapse of the Roman empire and the so-called dark ages which followed. Despite defects in theology and practice, Christianity would prove to provide the subsequent though much delayed impetus for eventual renewal of western culture and virtue of human endeavor.

To summarize, Constantine's heresy was the monolith—the holy Catholic church. Even later in the reformation (more than a millennium later), the principle of the monolith would live on—whether in the Catholic church of Rome or in the Reformation churches of Luther and Calvin. Each would espouse *one correct path* to Jesus, one way to salvation.

While Constantine certainly affected the course of Christian belief, his heresy was primarily a matter of style rather than substance. In practice, the imperial requirements associated with survival as Roman emperor would drive his actions at the moment when the church emerged from persecuted to dominance. As one recent author of church history puts it:

Constantine's contribution to the evangelization of the Roman empire and even beyond was *an immense, but not an unmixed, blessing.* Constantine moved from tolerance of all cults to favoritism of Christianity to open intolerance and efforts to make Christianity the religion of the empire. Not only so, but he sought to effect unity among the Christians, since, in his view, the unity and well-being of the empire depended on the concord in common faith and worship of all its citizens. Here he set Christianity on the track of persecution that has cast a shadow on its history ever since.[527]

Constantine's genius was that the church as monolith outlived the imperial empire. But like the empire, the hierarchical church eventually would run its course. What then, after the heretical malfeasance of this church-empire has outlived its usefulness? For that, we turn to a partial answer—the Protestant Reformation sparked by Martin Luther.

Supplement — Toward a New Testament Canon

For up to a century after Christ, oral tradition was favored over written works of Jesus and his disciples. This may be because church leaders still had direct connections with apostles or who had been in direct contact with apostles and others who had walked and talked with Jesus.

From Oral to Written Tradition. Preference for an oral tradition is most clearly indicated by the early church patriarch Papias who stated that he:

> "...did not imagine that things out of books would help me so much as the utterances of a *living and abiding voice*." [528]T

The earliest known definitive statement of an accepted body of New Testament writings comes from the Muratorian Canon, believed to have been originally composed *c.* 200 AD. All but five of the current 27 NT books were recognized; those initially excluded were Hebrews, James, 1 & 2 Peter, and 3 John.

In the third century, theologian Origen divided a variety of Christian writings into three categories: (a) widely accepted, (b) questioned or accepted with reservations, and (c) rejected. Origen made a strong case for inclusion of Hebrews. Works he *accepted with reservation* were James and the so-called "Catholic epistles" of 2 Peter, 2/3 John, and Jude.

Like Origen before him, Eusebius of Caesarea (*c.* 325) listed most of the present canon but referred to a few writings as disputed. Eusebius comments

---

[527] Hinson, *The Early Church,* 206.
[528] Eusebius, 3.39. Much of this supplemental information is derived from Eusebius *History of the Church.*

that the Roman church continued to deny Hebrews as the work of Paul. As with Origen, writings noted by Eusebius as "disputed" included James, Jude, 2 Peter, and 2/3 John.

Revelation also was questioned. While authorship is directly attributed right from the start of the Revelation account to "his servant John," there has long been scholarly and theological confusion as to who this John was.

Western churches were most concerned with James and Hebrews. The so-called "Catholic epistles" generally favored by Western churches included 1 & 2 Peter, 1/2/3 John and Jude.

Canonicity Testing. Criteria or tests increasingly applied to determine canonicity included:

- Authorship by an apostle or immediate follower—as inspired Scripture.
- Regular church usage.
- Consistency with orthodox Christian belief.

The latter test of consistency with orthodox belief came to the fore as the time of formal canonization acceptance drew closer.

Canon Acceptance. Added impetus toward formalization of an accepted set of New Testament writings emerged with the conversion of a Roman emperor (Constantine) to Christianity. As Christianity became the official religion of the empire, there were both ecclesiastical and political reasons for deciding which books were in and which were out.

A formal canon fit with the trend from a diverse and eclectic set of church doctrine and practices to the centralization of authority with the Roman Catholic church and ensuing papal authority. Politically, a clear set of accepted political works coincided with the empire's solidification of Constantine's sole rule.

The Synod of Laodicea (*c.* 363) is the first to take action regarding a New Testament canon, directing that only those books regarded as canonical should be read in church. Unfortunately, a detailed listing of books accepted by Laodicea is no longer available. However, it is known that the Laodicean Council did not consider Revelation as canonical.

In 367, Athanasius (Bishop of Alexandria and chief defender of the Nicene Creed) compiled a list covering all 27 books of the present New Testament canon.[529] In his annual Easter (or Festal) letter of 367 AD, Athanasius identified what should be included and not included in the New Testament.

In the spirit of nothing being taken away, Athanasius becomes the first known to list the current 27 books of the New Testament—although his order of NT books is somewhat different. In the spirit of preventing unwanted additions, Athanasius also listed books that deserve to be read but are not part of the New Testament canon and described apocrypha which he denounced as fabrications and heretical.

In 397, the complete canon of the New Testament (as known today) was ratified at the third Council of Carthage. The findings of the council were strongly influenced by Augustine of nearby Hippo. While Carthage represented a local rather than church-wide council, this event seems to have fixed the canon in the west. From 397 forward, the current list of 27 NT books appears to have been generally accepted—at least throughout the Latin church.

Though *accepted,* the New Testament of Athanasius, Jerome and the Vulgate would not be formally *canonized* for more than a millennium. It would take the reformist rantings of a medieval cleric—Martin Luther—to serve as the impetus by which an official listing of books approved for the New Testament would be finally and formally authorized by the Roman Catholic church (at the Council of Trent in 1546).

---

[529] Despite his general condemnation of non-canonical writings, Athanasius identified books including the Didache (or Teaching of the Apostles) and the Shepherd of Hermas as suitable for reading and instruction.

XI. Luther—Reformation Undone

Unless I am convicted by Scripture and plain reason, I do not accept the authority of popes and councils, for they have contradicted each other—my conscience is captive to the Word of God. I cannot and I will not recant anything, for to go against conscience is neither right nor safe.

...Here I stand. I cannot do otherwise. God help me!
Martin Luther before the Diet of Worms, 1521.

In 1517, an Augustinian monk posted a notice requesting a public discussion at Germany's Wittenburg University.[530] With these 95 Theses, 33–year-old monk Martin Luther declared an end to the 1,200 year era of holy Roman Catholic hegemony over Christian belief and practice.

The single Catholic church put in motion 12 centuries earlier by Emperor Constantine would now be faced with a challenger over an issue as old as the dispute between the apostle Paul and Jesus' brother James.

Was salvation from eternal damnation to be found as a matter of works or as a matter of faith?

For Luther, the immediate issue at hand related to the increasingly pervasive papal practice of selling indulgences—relief from the eternal damnation or purgatory in exchange for a monetary contribution. The application of much of this *pay for grace* theology included funding the construction of St. Peter's basilica in Rome.

The 95 Theses were aimed squarely at papal authority—both temporal and spiritual. Luther's thesis #5 launched the attack:

---

[530] Whether Martin Luther actually posted his theses on the door of the castle church in Wittenberg has been a matter of some debate. There is support for an alternative view that Luther sent copies of his 95 Theses to Archbishop Albrecht of Mainz and Bishop Jerome of Brandenburg.

The pope has *neither the will nor the power* to remit any penalties beyond those imposed either at his own discretion or by canon law.[531]

By the time he gets to Thesis #86, Martin has become somewhat more personal in his attack:

Again: since the pope's income today is larger than that of the wealthiest of wealthy men, why does he not build this one church of St. Peter *with his own money,* rather than with the money of indigent believers?[532]

The Reformation that Luther launched carries forward as the pivotal event of Christianity for the subsequent 500 years to this 21st century. Unfortunately, this reformation is incomplete. The Christian revolution was aborted—by none other than Luther himself.

Background of Martin Luther

The life of Martin Luther can be divided into distinct periods—as it has by numerous theologians and historians. At least three distinct phases can be identified—beginnings, reformation, church leadership and old age.

But we are getting ahead of the story. As with the other great pioneers (and potential heretics) of the faith profiled to this point, we now shift to Martin Luther—a child of the middle ages.

Luther's Beginnings. Martin Luther was born in Eisleben, Germany on November 10, 1483. His father Hans was a copper miner. The older Luther had high hopes for Martin to become a professional man, a lawyer. At age 17, his father picked the University of Erfurt, one of the finest universities of the time—as the place for Martin's college education—paid for by Hans.

This was not a good time for the young student, especially as friends of Martin and his family died of the plague. After graduating 30th in a class of 57, Martin received his master's degree. His father then arranged for Martin's entry into law school.

---

[531] Martin Luther, "Disputation on the Power and Efficacy of Indulgences," *Blue Letter Bible,* 1517,
https://www.blueletterbible.org/Comm/luther_martin/theses/95theses.cfm.
[532] Ibid.

On July 2, 1505, less than two months after beginning law school, Martin was traveling his way back to Erfurt from his parents' home and became caught in a violent thunderstorm. Luther was nearly struck by lightning and thrown to the ground. At this moment, he cried to Saint Anne to save him, vowing to become a monk if he escaped alive.

Priestly Role. Just over 2 weeks later, Martin Luther entered the Black Monastery on July 17—much to his father's displeasure. Martin saw this as perhaps the surest path to his own soul's salvation. As a grouping of Augustinian Hermits, the monastery was a strict though not austere order of mendicant monks.

In 1507, Luther was ordained and celebrated his first mass. The subsequent year he taught briefly at the new university in Wittenburg. In 1510, he and a traveling companion were sent to Rome to handle some of the orders' political affairs. Upon his return in April 1511, Luther was transferred to the newly constructed Black Cloister in Wittenburg.

In 1512, Luther received his Doctor of Theology degree. A year later, he became a lecturer on the Psalms. At age 30 (in 1513), he also became priest off-campus at Wittenberg's city church. Two years later, he was appointed vicar in charge of eleven Augustinian monasteries. That same year, he began a year of lectures on the subject of the New Testament book of Romans.

In 1516, plague struck Wittenberg. Luther stayed and the next year Johann Tetzel began selling indulgences on the borders of Saxony. This occurred through licensing action of Pope Leo X as a means to finance the construction of St. Peter's basilica in Rome.

Many of the customers for Tetzel's indulgences also were parishioners of Martin Luther. As one side effect of Tetzel's hard sell, Luther noticed fewer people coming to confession. He was outraged.

Reformation. On October 31, 1517, Martin Luther posted his *95 Theses* to protest the sale of indulgences. To elevate the level of protest, he also had a copy of the Latin text delivered to the archbishop, hoping to get an answer beyond that of a private disputation. Initially, Luther received little response, but in December Johann Tetzel wrote two sets of counter-theses after noticing a fall-off in the sale of indulgences.

Less than one year after the posting on the Wittenberg door, Luther was tried (in absentia) on charges of heresy in Rome. Pope Leo also issued the bull

Cum Postquam, outlining the church's doctrine on indulgences (in direct opposition to Luther).

By early 1519, Luther was ready to recant and even send a letter of apology to the pope. In March, he actually sent a letter to Leo X, stating it was not his intent to undermine the authority of the pope or church. However, Luther also entered into a debate with Johann Eck who was to become a leader in the counter-reformation. It was during this debate that Martin Luther denied the primacy of the pope and the infallibility of church General Councils.

In 1520, Luther completed three major works. The first was titled and addressed *To the Christian Nobility of the German Nation.* It debunked the *three walls* on which papal authority had rested. Martin stated that all believers are priests, there is no exclusive papal right to interpret the Scriptures, and a reformatory council of the church could be called by others than the pope.[533]

In 1521, Martin Luther was summoned by Emperor Charles V to appear before the Diet of Worms. During the second hearing, Luther made his position clear:

> Unless I am convicted by Scripture and plain reason, I do not accept the authority of popes and councils, for they have *contradicted each other*— my conscience is captive to the Word of God. I cannot and I will not recant anything, for to go against conscience is neither right nor safe. God help me.

As Martin neared the age of 40, in 1523, the first "Protestant" martyrs were burned at Brussels. In 1524, peasants revolted citing Luther's teachings and demanding more equitable economic conditions. Luther also stopped wearing the religious habit.

In 1525, Martin Luther wrote *Against the Murderous and Thieving Hordes of Peasants.* At the Battle of Frankenhausen, an estimated 50,000 peasant lives were lost. By the time the uprising was quelled, the death toll had increased to nearly 100,000. The peasants believed Luther had betrayed them.

---

[533] Luther's concept of a "priesthood of believers" finds its most direct NT reference in I Peter 2:9: "But you are a chosen race, a *royal priesthood,* a holy nation, God's own people, in order that you may proclaim the mighty acts of him who called you out of darkness into his marvelous light."

This same year, Martin Luther married former nun Katherine von Bora. They took up residence at Black Cloister, the former Augustinian monastery in Wittenberg.

Church Leadership and Old Age. Though married late at nearly age 42, Martin Luther clearly enjoyed family life. Over the next 9 years, Katherine gave birth to 6 children—two of whom would die before their father.

His love for family represents an ongoing legacy—reflected in the Christmas tree tradition begun with Martin's family. And he composed the most basic and beloved of the Christmas carols, "Away in a Manger."

As a composer, Luther also wrote the *Smart Songbook* and "A Mighty Fortress is our God" in 1527. He wrote doctrinal text for the new Lutheran church, including a *Small* and *Large Catechism.*

While Luther found marriage enjoyable, advancing age and, perhaps, job stress led to growing health issues. Within two years of marriage, Luther began to experience heart problems as well as long-standing digestive and intestinal difficulties. By 1538 (age 54), deteriorating health (including uric acid stones) and arthritis were affecting his ability to work and write. The next year, Katherine experienced a miscarriage; Martin was by her bed much of the time.

Advancing age also brought on more violently polemical writings, capped by his polemic *Against the Jews* in 1543. In 1545, Luther wrote *Against the Papacy at Rome founded by the Devil.* Less than one year later, Martin Luther died during a visit to Eisleben, the home of his birth. Death was attributed to heart failure. The date was February 18, 1546, and Martin was 62 years of age.

From Constantine to Luther

For a moment, it is useful to back up a bit. In one fell swoop, we have jumped forward 1,200 years in time between two very different sets of heresies—from the Roman emperor Constantine to the upstart Protestant Martin Luther. What happened between is often referred to as the *dark ages.* This indeed was a period of social and economic regression:

- From the life of the city back to the country.
- From an educated elite and middle class back to illiteracy of the masses.
- From religious pluralism and pantheism to monolithic monotheism.

- From widespread travel and communication back to parochial isolation.
- From a time of prosperity and *consumer surplus* back to survival.

Yet during this age of darkness there are distinctive rays of light. Individuals kept the flame of authentic Christianity alive, bridging the immense gap between the church of the early persecuted believers and the church's increasingly dominant cultural position throughout medieval Europe. While one could recount numerous individuals who played their part, two are of particular significance—influencing the thought and theology of Martin Luther.

Augustine of Hippo. One such individual was Saint Augustine. Just a generation after the Council of Nicaea, Augustine was born in 354 in the North African city of Thagaste to a pagan father and Christian mother. As a young man, Augustine took a concubine who bore him a son. After an interest in a Gnostic and Manichaean theology centered on the concept of a cosmic struggle between good and evil, Augustine turned to Christianity. The central controversy of this time period was occasioned by Donatist emphasis on the church as a *pure* body. Augustine saw just the opposite—a *mixed body*—where the wheat and the weeds would grow together.

As Augustine was writing his treatise *On the Trinity,* the Visigoths sacked Rome in 410. This was a shock to Constantinian Christians, who believed that God would protect the Roman empire if the people were faithful. Augustine responded by writing the *City of God*, arguing that God alone grants authority to kings and kingdoms. In his view, the church superseded the state—a concept that would be fully embraced and often enforced by the papacy.

In Augustine's time, church discipline meant the arrest and, in some instances, the death of North African Donatists. A millennium later, Augustine's logic would serve as spiritual justification for the Spanish Inquisition.

Origen Undone. A victim of the protracted debate between Arians and Nicenes of the fourth century proved to be the 3rd century theologian Origen. At first quoted by both sides of the Arian controversy, his perspectives increasingly came under attack. Origen's views on creation and resurrection were suspect, including Origen's doctrine of the pre-existence of souls, restoration of all things, and subordination of the Logos (or Incarnate Word of God).

In the late 4th century, Jerome translated the homilies of Origen to Latin and prepared the translation of what would become known as the Vulgate Bible. Initially a supporter of Origen, Jerome changed course to condemn Origen for his views of universal salvation and on the Trinity. While long deceased, Origen would be formally condemned by the council at Alexandria as a heretic in 399/400.[534]

Over the course of the next 1–1/2 centuries, the Origenist controversy continued to smolder. In 553, Origen was again condemned and anathematized as a heretic by the Second Council of Constantinople. Augustine would become the pre-eminent theologian of the western church while Origen's philosophy would continue to undergird Eastern Christianity.

Split of East and West. For centuries, western churches (led by papal authority in Rome) and eastern counterparts (centered in Constantinople) had participated together as one Catholic church. However, there were issues—cultural, political and theological—leading to increasing friction. A key theological controversy arose related to what is known as the Filioque, a Latin term meaning "from the son."

The eastern position affirmed the original Nicene concept of 325 AD that the Holy Spirit originates from the Father alone. The western position increasingly gravitated to the concept that the Holy Spirit originates from the "Father and the Son."

In 1054, the final split (known as the Great Schism) was sealed between churches of the east and west. Long-standing issues came to a head when a new emperor of the Holy Roman Empire, Constantine IX (1042–1055) demanded that the patriarch of Constantinople acknowledge the authority of Rome. This the patriarch Cerularius would not do.

As a result, churches in Western Europe, under the authority of the Catholic pope at Rome, separated from the churches in the Eastern Roman (or Byzantine) Empire, under the authority of the patriarch (bishop) of Constantinople. Cerularius was excommunicated from the Roman church on July 16, 1054.

---

[534] Origen had become intrigued with *subordinationism,* the concept that Jesus represents a being that is distinct from and subordinate to God the Father—a concept that found more favor in eastern than for western Christendom.

The churches of the Eastern Empire have come to be known by the term of the Eastern Orthodox church. The word orthodox was intended to mean correct teaching or right belief.

Reformation Incomplete

Returning to Luther's era, the Protestant reformation of the 16th century did not spring forward by happenstance. Growing discontent with the church existed throughout the Holy Roman Empire—especially Germany.

Underpinnings. As one church historian has written:

> The Renaissance papacy invariably lived beyond its means and was often on the edge of bankruptcy, not least because it required immense sums to maintain its political standing in Italy. To meet expenses, the papal Curia devised new and more oppressive taxes, fees, and fines which bore heavily on the higher clergy who, in turn, passed them on to the lower clergy and, ultimately, to the laity. Rome became a byword, especially in Germany, for venality and avarice.[535]

Moral and ethical lapses covered a range of clerical abuses including the increasing sale of ecclesiastical indulgences, nepotism, absenteeism, and concubinage. Parish clergy were often minimally educated and impoverished—a more obvious shortcoming as the general population became more literate and urban.

Popular religion had become less enabling, more oppressive. Great emphasis was placed on prospects for personal salvation versus fear of torments ranging from purgatory to eternal damnation. Only a faith that demonstrated strong performance of works could achieve salvation. No one could be sure that he or she had done enough.

Behind the day-to-day concerns, there were deeper psychological underpinnings. The 20th century psychologist Erik H. Erikson wrote about *Young Man Luther,* observing that "his young manhood is one of the most radical on record." In his work, Erikson comments on this passing from the medieval era:

---

[535] Williston Walker, *A History of the Christian Church,* 419.

It has been said that Descartes' "I think, therefore I am" marked the end of medieval philosophy, which began with St. Augustine, who saw in man's ability to think the proof not only of God's existence, but also of god's grace. Augustine thought that man's "inner light" is the realization of the *infusio caritatis,* so that we may speak of a *caritative* or *infused identity.* It is precisely because Augustine centered all his theology in faith that Luther called him the greatest theologian since the apostles and before Luther.[536]

Luther himself saw his role as one of learning by doing. He wrote:

I did not learn my theology all at once, but had to search constantly deeper and deeper for it. My temptations did that for me, for no one can understand Holy Scripture without practice and temptations…It is not by reading, writing, or speculation that one becomes a theologian. Nay, rather, it is living, dying, and being damned that makes one a theologian.[537]

Loose Ends. As early as 1522, there were signs that Luther's reformation was not prepared to go all the way. A fiery fellow monk, Gabriel Zwilling, was denouncing the tradition of the Catholic mass and urging the abandonment of clerical vows. Another associate, Karlstadt, opposed the use of pictures, organs and Gregorian chant in worship services; he also took a wife.

To restore public order in Wittenberg, the city government asked Luther to return. He did and preached against Karlstadt—who was forced to leave the city. The old order of worship was reinstated. In this, Luther's core conservative bent became ever more obvious:

He opposed not merely the Romanists, as heretofore, but those partisans of the revolution who would move, as he believed, too rapidly. The separations within the reform party itself had begun.[538]

---

[536] Erik H. Erikson, *Young Man Luther: A Study in Psychoanalysis and History*, 9th printing (New York: W. W. Norton, 1962), 183.
[537] *Gems of Luther* (trans. by P.C. Hirschfeld, ed. 1838), https://libquotes.com/martin-luther/quote/lbb5l1v, accessed February 8, 2024).
[538] Walker, *History of the Christian Church,* 434.

Karlstadt went on to espouse more radical views, denying the value of education, living like a peasant, destroying images and rejecting the physical presence of Christ in communion.

Even more radical was Thomas Muntzer, a former Catholic priest who broke openly with Luther in 1523. He opposed the "easygoing flesh of Wittenberg," advocated violent revolution to overthrow clerical and secular authority.[539] Perhaps not surprisingly, Muntzer subsequently became a leader in the peasant revolt.

Peasants Revolt. The uprising started in southwestern Germany in mid-1524. In February 1525, Swabian peasants (in southwestern Germany) put forward a series of twelve articles covering both spiritual and economic concerns, among these items demanding:

- The right for a community to hire and fire its own pastor
- Abolition of grain and livestock tithes
- Abolition of serfdom
- Reservation of hunting in the forests to the poor
- Elimination of forced, unpaid labor
- Fair rents
- Common lands restored
- Death taxes abolished

Martin Luther initially took an even-handed approach toward both sides, blaming peasant discontent on "wild and dictatorial tyrants."[540] However, he came to view political revolution as the greater evil, tantamount to rebellion against God. In writing *Against the Robbing and Murdering Hordes of Peasants,* Luther advocated crushing the revolt by force of arms.

Despite the loss of some appeal to the masses, the Lutheranization of Saxony was proceeding. As church historian Williston Walker has written:

---

[539] Walker, 437.
[540] Martin Luther, *Luther's Works, Volume 46: Christian in Society III*, 46:20.

In a word, a Lutheran state church, coterminous with the electoral territories and having all baptized inhabitants as its members, was *substituted* for the old bishop-ruled church.[541]

Another threat to the Protestant hegemony of Luther came with Swiss born Ulrich Zwingli. Whereas Luther held to the Catholic belief that the body and blood of Christ are substantially present in the bread and wine, Zwingli denied any possible bodily presence. To Zwingli, Luther's insistence on the corporeal presence of Jesus was essentially an illogical remnant of Catholic superstition. To Luther, Zwingli and his supporters were not Christians.

Halting Reformation. So, here we have it. The leader of the Reformation was unable to go the distance. Like Paul before him, Martin Luther:

- Advocated the saving power of grace, but re-established a new church authority emphasizing performance via a new set of Protestant works and dogmas.
- Preached the priesthood of believers over papal authority, then implemented a new Lutheran hierarchy intolerant of internal and external dissent.
- Threw off papal authority, but left the creed of Nicaea essentially intact.
- Stressed the importance of individual faith over collective belief, but rejected the role of individual reason with equal vehemence.[542]
- Was himself condemned, then turned and advocated the persecution of those sometimes fellow travelers with whom he disagreed.

For a brief moment, a new window of Christian opportunity was opened. In wafted the fresh thought of a Jesus movement that might be tolerant of different, even highly personalized, interpretations of who God is and the most appropriate human response.

---

[541] Walker, 440.

[542] Luther seemed to believe that reason was destructive of faith—a fear that was to be played out as the period of enlightenment gave way to the ascendancy of rational scientific thought.

Reconciliation Thwarted. As earlier noted, in 1519 Martin Luther had agreed to keep silent on the ecclesiastical questions in dispute if his opponents would do the same. The case would be submitted to German bishops and Luther would write a letter indicating continued fealty to the pope.

But then in June and July, Martin Luther was drawn into a series of debates with Johann Eck at Leipzig.

Eck cornered Luther, forcing him to proclaim the fallibility not only of the pope, but of general church councils. Positions hardened and a papal bull of condemnation was issued on June 15, 1520.

There was still another chance. As late as 1522, Pope Adrian VI (as successor) had acknowledged the excess and greed of the papal court under his predecessor, Leo X. This was the first formal apology in the history of the church.

However, shortly before, on April 17, 1521, Martin Luther had appeared before the emperor and Reichstag at Worms and was asked whether he would recant. Luther asked for time to consider. He acknowledged that he had written and spoken too strongly in opposition to some persons.

But then Luther slammed the window shut. To the emperor, he said he could not retract unless convicted he was wrong "by the testimony of the Scriptures or by clear reason."[543]

The die was cast, permanent separation was the inevitable result. Even though the emperor cut the discussion short, Luther felt impelled to drive the wedge in further, reportedly proclaiming:

Here I stand. I cannot do otherwise. *God help me*. Amen.[544]

A month after his journey home from Worms, Martin Luther was formally put under the ban of the empire—ordered to be seized for punishment and have his books burned. That Luther survived is credit to the vigor of the territorial ruler, Frederick the Wise, who refused to buckle to imperial edict.

Those who followed Martin Luther drove the wedge in further. Most notable of these is John Calvin who perfected the concept of a Protestant *work ethic*. Following in Luther's footsteps, he solidified the position of salvation

---

[543] *Luther's Works,* 32:112.
[544] Philip Schaff, *History of the Christian Church, Vol VII Modern Christianity: The German Reformation,* 55.366, https://ccel.org/ccel/schaff/hcc7/hcc7.ii.iii.xxv.html (accessed February 9, 2024). An account of the Diet of Worms.

unto righteousness. As Calvin said: "We are justified not without, yet not by works."[545]

The Catholic response hardened; in reaction, so did the Protestant. The result was a legacy of religious wars and dueling denominationalism. Each offshoot, each new denomination, felt the seemingly irresistible urge to claim its interpretation, its authority as the only path to truth.

Reformation Legacy. Half a millennium later, we live in the shadow of Martin Luther's protest and ensuing reformation. Martin's heresy was not the doctrine of salvation by grace; Martin merely uncovered what Paul had written 1,500 years earlier.

Rather, Luther's undoing was his inability to put the theology of a priesthood of believers *into practice*. His heresy was the reinvigorated imprimatur for Christianity—Protestant or Catholic—to continue down the same path of intolerance and repression that continue to obscure the diversity and true eclecticism of Jesus' message.

For Roman Catholics, there is a related heresy—the transfer of Christian idolatry from hierarchy and tradition to *sola scriptura* (the Word). The author of *Constantine's Sword: The Church and the Jews* puts it this way:

> To Luther, Bible readers are individuals who submit to the Word of God as each one understands it, but also as each one bows before it. Luther rejected what appeared to him to be the church's idolatry of its own hierarchy, but despite his best intentions, he replaced it with a deference to the Word that slips all to easily into an idolatry of its own.[546]

Part of the reason for Martin Luther's inability to shake the Catholic tradition of religious and cultural intolerance comes from his own proclivity to long bouts of depression. This natural predisposition was reinforced by preoccupation with the wrath of God. During a bout of this black horror, Luther could not bear to read Biblical words such as those of Psalm 90: "For we are consumed by your anger; by your wrath we are overwhelmed."[547]

---

[545] John Calvin, *Institutes*, 3.16.1.

[546] James Carroll, *Constantine's Sword: The Church and the Jews: A History* (New York: Houghton Mifflin Company, 2001), 559.

[547] Psalm 90:7.

The early 21st century religious commentator Karen Armstrong offers this commentary:

> Throughout his career, Luther saw death as an expression of God's wrath. His theology of justification by faith depicted human beings as utterly incapable of contributing to their own salvation and wholly reliant on the benevolence of God. It was only by realizing their powerlessness that they could be saved. To escape his depressions, Luther plunged into a frenzy of activity, determined to do what good he could in the world, but consumed also by hatred.
> *Luther's rage* against the Pope, the Turks, Jews, women, and rebellious peasants—not to mention every single one of his own theological opponents—would be typical of other reformers of our own day, who have struggled with the pain of the new world and who have also evolved a religion in which the love of God is often balanced by a hatred of other human beings.[548]

Luther's inability to trust in a priesthood of believers, in individual reason, came as the result of his own insecurities—of a fatalistic view of life and eternity. Because Luther's God was a deity of vengeance, Martin Luther similarly gave himself license to wreak havoc on those with whom he disagreed.

As with the church he had dedicated his life to tear down, this revolutionary reverted to what he earlier had disdained—a priesthood of one. Papal authority was no more. In its place would be substituted Luther the new religious autocrat—for Lutherans and by translation to many of the offshoot Protestant faiths, especially those that would become religions of the state.

Peculiarities of Martin Luther

Much like the apostle Paul, Martin Luther was a man of uncommon intellect and authority. One did not cross Luther lightly. Yet it is precisely the power of the man from which spring forth distinctive Luther eccentricities—some amusing, others downright disastrous. Three are of note here—the printed word, vulgar Luther, and Lutherly exclusion.

---

[548] Karen Armstrong, *The Battle for God* (New York: Alfred A. Knopf, 2000), 65.

The Printed Word. Like the apostle Paul, Martin Luther came on the scene at an especially propitious time in global history—especially for western civilization. Paul benefited from remarkable access to the Roman world of the Mediterranean due to empire-wide rule of Roman law, common language and relative ease of travel.

Luther piggy-backed on the recent invention of the printing press to create the world's first media market. He would make the printed Bible and a wide range of publications available to the masses—in the common language of the day. As expressed by the author of a book titled *Brand Luther,* Martin Luther's book designs:

> ...clothed Luther's works in a new and distinctive livery, immediately recognizable on a crowded bookstall. The result was the development of a form of a book that was itself a powerful representative of the movement—bold, clear, and responsibly distinct from what had gone before. This was Brand Luther, and its success lay at the heart of the tumultuous events that convulsed his homeland in the years after 1517. It lies at the heart of Luther's success, and of the transforming impact of the Reformation.[549]

The Vulgar Luther. If lucky timing and genius were instrumental in Luther's rapid rise to continent-wide recognition, two other qualities contributed immensely to his offsetting failings—the first of which can be termed as Luther's pronounced vulgarity. Much of Martin's vulgar commentary focused on the digestive and excretory systems—where Luther himself often experienced physical challenges.

Luther was particularly haunted by the presence of the devil—who manifest himself in obscene ways. Even a few days before his death, Luther believed he saw the devil sitting on a rain pipe outside of his window, exposing his behind to Martin.[550] This lifelong obsession with demonology may be a partial explanation for Luther's scatological defense. It is the psychologist/historian Erik Erikson who writes:

---

[549] Andrew Pettegree, *Brand Luther: 1517 Printing, and the Making of the Reformation* (New York: Penguin Books, 2016) xiii-xiv.
[550] Erikson, *Young Man Luther,* 59.

That the devil can be completely undone if you manage to fart into his nostrils is only one of those, shall we say, homeopathic, remedies which Luther, undoubtedly on the basis of a homegrown demonology, advocated all his life.[551]

In the melancholy mood of his later years, Luther would express what psychoanalyst Erikson describes as his "depressive self-repudiation in anal terms." The example Erikson gives is of Luther at the dinner table, expounding:

I am like ripe shit, and the world is a gigantic asshole. We probably will let go of each other soon.[552]

Lutherly Exclusion. The Augustinian monk who railed against the egotistical excesses of the papacy increasingly came to emulate similar patterns of disfavor, then persecution for those *out of synch* with his own expectations.

On the canonical level, a particular target of Martin Luther's ire was the New Testament epistle of James. The epistle's assertion that "faith without works is dead" absolutely rubbed Martin the wrong way (much as James views had aggravated the apostle Paul centuries earlier). Luther commented that James was "a right strawy epistle" and questioned whether a book of such inferior worth even belonged in the New Testament.[553]

On a more practical human and societal level, Luther's disfavor had more catastrophic consequences. His ultimate condemnation of the Peasants' Revolt would lead to the loss of about 100,000 lives. His withdrawal of guidance to mitigate unnecessary revolutionary bloodshed would be a regret he would acknowledge late in life.

Luther would part company with other reformation leaders over matters of theological substance and style. Examples include the Swiss reformer Ulrich Zwingli, especially over differences in interpretation of the eucharist as literal

---

[551] Erikson, 61–62.
[552] Erikson, 206.
[553] Luther also questioned the New Testament canonicity of Hebrews, Jude and Revelation.

(Luther) versus symbolic (Zwingli) and with John Calvin over a theology of justification by faith (Luther) versus the sovereignty of God (Calvin).

Particular venom was directed toward a religious splinter group—the Anabaptists. The term "Anabaptist" was one coined by its opponents, meaning re-baptizers. In reality, Anabaptists (also known as Swiss Brethren) recognized one baptism only—for consenting adults rather than infants. They also opposed the establishment of a state church.

Luther initially supported just banishment of Anabaptists. By 1535, his mood changed radically, allowing even for the possibility of executing Anabaptists who disrupted the public order and refused to stay in banishment.

And in a sentiment with far-reaching and yet more disastrous consequences, Martin Luther came to advocate severe repression for the Jewish population in Germany. Early in his career, Luther had appeared sympathetic to Jewish resistance to the Catholic church, writing:

The Jews are blood-relations of our Lord; if it were proper to boast of flesh and blood, the Jews belong more to Christ than we. I beg, therefore, my dear Papist, if you become tired of abusing me *as a heretic*, that you begin to revile me as a Jew.[554]

But then, just three years before his death, Martin Luther wrote *Against the Jews*, offering suggestions to:

Burn down their synagogues, forbid all that I enumerated earlier, force them to work, and deal harshly with them, as Moses did in the wilderness, slaying three thousand lest the whole people perish.[555]

---

[554] Martin Luther, *On The Jews and Their Lies*, 1543, trans. Marin H. Bertram. AAARGH Internet, 2009, p.2.
https://www.prchiz.pl/storage/app/media/pliki/Luther_On_Jews.pdf
(accessed February 8, 2024).

[555] Martin Luther, *The Jews and their Lies (1543),* excerpts from the Jewish Virtual Library, https://www.jewishvirtuallibrary.org/martin-luther-quot-the-jews-and-their-lies-quot (accessed February 8, 2024).

This is strong language—even for a polemical time—and Luther justifiably shares a significant measure of responsibility for ensuing events including the 20th century holocaust four centuries later.

Martin Luther in Summary

With Martin Luther, we profile the last of the great pioneers—as viewed by some—or heretics of Christianity—as viewed by others. Luther took his historic stand at Wittenburg—placing himself in opposition to the combined weight of more than a millennium of accreted Catholic dogma and practices. His 95 Theses unleashed the force of a discontented populace, setting faith and reform politics against corrupt papal authority and the economic hegemony of a single European church-state.

From a 16th century perspective, Luther's heresies involved matters of both substance and style. The substance involved correction of abuses of the then established universal (Catholic) church. Luther's pugnacious style proved critical to its success—a style involving both ecclesiastical and political intrigue.

More so than other pioneers of the Christian faith (excepting only Constantine), Martin Luther changed not only the church, he also altered the state. The economic and social energies unleashed by the Reformation heralded the end of feudalism, the triumph of capitalism, the resurgence of education, and eventually the swelling tide of democracy.

As with our other early Christian pioneers, there are pros and cons associated with Martin Luther's reformation. The 20th century psychologist Erik H. Erikson has put what might be considered as a more positive spin on Luther's contribution to the modern age, writing:

> He (Luther) is revered as a voice of *genuine inspiration*, or made out to be the tool of a conspiracy of crude economic forces which were in need of a bit of evangelical polish. Be all this as it may, Luther was the herald of the age which was in the making and is—or was—*still our age* the age of literacy and enlightenment, of constitutional representation, and of the freely chosen contract; the age of the printed word which at least tried to

say what it meant and to mean what is said, and provided identity through its very effort.[556]

As Erickson also has noted, there is also a dark side to Luther's legacy. If the 21st century still resonates in the freedom and dynamic energy released by of these tidal forces, it also remains imprisoned within the socio-religious-cultural-political fortress that Luther reinforced. To the dominant church of his era, Martin Luther's perceived heresy came in his challenge to papal authority.

To those who value the divine, Luther's heresy was the claim of salvation through grace, not works. But these heresies were nothing new; Luther was merely rediscovering and again unleashing the power of a pioneering Pauline ministry as experienced 1,500 years earlier.

Luther would unwittingly unleash a diverse horde of *protestants,* those who protest against the established order in favor of both spiritual and cultural reform. The question is: did the protest pay off in meaningful change and improvement over what came before? The answers are decidedly mixed.

The reformation of *protestants* that Luther launched carries forward as the dominant event of Christianity over the subsequent 500 years to this 21st century. Unfortunately, this reformation feels incomplete. In effect, the Christian Renaissance was aborted—by none other than Luther himself.

For those living through an ensuing five centuries of Luther's legacy, the real heresy lies in his failure to complete the Reformation he started. Luther failed to throw off the shackles of Nicaea, to accept and celebrate diverse interpretations and marketability of the Jesus message, and to center a revived church on the message of creative conflict resolution rather than monolithic dogmatic uniformity. By inability to effect a true priesthood of believers. That time, that fulfillment of reformation, has yet to come.

Supplement — Pre-Post Luther Theologians

Space is limited but in the spirit of our 12 Christian pioneers, here are thoughts as to notable theologians and pastoral practitioners—illustrating the diversity of belief and practice from Constantine to today.

From Constantine to Luther. This listing chronologically spans 12 centuries, from the 4th-15th:

---

[556] Erikson, *Young Man Luther,* 224.

- **Jerome**—4th century ascetic, translator of commentaries and the Bible to the Latin Vulgate
- **John Chrysostom**—archbishop of Constantinople, critic of abuse by church and political elders
- **Augustine**—immensely influential to western Christian theology, both Catholic and Protestant
- **Nestorius**—condemned for advocating Christ as two distinct beings—one divine, one human
- **Gregory the Great**—bishop of Rome, instituting the mission to convert Anglo Saxons to Christ
- **Bede**—English monk, Bible historian, known as the "Father of English History" and AD dating
- **Anselm**—Archbishop of Canterbury, exiled twice, known for "faith seeking understanding"
- **Francis of Assisi**—founder of Franciscans with vows of poverty, chastity and obedience
- **Thomas Aquinas**—Dominican theologian, reconciling Aristotelian philosophy with Christianity
- **William of Ockham**—Franciscan friar, known for Occam's razor seeking the simplest solutions
- **John Wycliffe**—dissident Catholic theologian who openly criticized wealth of the Church
- **Jan Hus**—Czeck theologian opposing sale of indulgences, excommunicated, burned at the stake
- **Thomas a Kempis**—devotional writer advocating perfection by following the example of Jesus
- **Desiderius Erasmus**—wrote new Latin/Greek New Testaments, advocated religious tolerance
- **Thomas Cranmer**—Archbishop of Canterbury, English Reformation leader, burned at the stake
- **Ignatius of Loyola**—founder of Jesuits emphasizing missionary work, led counter-reformation
- **John Calvin**—reformation counterpart in Geneva to Luther, taught predestination

From Luther to Present. Covers a shorter span of 6 centuries with more voices from the 15th-21st:

- **Michael Servetus**—Theologian/physician, opposed trinitarianism, burned at the stake in Geneva by consent of John Calvin
- **John Knox**—Calvinist minister, leader of Scottish Reformation, opposed Mary Queen of Scots
- **Jacob Arminius**—Dutch reformed minister advocating free will over Calvinist predestination
- **John Milton**—English poet best known for *Paradise Lost*—the fall and redemption of humanity
- **Richard Baxter**—non-conformist minister known as "chief of English Protestant Schoolmen"
- **George Fox**—founder of Society of Friends (Quakers), pacifist dissident, repeatedly jailed
- **Jonathan Edwards**—American puritan, preached "Sinners in the Hands of an Angry God"
- **John Wesley**—English revivalist, founder of Methodism, traveled England and America
- **George Whitefield**—With Wesley, Methodist preacher but Calvinist vs Wesley's Arminianism
- **Frederick Hegel**—German philosopher pushing a dialectic of Jesus transcending virtue and vice
- **Charles Finney**—Presbyterian minister, leader of 2nd Great Awakening, also an abolitionist
- **Mary Baker Eddy**—founder of the Christian Science movement based on science and health
- **Charles Spurgeon**—the "Prince of Preachers," opposed liberalism of the British Baptist Union
- **Dwight L. Moody**—American/British evangelist starting 1870s—addressing 100+ million
- **Billy Sunday**—baseball player turned early 20th century evangelist, supported prohibition
- **C.S. Lewis**—British theologian and writer encompassing religious treatises and popular fiction

- **Dietrich Bonhoffer**—Lutheran writer on *Cost of Discipleship*, executed as anti-Nazi dissident
- **Francis Schaeffer**—American/Swiss evangelical supporting historic faith over modernism
- **Billy Graham**—American evangelist hosting large crusades, bipartisan friend of U.S. presidents
- **Karen Armstrong**—left convent for popular writing with liberal, comparative religious focus

XII. Jesus—Conflicted Christianity

Do you think that I have come to bring peace to the earth?
No, I tell you, but rather division!
From now on five in one household will be divided,
three against two and two against three;
they will be divided:
father against son and son against father, mother against daughter and
daughter against mother, mother-in-law against her daughter-in-law and
daughter-in-law against mother-in-law.
Jesus, from Luke 12:51–54 [557]

We each have our own personal image or metaphor for Jesus. To some, he is the great shepherd. To others, the Son of God or maybe Son of Man. Or how about the way, the truth and the life? The word? The teacher, healer? The Christ? King of the Jews?

Without discounting any of these possibilities, another alternative is offered for consideration. This is of Jesus as the first and last of those who have been alternatively characterized by some as pioneers of Christianity, to others as heretics—outside the mainstream of the culture and religion of their time on this earthly orb.

From Matthew to Luther. We began this excursion into these selected great pioneers (and associated heresies) of Christianity with the writers of the New Testament gospels. Continuing from those connected with Jesus during his earthly ministry down through the centuries to Martin Luther, the central argument has been that each of these 11 proto-Christian figures introduced some new and significant twist to the Christian faith—challenging the orthodoxy of their time (and often ours as well).

---

[557] Similar references at Matthew 10:34–36 and the non-canonical Gospel of Thomas 16. See also Micah 7:5–6.

The resulting legacy has been one of on-going dissension and conflict within the Christian ranks—from the 1st century through the 21st. A simple question is posed: *Is this conflict intended or unintended?*

A Jesus of Conflict? To answer the question, we must travel back to the source—back to the very person of Jesus, the reputed son of the living God.

In exploring the first 11 pioneers, we have viewed Jesus through the eyes of others. This includes both those who were Jesus' contemporaries and those who came later.

Now we take the last step—stripping back the layers of time and tradition to see Jesus as he was. And when we take this step, we discover that *conflicted Christianity* comes as no accident. The conflicts are there because that is what Jesus intended. He wanted it that way.

Restated, the argument presented here embodies three distinct but related themes:

- While early New Testament era authors and subsequent pioneers each offered their own spin on Jesus' life, the reported conflicts reflect something far deeper—seemingly contradictory statements and actions by the historical Jesus himself.
- Jesus intentionally set up situations of conflict and contradiction.
- We can never fully experience the kingdom of God without living through these contradictions—both individually and collectively.

Jesus stands as the first and last of the Christian pioneers. Jesus delivered a message that was uncomfortable to the ruling elites of his day. For this, he was executed. Even today, 20 centuries later, Jesus points to a path, a way of life that most of humanity is inclined to avoid or ignore.

A primary thesis is this—*Jesus intended conflict.* This was the god-man who desired that we be fully immersed in the turmoil—even through the rough and tumble of life.

And there is a purpose—that we wrestle with the contradictions, draw new understanding synthesized for changing times, and apply the understanding in the here and now of daily lives. When we fail to grasp the message, we miss the full wonder of God's kingdom—a kingdom that is emerging but also here among us in the here and now.

On these pages, we outline this alternative view of Jesus. For a few moments, keep an open mind. Whatever your perspective, prepare to be challenged!

Background of Jesus

As with our other pioneers of Christian faith and practice, it is useful to start with what we know about Jesus, then move to the more important and challenging aspects of the purposes of his earthly mission.

Who Was Jesus? From an historical perspective, we know nothing about Jesus except from what others have written about him. Jesus left no video or social media posts, no autobiographical writings, not even a drawing of his likeness.

No New Testament (or secular) writer of the first two centuries AD approached the task of reporting Jesus' ministry in a fully objective fashion. As is evident with the New Testament writers profiled, each was telling his (or her) own story. Each put their own spin on the message—by choosing specific incidents (and words) to include or exclude.

So, is it really possible to strip back the accretions of time and tradition and find the real historic Jesus? The answer is both yes and no.

Yes, it is possible to piece together a portrait of the man from what others have written about Jesus—biases and all. *No,* it is not possible to totally eliminate those biases and potential distortions of the record as it has been received. However, the risks are greatly reduced when we look to *multiple accounts*—both within and outside the New Testament canon.

And for this topic—that of conflicted Christianity—there is an even better option. We can simply take and absorb each account on its own merits. If even a single author reports that Jesus contradicted himself, we need not worry about different *spins* between writers. Maybe something else really is going on.

Tradition of the Historic Jesus. The essentials of the historical Jesus can be gleaned from a variety of both historical and credal documents passed down through two millennia. Consider first the creed formulated under the direct supervision of the Roman emperor Constantine at the Council of Nicaea in 325 AD:

We believe in...

…One Lord Jesus Christ, the Son of God. Who for us men and for our salvation came down and was incarnate, was made man, suffered, and rose again the third day, ascended into heaven, and is coming to judge living and dead.[558]

When it comes to the historical Jesus, stripping down the Nicene Creed to its bare essentials is very simple. Jesus was the Son of God, became human, died, was resurrected, ascended to heaven, and is coming again.

The Josephus Account. Now consider a different formulation, ostensibly from a more dispassionate and unlikely non-Christian source, that of a first-century Jewish military leader, traitor and historian known as Flavius Josephus:

Now, there was about this time Jesus, a wise man, if it be lawful to call him a man, for he was a doer of wonderful works—*a teacher of such men as receive the truth with pleasure.* He drew over many to him both many of the Jews, and many of the Gentiles. He was [the] Christ; and when Pilate, at the suggestion of the principal men among us, had condemned him to the cross, those that loved him at the first did not forsake him, for he appeared to them alive again the third day, as the divine prophets had foretold these and ten thousand other wonderful things concerning him; and the tribe of Christians, so named from him, are not extinct at this day.[559]

The essentials as recounted by Josephus parallel those of the Nicene Creed in several key respects. Jesus was an actual human, died on a cross, and reappeared. Josephus also calls Jesus a doer of wonderful works (miracles?), a teacher, and as the source for a movement involving people who came to be known as Christians.

For some, this extraordinarily brief account of Josephus is viewed as too short for such an important figure and by others questioned as a possible later

---

[558] Eusebius, *A New Eusebius,* 366.

[559] Josephus, *The Antiquities of the Jews,* Book 18 Chapter 3 (separate numbering as 18.63–64), as translated by William Whiston. Some modern scholars suggest this text may have been altered in later manuscripts, but there is no definitive evidence either for or against this proposition.

addition or redaction to the works of Josephus. There may be a more logical explanation of what Josephus has in mind.

The amount of press Josephus gives to Jesus is much skimpier than what he gives to Jesus' cousin John the Baptist and to Jesus half- or stepbrother James. Historian Josephus also was a consummate politician—an adherent to the *great man school* of human history. The execution of John the Baptist figures as an historically significant political event for 1st century Palestine. Josephus cites the Baptist's beheading as the reason for the subsequent defeat in battle of Herod Antipas by King Aretas IV of Nabataea. Herod had divorced the daughter of Aretas in favor of Herodias who had been married to another half-brother Herod II—a divorce which the Baptist had publicly condemned.[560]

As described in an earlier chapter, James the *brother* of Jesus was similarly a significant figure in 1st century Palestine, widely respected by early Christians as well as non-converts. His execution at the direction of the Jewish Sanhedrin during a time when Judea was between Roman procurators (governors) became a major political event—with Rome removing the high priest due to the ruckus raised by those who believe James' execution to be a miscarriage of justice. As suggested by the Jewish historian Josephus, it signaled to Rome the inability for Judaic leadership to exercise responsible governance, planting the seeds for the broader Jewish rebellion that emerged shortly thereafter.[561]

While the Josephus writings generally occur in chronological sequence, the Jesus paragraph is sandwiched in between what appear to be unrelated events.[562] Just preceding the Jesus paragraph Josephus describes an ill-fated effort of Pontius Pilate to bring a water aqueduct into Jerusalem by appropriating "sacred money" leading to an uprising to which Pilate responded by bludgeoning a gathered crowd of protestors.

Immediately following the Jesus paragraph is another unrelated event—the sad tale of a virtuous Roman woman named Paulina who is tricked into

---

[560] Josephus details the execution of John the Baptist and aftermath in *Antiquities*, Book 18.3 (18.109–119).

[561] James' execution and aftermath is described by Josephus in *Antiquities*, Book 20.9 (20,197–223).

[562] These four unrelated stories regarding Pilate, the single paragraph note about Jesus, the tale of Paulina and that of Fulvia are covered together in one chapter from Josephus, *Antiquities of the Jews,* Book 18.3 (18.55–84).

sleeping with an impostor at the Temple of Isis in Rome. The ensuing scandal catches the attention of the Roman emperor Tiberias who crucifies complicit temple priests, banishes the perpetrator of the rape and destroys the temple of Isis.

Josephus then follows this story with another unusual narrative of a scheme by a Jew and accomplices to defraud a Roman woman named Fulvia who was interested in Judaism, wanting to send purple and gold to the Jewish temple at Jerusalem. The fraudsters took and spent the money for their own purposes. This event also aroused the ire of emperor Tiberias who then banishes all Jews from Rome—all for the wickedness of four men.

What appears to be the case is that Josephus has four rather remarkable stories to tell but doesn't quite know if or where they fit in with the rest of his sweeping narrative of Jewish history and politics. He cannot easily disregard theses accounts, so he force fits them into one rather disjointed series of four abbreviated sidebar excursions.

One last clue to the seeming cluelessness of Josephus. He introduces the Jesus paragraph with this rather abrupt transition, saying "Now there was about this time Jesus, a wise man..." While Josephus gives no indication that he was a follower of Jesus as Christ, he clearly respects him...just not sure how to place him in the pantheon of Jewish history.

Other Historical Accounts. Jesus also is mentioned as an historical figure by two Roman figures of the first and early second centuries—Roman historian Tacitus and politician Pliny the Younger. As indicated by their disparaging statements, neither could be considered as friends of the nascent Christian movement.[563]

Beyond these early cryptic secular formulations, most of what can be gleaned about Jesus' life is found in the four Gospels of the New Testament—supplemented by other writings of the canonical New Testament. The apostle Paul provides few clues in his letters about Jesus' life—describing only

---

[563] Tacitus, *Roman Annals*, 15.44 records that in about 115–117 AD emperor Nero had attributed burning of Rome in 64 AD to Christians. In his writings, Tacitus refers to "a class hated for their abominations, called Christians by the populace." He also describes Christians as having a "hatred of mankind."
Pliny the Younger was governor of Bithynia. At about 111–113 AD, he reported to emperor Trajan that "the contagion of that superstition (Christianity) has penetrated not only the cities but also the villages and farms." From Pliny, *Epistulae*, X.96.

selected events surrounding his death and resurrection. Other early information is available from non-canonical sources (including self-named Gospels) of the first two centuries, at least some of which are of dubious historicity.

So, the essentials of what we can know with some reasonable certainty from both the Biblical and non-Biblical accounts can be summarized as follows:

- Jesus was born in Bethlehem to a woman named Mary (reputedly a virgin) and betrothed to a man named Joseph (as indicated by two of the four Gospels—Matthew and Luke). By Matthew's account, Jesus' birth is placed near the end of the reign of Herod the Great (about 4 BC). Luke's account appears to be somewhat in conflict, placing Jesus' birth at the time of a Roman census authorized when Quirinius was governor of Syria (ostensibly about 6–7 AD).[564]
- After a brief sojourn by his parents to Egypt, Jesus apparently was raised in the Galilean village of Nazareth (Matthew and Luke), about which little is known except that Jesus apparently traveled to the temple in Jerusalem at age 12 (recounted only in Luke).[565]
- When Jesus was about 30 years old, he began a period of ministry that extended over about three years.[566] Prior to beginning his ministry, he relocated his residence from the hill town of Nazareth to the Sea of Galilee fishing community of Capernaum.
- The three synoptic Gospels (Matthew, Mark, Luke) place most of this ministry in Galilee, while most of the events recounted by John's Gospel occur to the south in Judea. Jesus ministers primarily to Jews, though some brief but pivotal encounters with non-Jewish individuals also are recounted. All four gospel writers indicate that Jesus' ministry begins about the time of his baptism by the person known as John the Baptist in the Jordan River.

---

[564] This apparent conflict in dating of the birth of Jesus is potentially solved if Quirinius served two separate terms as governor, which some have suggested.

[565] Other more fanciful accounts of Jesus' youth are provided by the non-canonical *Infancy Gospel of Thomas*, part of the Nag Hammadi library.

[566] Luke 3:23 indicates that "Jesus was about thirty years old when he began his work."

- Jesus' status within Jewish society of the 1st century was subject to questioning and ridicule—because of the insignificance of his home town Nazareth and questions about his paternal parentage.[567]
- All four Gospels report that Jesus' message was increasingly opposed by certain segments of the Jewish religious establishment, notably the sects of the Pharisees and Sadducees together with scribal authorities.
- All four New Testament Gospels (and most of the non-canonical Gospels) also report that Jesus performed both healing and nature miracles. Two of four Gospels (Matthew and Luke) feature Jesus as an inveterate story teller of parables.
- All four Gospels provide an account of Jesus' death and subsequent apparent resurrection. Two Gospels (Matthew and Luke as well as Acts) clearly indicate that Jesus then ascended to heaven, as do later (but apparently not the earliest) extant manuscripts of Mark's gospel.

There are a variety of other items taken for granted by many Christians but about which the New Testament Gospels are not as clear or consistent. These include questions relating to the divinity and messiah mission of Jesus, personal salvation, social reform, heaven and hell, and second coming (or future eschatology).

The Missing Years. There has long been considerable speculation as to what Jesus did between the years of his childhood and his call to active itinerant ministry about 30 AD. Mark's gospel provides a clue; he had followed his father's footsteps as a carpenter.[568]

While the consensus position is that Jesus' ministry occurred over about three years, there are alternative views. One view is that the ministry of Jesus spread over a much longer time than three years. A 21st century writer, for example suggests that Jesus began an apprenticeship with John the Baptist,

---

[567] At John 7:52, the chief priests and Pharisees admonish Nicodemus saying: "Search and you will see that no prophet is to arise from Galilee." At John 8:19, Jewish leaders ask Jesus: "Where is your Father?" suggesting doubts as to his paternal parentage, i.e. as a Galilean *mamzer*. Earlier, the disciple Nathanael had commented at John 1:46: "Can anything good come out of Nazareth?" Thomas 105 has Jesus offering a description of the "child of a whore," possibly though not definitely in reference to himself.

[568] Mark 6:3.

then was involved in a gradually widening ministry over the course of more than a decade prior to his crucifixion.[569]

Conflicted Christianity

For two millennia, theological and doctrinal debates over the life, teachings and actions of Jesus have been predicated on the notion that there is but *one truth*. Where there may appear to be two conflicting statements, orthodoxy demands that truth must be reconciled through *harmonization*.

Seeming contradictions are to always be reconciled, no matter how problematic or bizarre the resulting explanation. The contradictions are primarily of two types:

- Internal inconsistencies noted *within* the accounts of each individual NT author.
- Inconsistencies *between* different NT authors.

Conflicts Within Gospel Accounts. Conflicts between gospel accounts are more often noted than those conflicts internalized within a single New Testament gospel. Yet it is these internal conflicts that are of most interest—because they appear to portray Jesus often at war with himself.

Virtually all of the New Testament Gospels and some of the non-canonical writings provide vivid examples of a *conflicted Jesus*.[570] In the *Gospel of Mark* alone, at least 15 different sets of conflicting statements attributed to Jesus can be found.[571]

Here is an example. Speaking to a rich man, Jesus invokes the Mosaic commandment to: "Honor your father and mother."[572]

Yet, just moments later, Jesus admonishes Peter his disciple:

---

[569] Bruce Chilton, *Rabbi Jesus: An Intimate Biography,* (New York: Random House), 2000, xv. Chilton also suggests that Jesus may have been born at a different Bethlehem in Galilee (near Nazareth) rather than the better known Bethlehem of Judea.

[570] Interestingly, the New Testament writings of Paul and James do not provide similar examples of Jesus making clearly contradictory statements.

[571] See www.jesustheheresy.com, *Contrasting Accounts of Jesus,* 91–93, for a complete listing.
https://www.jesustheheresy.com/#/contrastingaccounts/.

[572] Mark 10:19.

Truly, I tell you, there is no one who has *left house or brothers or sisters or mother or father or children or fields,* for my sake and for the sake of the good news, who will not receive a hundredfold now in this age—houses, brothers and sisters, mothers and children, and fields, with persecutions—and in the age to come eternal life.[573]

The Jesus of Matthew and Mark also appears to *flip-flop* on the question of whether to accept and heal a non-Jew. As told in Matthew (and illustrated by the cover to this book), this encounter is worth recounting in its entirety:

Jesus left that place (Gennesaret) and went away to the district of Tyre and Sidon. Just then a Canaanite woman from that region came out and started shouting, "Have mercy on me, Lord, Son of David; my daughter is tormented by a demon." But he did not answer her at all. And his disciples came and urged him, saying, "Send her away, for she keeps shouting after us."
He answered, "I was sent *only to the lost sheep of the house of Israel.*" But she came and knelt before him, saying, "Lord, help me." He answered, "It is not fair to take the children's food and throw it to the dogs." She said, "Yes, Lord, yet *even the dogs eat the crumbs* that fall from their masters' table."
Then Jesus answered her, "Woman, *great is your faith!* Let it be done for you as you wish." And her daughter was healed instantly.[574]

Why did Jesus change his mind and help this Canaanite woman? One interpretation is that he was testing to see how badly she wanted healing—pushing her buttons. A second explanation is that he was persuaded and changed his mind by the strength of her logic. A third and related explanation would be that Jesus was confronted by his own prejudicial attitudes toward non-Jews. He comes across as confused by the contradiction between his belief and her assertion, leading Jesus to reconsider his own xenophobia.

---

[573] Marl 10:29–30.

[574] Matthew 15:21–28. A parallel passage is found at Mark 7:24–30. The Greek for "dogs" is perhaps more appropriately translated as "little dogs," still uncomplimentary but with perhaps with lesser bite.

No matter what the explanation, here is a picture of Jesus who might be considered as disingenuous or as conflicted by his own varied personal beliefs and emotions. In any event, much as Moses prevailed in dialogue with God to prevent destruction of Jewish migrants traveling from Egypt to Canaan, the Canaanite woman similarly accomplished a change of heart and action via her deprecating but assertive stance toward Jesus.[575]

Luke's Jesus is conflicted over money. One the one hand, Jesus espouses charity and forgiveness of debts:

If you lend to those from whom you hope to receive, what credit is that to you? Even sinners lend to sinners, to receive as much again. But love your enemies, do good, and lend, *expecting nothing* in return.[576]

But, Luke's Jesus appears to be disseminating a different message regarding financial stewardship in a parable. The punchline goes like this:

Why then did you not put my money into the bank? Then when I returned, I could have collected it *with interest*.[577]

Does Jesus support lending for a return on investment? As Luke relates, the answer would appear to depend on the day and the circumstance. Or maybe we as the audience need to consider the circumstances of each situation before deciding on a tailor-made course of action—when to invest wisely versus to give without expectation of return.

For the three synoptics, the ambivalence of Jesus' message is focused more on the present material world. The *Gospel of John* also provides evidence of tension between what might be considered as a *soft* versus *hard* Jesus. However, John's emphasis is more on the future and the spiritual.

For example, to the sellers in the temple, Jesus shouts:

Stop making my Father's house a marketplace![578]

---

[575] Exodus 32:11–14.
[576] Luke 6:34.
[577] Luke 19:23.
[578] John 2:16.

In this instance, Jesus is very much concerned with protecting the sacredness of a temple at a physical location—in Jerusalem. But, to a Samaritan woman, Jesus seems to convey a different message:

> Woman, believe me, the hour is coming when you worship the Father neither on this mountain (Gerizim) nor in Jerusalem.[579]

In this latter case, Jesus seems to show disdain for the Jewish temple—the symbol of an age about to pass away. Again, which is it? Is God to be worshipped at one place? Or everywhere? One might reasonably ask: Will the real Jesus please stand up?

Alternatively, one might conclude that we are really passing from one era of OT worship at one place to an expectation of post-temple NT worship everywhere.

As if confusion about where to worship is not enough, Jesus also fuels an ageless debate as to whether sin causes disease. To a man Jesus heals and finds later at the temple, Jesus says:

> See, you have been made well! Do not sin anymore, so that *nothing worse happens to you.*[580]

But in talking of a blind man, Jesus clearly decouples illness from sin. He observes:

> Neither this man nor his parents sinned; he *was born blind so that God's works might be revealed* in him.[581]

In this case, the purpose of disease is not punishment, but glorification of God—albeit at the obvious multi-year expense of this individual's well-being. So, once again—does illness occur as a result of sin or for other reasons? The apparent answer—it depends!

Conflicts Between Gospel Accounts. Conflicts between gospel accounts have been more widely cited—in large part due to varying chronologies as well

---

[579] John 4:21.
[580] John 5:14.
[581] John 9:3.

as details of Jesus' ministry provided by the four gospel writers. An example of a doctrinal conflict is most simply illustrated by Matthew's "Blessed are the poor *in spirit*" versus Luke's more abbreviated and pointed statement of "Blessed are the poor."[582]

So, is Jesus' blessing directed at those who are poor in material possessions or poor in spirit? In this case, the answer seems to depend on the discretion of the person telling the story. Or the day on which the story occurs.

Throughout his gospel, Luke places special priority on assistance to the poor. Mark takes a different tack, quoting Jesus as saying:

> For you always have the poor with you, *and you can show kindness to them whenever you wish,* but you will not always have me.[583]

Matthew has Jesus making the same statement, only a bit more hard hitting by deleting the *italicized* phrase noted above. In his account of this same incident of the anointing of Jesus, Luke avoids the entire comment about the inevitability of poverty.

John's Gospel takes a tack similar to Matthew, but adds the parenthetical note that it was Judas Iscariot who had raised the question of extravagant spending to anoint Jesus:

> ...not because he (Judas) cared about the poor, but because he was a thief; he kept the common purse and used to steal what was put into it.[584]

John attempts to shift the focus away from the appropriateness of the anointing to Judas' evil motive of theft from the common fund. But Jesus avoids Judas' treachery by shifting the focus to the question of extravagance versus alleviating poverty. He shuts down the conversation, tersely saying:

> Leave her alone. She bought it so that she might keep it for the day of my burial. You always have the poor with you, but you do not always have me.[585]

---

[582] See Matthew 5:3 and Luke 6:20.
[583] Mark 14:7.
[584] John 12:6.
[585] John 12:7–8.

For three of four gospel writers, in this case with crucifixion looming, extravagance trumps alleviation of poverty (which certainly would not have made much difference on a mass level). One writer (Luke) places the focus of his narrative on the role of a sinner being involved. And even for the three who agree on the priority of the anointing, each account has its own twist.

As might be expected, Mark offers the most direct support for the primacy of anointing, trumping alleviation of poverty by Jesus. Matthew softens this by saying there are other times and ways to address poverty. And John partially deflects the issue away from the question of poverty to that of the thievery of Judas.

Mark's statement that "the Sabbath was made for humankind, and not humankind for the Sabbath" is *softened* by both of the other synoptics to read more simply as: "...the Son of Man is Lord of the Sabbath."[586]

There also are interesting differences in the way that the early Sunday visit to Jesus' tomb is handled. None of the four Gospels seem to agree on specifically which women made the visit.[587] Of greater interest, the three synoptics describe the reactions of these early morning visitors quite differently.

Early manuscripts of Mark's gospel (ending at verse 8 of chapter 16) clearly have the women fleeing from the tomb in "terror and amazement." What comes next? The earliest manuscripts of Mark don't say but leave the audience hanging.

Matthew describes a somewhat more complex emotion of "fear and great joy." Luke simply comments that women were "returning" from the tomb to relay the information to the disciples and others, with no other mention of accompanying emotion specifically noted.

With John there is a more complicated, nuanced account. Mary Magdalene visits the tomb first, runs to Peter and the "other disciple"). Then the action returns to Mary who has separate encounters with two angels, then a gardener who turns out to be the risen savior.

---

[586] Matthew 12:8, Luke 6:5.

[587] Mark has Mary Magdalene, Mary the mother of James and Salome visiting the tomb; for Luke it is Joanna and the other women as well as Mary Magdalene and Mary the mother of James. For Matthew, the visitors are solely Mary Magdalene and the "other Mary" (not specified). For John, the only woman identified is Mary Magdalene.

More than the other synoptics, Luke exhibits a tendency to downplay (or soften) some of the conflicts,[588] Mark has Jesus saying that he talks in parables, in part, so that those "outside:"

> …may indeed look, but not perceive, and may indeed listen, but not understand, *so that they may not turn again and be forgiven.*[589]

Luke deletes this hardened (*italicized*) portion of the above noted statement.

Mark's Jesus is blunt with the disciples in a storm tossed boat: "Have you still no faith?"[590] Matthew softens this somewhat to "you of little faith."[591] Luke goes further to simply ask: "Where is your faith?"[592] Of the three accounts, clearly Mark's is the most pejorative—especially as only Mark inserts the accusatory term "still" in the question. Jesus is clearly exasperated with what Mark's gospel perceives to be a gaggle of dimwitted disciples.

In a similar or perhaps different account of a woman ("a sinner") anointing Jesus as described in Luke's gospel, the concern of the Pharisee host is more with Jesus letting a sinner touch him than with the question of whether this is an appropriate use of an expensive anointing.[593]

While a reading of Mark provides perhaps the most distinctive differences between a *soft* and a *hard* Jesus, Matthew and Luke also offer some passages unique to their respective Gospels. For example, Matthew is notable for contrasting God's emphasis on love and care versus uncertainty and strife. Luke tends to present conflicts in more practical and everyday terms—including examples associated with lending or saving and the personal sacrifices involved in following Jesus.

---

[588] Luke's willingness to disregard or downplay conflicts also carries over to the book of Acts, exemplified by glossing over the details of what happened in the transition of church leadership from Peter to James to Paul.
[589] Mark 4:12.
[590] Mark 4:40.
[591] Matthew 8:26.
[592] Luke 8:25.
[593] Luke 7:36–50.

In short, the gospel writers consistently portray Jesus differently in terms of theology, politics and humanity. Is this simply because each writer is injecting his own unique bias or *spin* into the account?

Or could these differences also reflect genuinely different faces of the same Son of Man? A rabbi who could be both *hard and soft*, who preached both a personal and social gospel.

The answer may be neither and both. Each gospel writer sought to explain this conflicted Jesus in terms that met with their understanding of underlying events in a manner that also would be understandable to the intended audience. It is not surprising that each author would find a different means to fit their particular spin to interpret the meaning(s) of this unique ministry.

Non-Canonical Gospels. Turning to accounts outside the canonical New Testament, some writers offer relatively cohesive pictures. Others present a collage of what may include more discordant elements. This is especially true of the *Gospel of Thomas.*

For example, the Jesus of Thomas sends mixed signals about the priority placed on reconciliation with those believers who fall by the wayside. In strong language unique to this non-canonical gospel, Jesus is quoted as saying:

> Damn the Pharisees! They are like a dog sleeping in the cattle manger: the dog neither eats nor [lets] the cattle eat.[594]

But, this is the same Jesus who can tell this parable of the lost sheep with a straight face:

> The [Father's] imperial rule Kingdom is like a shepherd who had a hundred sheep. One of them, the largest, went astray. He left the ninety-nine and looked for the one until he found it. After he had toiled, he said to the sheep, *'I love you more than the ninety-nine.'*[595]

In the first instance, the Jesus of *Thomas* is dismissive of all religious folks who stray from God's kingdom through their own hypocrisy. In the second, Jesus the savior looks to pursue and restore any who inadvertently or purposely stray from the fold.

---

[594] Thomas 102.
[595] Thomas 107.

The *Infancy Gospel of Christ* is striking for what it presents as wildly contrasting *actions* of the young Savior. The author claims that Jesus as a youth withers the hand of a boy who drains a pond Jesus made; another boy is struck dead just for bumping into Jesus.[596]

Later, after receiving a scolding from his father (Joseph), Jesus evidences a change in attitude toward actions of healing. He resurrects a child who fell from a roof, heals a young man's foot, heals a snake bite of brother James, and restores life to a construction worker.[597]

It is not surprising that Jesus' apparent ambiguity would create confusion among even his closest relatives and followers. For example, the writer of *Secret James* expresses the frustration of at least one disciple, in this case the anxiety of lead disciple Peter who is telling Jesus:

Sometimes you urge us on toward heaven's domain, *yet at other times* you turn us away, Lord. Sometimes you make appeals, draw us toward faith, and promise us life, *yet at other times you* drive us away from heaven's domain.[598]

This represents a clear example of disciples' difficulty in interpreting seemingly conflicting statements from Jesus—albeit from a non-canonical source. In at least this instance, the reply of Jesus is of little direct help. Rather, Jesus faults the disciples' lack of understanding. What's more, the response appears directed toward the wrong person in his own brother James rather than Jesus' critic Peter—as Jesus expresses what may be pent-up frustration about James' past disregard for Jesus' divine earthly mission:

I have offered you faith many times; moreover, I have made myself known to you, James, and you have not understood me.[599]

The Persona of Jesus Amid Conflict. "Persona" denotes the *public* role or personality that a person assumes or is perceived to assume. With Jesus, all we have available is a persona derived from the now public accounts of four gospel

---

[596] Infancy Thomas, 4:1–2.
[597] Infancy Thomas, Chapters 9, 10, 16, 18.
[598] Secret James 9:1.
[599] Secret James 9:2.

writers coupled with other New Testament books and some early though non-canonical writings.

So, how does Jesus handle himself in messy situations? What is his persona amid conflict? Not surprisingly the answer once again is "it depends." Consider the following types of situations:

- **Jesus can step over potential conflict with a short but pointed rebuke.** For example, when the disciples attempt to shunt children aside, we hear the gentle shepherd calling out: "Let the little children come to me, and do not stop them; for it is to such as these that the kingdom of heaven belongs."[600]
- **There are times when Jesus is seemingly oblivious to conflict around him**—until he is called up short by the cries of others. This is classically illustrated with Jesus asleep in the bottom of a boat even as storm weather surges and his disciples are terrorized. Jesus is awakened with the plaintive question: "Teacher, do you *not care* that we are perishing?"[601]
- **Jesus sometimes exhibits an uncanny ability to defuse conflict by cutting to the quick of an issue.** This has the effect sometimes of shaming others in the process. This occurs, for example, when the scribes and Pharisees bring Jesus a woman caught in adultery. Jesus calms a potentially murderous situation with one request: "Let anyone among you who is without sin be the first to throw a stone at her."[602] For the wayward woman, God's grace is extended freely even when it may appear to go beyond what is deserved. The case can be made that Jesus is calling for the law to be applied consistently with non-malicious, impartial witnesses. In effect, this case failed for lack of witnesses.[603]
- **There also are times when Jesus manages to sneak away from (or rise above) conflict.** This is perhaps best exemplified as he "passed

---

[600] Matthew 19:14.
[601] Mark 4:38.
[602] John 8:7.
[603] See Deuteronomy 19:15–19 for Mosaic law regarding required testimony of witnesses.

through" a crowd even as they were ready to throw him from a cliff (in his own hometown).[604]

- **Sometimes Jesus intentionally creates conflict.** He sets himself in direct (even seemingly needless) opposition to others—clearly exemplified in his interaction with the Canaanite woman. This approach also occurs, for example, as Jesus calls out "…woe to you, scribes and Pharisees, hypocrites! For you lock people out of the kingdom of heaven." And again, "Woe to you, scribes and Pharisees, hypocrites! For you cross sea and land to make a single convert, and you make the new convert twice as much a *child of hell* as yourselves."[605]

- **Finally, there are times when Jesus refuses to directly engage in conflict—even in self-defense.** At his trial, he is asked by Pilate: "Are you the king of the Jews?" The first time Jesus replies: 'Do you ask this on your own, or did others tell you about me?' The second time Pilate asks the question, Jesus responds: 'You say that I am a king. For this I was born, and for this I came into the world, to testify to the truth. Everyone who belongs to the truth listens to my voice.' The third time Pilate asks the question comes after this procurator has agreed to release Barabbas at the request of the assembled crowd. This time Pilate asks Jesus, 'Where are you from?' Initially, Jesus does not answer. Pilate presses and this time Jesus both opines and lets Pilate off the hook: 'You would have no power over me at all unless it were given to you from above; therefore the one who handed me over to you is guilty of a greater sin.'[606]

So, why does Jesus respond to conflict one way in one situation, another in another situation. Several possibilities are suggested: a) his responses are part of a larger strategic game plan; b) responses are based on Jesus perception

---

[604] Luke 4:28–30.
[605] Matthew 23:13,15.
[606] The first question and Jesus' response in recorded by all three synoptic gospels. In John's gospel, Jesus gives a somewhat different response: "Is this your own question, or did others tell you about me?" Only John's gospel records the second and final verbal exchange between Pilate and Jesus. Excerpted from John 18:29–19:11.

of specific situations of the moment; c) responses are random; or d) some combination of the above.

The strongest scriptural support is indicated for option (d)—a combination of reasons. It is the unknown writer of Hebrews who provides a reason why. He explains the unique role of Jesus as both high priest and yet fully human, observing:

> For we do not have a high priest who is unable to sympathize with our weaknesses, but we have one who in every respect has been tested as we are, yet without sin.[607]

So, Jesus' response to conflict is much the same as when he himself sometimes creates conflict—in widely if not wildly different ways. He responds situationally much as most of humanity also responds—meeting each individual at their own level of understanding. If the writer of Hebrews is correct in suggesting that these responses to conflict can diverge but yet be without sin, that becomes a possibility that also may prove to be extraordinarily liberating.

Contradictory Actions of Jesus

Not only do we have Jesus responding differently to external conflict in varying situations, but this is a person who can take contradictory actions even when the circumstances are seemingly similar. With the exception of Mark, the four Gospels of the New Testament canon devote the majority of their respective narratives to the *words* of Jesus. But, as the colloquialism goes, "actions speak louder than words."

And so, we turn to the actions of Jesus. Do they show a pattern of conflicted behavior that corresponds with his spoken statements? The answer is a decided *yes*. Look at the earthly record of an individual who:

- Walked away from his parents at age twelve but at age 33+/-made sure to entrust his mother into the care of a beloved disciple at the time of his crucifixion.

---

[607] Hebrews 4:15.

- Drove the money-changers from the temple with a whip and then submitted days later to Jewish and Roman authorities without any resistance.
- Encouraged children but cursed a fig tree.
- Could command center stage with a Sermon on the Mount but yet slip through a crowd ready to stone him.
- Repulsed a Gentile woman seeking healing, then relented after she persisted.
- Performed healing and natural miracles in both urban and rural venues, but not in his own home town (of Nazareth).
- Deliberately set his face to Jerusalem and the accompanying expectation of death but then asked Father God to consider reversing this previously agreed course of action.

Some might suggest that these are contradictions in appearance only. Seemingly conflicting events may actually hide deeper meaning—and so really represent a consistent manifestation of Jesus' holy nature. For example, Jesus driving the money-changers from the temple represents a righteous anger appropriate for this event but not for Jesus' later arrest and trial. At the trial, the divine imperative for submittal to the foreordained outcome of crucifixion comes to outweigh any consideration of an angry response.

But then, how does one explain Jesus' ability to work miracles everywhere but Nazareth? Was he simply too nervous to do the miracle thing around those who had known him since childhood? Or was he *unmasked* by those (possibly even members of his own family) who knew the real Jesus and perhaps at that time judged him a charlatan?

Why All The Contradiction?

Are the contradictions real or only apparent? Are they to be explained away, to be *harmonized,* as has been the goal of mainstream Christian theologians since the first century.

The Real Message. What if these efforts to "make sense of it all" are missing the real message? A message with three parts:

1. **While early New Testament era authors each gave their own spin to Jesus' life, the reported conflicts reflect something far deeper—**

contradictory statements and actions by the historical Jesus himself. Conflict and contradiction run throughout Jesus' ministry—both in word and deed. Early Christian writers felt compelled to report at least some of the major conflicts as they occurred—because Jesus' actions and his teachings simply could not be explained otherwise.

2. **Jesus intentionally set up situations of conflict and contradiction.** The gospel text gives clear clues that Jesus intentionally set up conflict, purposefully making those around him uncomfortable. After all, it was Jesus who deliberately refused to see his mother, brothers and sisters when they traveled to see him. And it is Jesus who says that he speaks in parables—specifically so that his listeners will not necessarily understand his message. Jesus serves up the contradictions. At times, he offers hints of resolution. However, the gospel accounts often fall short, leaving the hearer and the reader with the opportunity to create a personal synthesis—applied to the needs and opportunities represented by each situation as it arises.

3. **We can never fully experience the kingdom without living through the contradictions—both individually and collectively.** This statement involves the greatest leap from the Jesus of the New Testament to the Jesus of today. Jesus is making his listener—then and now—reach for understanding and then for considered action.

Resolving Division. The primary question of this chapter is: how can a good God say that he came to bring not peace to the earth but rather division?[608] It seems that Jesus is simply acknowledging what occurs naturally as the result of exercising free will—in a fallen world.

However, there is a way out, the way of reconciliation. That pathway is illustrated by Luke 12. At the end of a discourse by Jesus, he concludes:

> And why do you not judge for yourselves what is right? Thus, when you go with your accuser before a magistrate, on the way make an effort to settle the case, or you may be dragged before the judge, and the judge hand you over to the officer, and the officer throw you in prison. I tell you, you will never get out until you have paid the very last penny.[609]

---

[608] Per Luke 12:51.
[609] Luke 12:57–59.

Matthew's account indicates that Jesus immediately follows this warning of bringing not peace but a sword with the following added comment—a resolution of sorts:

> Whoever loves father or mother more than me is not worthy of me; and whoever loves son or daughter more than me is not worthy of me; and whoever does not take up the cross and follow me is not worthy of me. Those who find their life will lose it, and those who lose their life for my sake will find it.[610]

From both Luke and Matthew, the message is clear. Expect conflict but realize there is a way through. That is by settling conflict as quickly as possible—otherwise yet worse may happen. And be prepared to bring the burden of the cross to follow Jesus Christ—recognizing that risking our life for the savior can at times become the only way to find the way through. The Jesus of Matthew puts it this way:

> Ask, and it will be given to you; search, and you *will find*; knock, and the door will be opened to you.[611]

Before Jesus appeared bodily on the scene, the Hebrew Scripture attributed to the OT prophet Micah offers a similar context of teaching about conflict and its resolution:

> Put no trust in a neighbor; have no confidence in a friend; guard the doors of your mouth from her who lies in your arms; for the son treats the father with contempt, the daughter rises up against her mother, the daughter-in-law against her mother-in-law; a man's enemies are the men of his own house.[612]

Micah immediately goes on—offering resolution and solution, stating:

---

[610] Matthew 10:37–39.
[611] Matthew 7:7, repeated in identical form by Luke 11:9.
[612] Micah 7:5–6.

But as for me, I will look to the Lord; I will wait for the God of my salvation; my God will hear me. Rejoice not over me, O my enemy; when I fall, I shall rise; when I sit in darkness, the Lord will be a light to me.[613]

And some years after Jesus' resurrection, the non-canonical Gospel of Thomas etches the words of Jesus in even bolder relief: "Those who seek should not stop seeking *until they find*. When they find, they will be disturbed. When they are disturbed, they will marvel, and will rule over all."

Settle quickly, look to the Lord who hears and acts, seek and find. God is there in and through it all. But it's not a one-way street. He looks for and supports our active participation.

Jesus in Summary

Jesus has been portrayed in countless ways over 20+ centuries—in forms ranging from the written word to artistic renditions. He is shown as the gentle shepherd, the embracer of children, the suffering Messiah and, yes, as the scourge of the sellers conducting their trade at the temple.

These images typically convey a single theme, a simple agenda. They sketch a Jesus of purpose, often of single-minded intent. Too seldom are the complexities—or the internal conflicts—of this man/god adequately captured in a single portrait.

To the Judeo-Greco inhabitants of 1st century Palestine, Jesus represents a pioneering conundrum. The historian Josephus—well acquainted with both Jewish and Roman culture—was as perplexed as others in summarily commenting that this was something of "a wise man, *if it be lawful* to call him a man."[614]

Jesus was out of the mainstream—a heretic to some—on matters related both to substance and style. He articulated belief in a kingdom both here and yet to come—both fulfilling and replacing the Jewish Torah. Jesus did it with style—his practice—involving supernatural healing, nature miracles, often difficult to understand teaching, challenging the authorities of his day.

---

[613] Micah 7:7–8. Micah goes on to elaborate yet further through to the end of the chapter to conclude his book.
[614] Josephus, *Antiquities of the Jews,* 18.63–64.

It is this ambiguity of being and purpose that made it so difficult for his disciples to answer the question: "Who do you say that I am?" Yet it is the underlying conflict within the man that continues to perplex even those who have come to inhabit this earth twenty centuries later. For most, the objective has been to smooth out the rough edges, to "harmonize" the Gospels.

Yet, the question has been posed: what if these efforts to "make sense of it all" are missing the real message? That this is a Jesus of deliberate, often bewildering conflict.

There is an answer—challenging but conceivable. The answer is that Jesus may have been delivering a totally unexpected message—a message with three parts:

1. While early New Testament era authors each gave their own *spin* to Jesus' life, the reported conflicts reflect something far deeper—contradictory statements and actions by the historical Jesus himself.
2. Jesus intentionally set up situations of conflict and contradiction.
3. We can never fully experience the kingdom without living through the contradictions—both individually and collectively.

The answer is summarized yet more succinctly by the unknown author of Hebrews, who puts it this way:

Therefore, since we are surrounded by so great a cloud of witnesses, let us also lay aside every weight and the sin that clings so closely, and let us run with perseverance the race that is set before us, looking to Jesus the *pioneer and perfecter* of our faith, who for the sake of the joy that was set before him endured the cross, disregarding its shame, and has taken his seat at the right hand of the throne of God.[615]

---

[615] Hebrews 12:1–2. The KJV terms Jesus as "author and finisher" of faith. At least 15 translations including the International Standard Version (ISV), New English Translation (NET), and New International Version (NIV) as well as the NSRV use the term "pioneer" in place of the traditional "author." Unlike Hebrews 2:20 which is translated from the Greek "aitios" as "pioneer,' in this case "pioneer" is a translation of the Greek "archegos."

Jesus pioneered by going outside the mainstream, by disrupting traditional views of what God's kingdom is and will be about. He perfects our faith by coming alongside humans to help finish the course—to reach closure.

As Jesus lived in and through conflict, he requests as much of those who follow behind. We are asked to work out our salvation via conflict—both personal and familial. So that, like the pagan, Canaanite woman who was initially rebuked by Jesus, we persist until the master relents, saying:

Let it be done for you as you wish.[616]

Supplement — The Secular Legacy of Jesus

After his death, resurrection and ascension, the effects and the memory of Jesus lived on—in ways including but extending well beyond the theological.

Surprisingly, the ramifications extended even to the realm of politics. Three major figures eventually would be affected by the manner in which the Jesus issue had been handled—Caiaphas, Pontius Pilate, and Herod Antipas.

Caiaphas' influence within the Sanhedrin waned after Jesus' execution. The first bad omen for the high priest was the tearing of the large tapestry in front of the Holy of Holies at the time of Jesus' death.

Caiaphas continued to wage war on the followers of Jesus, as recorded by the Acts of the Apostles, but had increasing difficulty making his charges stick. The apostles were threatened and flogged but persisted in teaching and preaching Jesus as Messiah both "in the temple and at home."[617]

History records that the trial, death and reported resurrection of Jesus made an impact on the Roman procurator of Judea, Pontius Pilate. Matthew's gospel records that the procurator's wife had a bad dream and advised her husband not to condemn Jesus.[618] This same writer suggests that Pilate washed his

---

[616] Matthew 15:28.

[617] Acts 4:42.

[618] Matthew 27:19. Pilate's wife was Claudia Procula, indicated by historical references as the illegitimate daughter of Julia, the only natural offspring of Augustus Caesar. Julia had numerous lovers and married Tiberius as her third husband. She was banished from Rome by Augustus for her lewd behavior. After Tiberius ascended the throne, he adopted Claudia as his own daughter.

hands of the matter, saying: "I am innocent of this man's blood; see to it yourselves."[619]

The NT church historian Eusebius goes further, indicating that Pilate even reported the death and apparent resurrection of Jesus, widely known throughout Palestine, back to the Roman emperor Tiberius. According to this account:

> ...Pilate knew all about Christ's supernatural deeds, and especially how after his death He had risen from the dead and was now generally believed to be a god.[620]

Some believe these incidents were contrived to absolve the Roman government and unfairly blame the Jewish leadership for Jesus' execution by crucifixion. However, the historical record also makes it clear that Roman authorization was required for execution, whether or not at the instigation of others.

In any event, Pilate appears to have continued with ill-advised, intemperate attacks against the population of his Judean protectorate. The final straw came when he ordered a large number of Samaritans seeking the sacred vessels of Moses killed at Mount Gerizim.[621] In about 37 AD, the Roman legate to Syria, Vitellius, dismissed both Pontius Pilate and the high priest Caiaphas.[622]

Most likely, Pilate retired to Italy, avoiding the further wrath of Tiberius due to the emperor's untimely demise.[623] Caiaphas probably became an ordinary member of the Sanhedrin.

---

[619] Matthew 27:24.

[620] Eusebius, *History of the Church,* 2.2.

[621] Other anti-Jewish actions of Pilate included bringing images of Caesar into Jerusalem and threatening the execution of Jewish leaders who "bared their necks," Pilate also appropriated funds from the Temple treasury (Corban) to fund construction of water aqueducts.

[622] As recorded by Josephus, *Antiquities of the Jews,* Book 18, Chapter 4 (18.88–89). Josephus records that Pilate served for 10 years as procurator in Judea. He was ordered to Rome to answer the accusations of the Jews before the emperor, but Tiberias died before Pilate arrived back in Rome.

[623] In his *History of the Church* 2.7, Eusebius writes that Pilate later committed suicide. However, this assertion has been questioned by some as an example of wishful thinking.

Herod Antipas, ruler of Galilee, also met with misfortune. First, he was put up to a war with the king of Nabataea by his first wife—due to Herod's dalliance with Herodias.[624] Fifteen years after the beheading of John the Baptist, the army of Antipas was destroyed. As the historian Josephus would later write, Herod's defeat "…came from God, and that very justly, as a punishment of what he did against John that was called the Baptist."[625]

The troubles of Herod Antipas were not over. Egged on by his misappropriated new wife Herodias, Herod traveled to Rome in 39 AD to be granted title as king of Perea as well as Galilee. But then, the new emperor Caligula banished Antipas to Spain in response to charges raised by Herod Agrippa, brother of Herodias.[626]

Jesus' growing band of post-resurrection followers would also provide fodder for another Roman emperor just one generation later. Nero would blame the conflagration of Rome in 64 AD on the subversive band of those who had become known as Christians.[627]

Jesus' legacy would reach beyond even theology and politics to other forms of human endeavor. Take art, for example.

In the fourth century, Eusebius would write that he had personally seen both a statute and colored portrait of "Christ himself." The statute reportedly was erected by the woman who had been healed by Jesus of hemorrhages.[628] Eusebius describes his personal encounter with the statute and its owner like this:

> Her house was pointed out in the city (Caesarea Philippi), and a wonderful memorial of the benefit the Savior conferred upon her was still there. On a tall stone base at the gates of her house stood a bronze statue of a woman, resting on one knee and resembling a suppliant with arms outstretched. Facing this was another of the same material, an upright figure of a man

---

[624] Herodias was first married to Herod Phillip.

[625] Josephus, *Antiquities,* Book 18, Chapter 5 (18:116).

[626] Agrippa had flattered the as yet private citizen Gaius Caligula, praying "the sooner to see Tiberius dying…" This was reported on by one of Agrippa's domestics to Tiberius who then had Agrippa imprisoned and tortured for six months until the death of Tiberius. From Josephus, *Jewish War,* Book 2, Chapter 9 (2:179–180).

[627] As documented by the Roman historian Tacitus.

[628] The account of the healing is recorded at Mark 5:24–34.

with a double cloak neatly draped over his shoulders and his hand stretched out to the woman. Near his feet on the stone slab grew an exotic plant, which climbed up to the hem of the bronze cloak and served as a remedy for illnesses of every kind. This statute, which was said to resemble the features of Jesus, was still there in my own time, so that I *saw it with my own eyes* when I resided in the city.[629]

---

[629] Eusebius, *History of the Church,* 7.18.

Epilogue

And so, we reach the end of a nearly two millennia long tour of a dozen Christian pioneers. Rather than focusing on those condemned by ecclesiastical orthodoxy, our attention has turned more toward reputed pillars of the church. To some whose views would be canonized—albeit at times considered as outside the mainstream—essentially heretical.

The trail of Christian pioneers can be traced to the writers of the New Testament Gospels. Matthew wrote in an attempt to prove that Jesus was the subject and the fulfillment of Old Testament prophecy. His was a (largely failed) campaign to bring Christianity back within the fold of Judaism.

One and one-half millennia later, Martin Luther wrote and spoke in opposition to the then dominant (or Catholic) church—at least of western Europe. Luther succeeded in positing a new form of Christian experience—re-establishing a Pauline primacy of faith over works.

However, Luther's reformation failed when it came time to turn the authority of the church on its head—a move toward a true priesthood of all believers. Rather, early reformist churches too often reverted to substitute one authoritarian and hierarchical system—one set of dogmas—for another.

In between Matthew the taxman and Martin the monk, we have profiled nine other pioneers of the Christian faith:

- The other gospel writers—Mark, Luke, and John.
- A triad of early Christian leaders—Paul, James and Peter.
- Two relegated to the fringes of acceptability—Thomas and Mary.
- And the first to marry church and state—Emperor Constantine.

Each was viewed at some point and by some audiences as heretical—in conflict with orthodoxies of their time. The author and the finisher of this chain of perceived heresy is none other than Jesus. He is the one who posited the first heretical views of the nascent Christian movement—teachings and actions viewed as antithetical to Judaism and for which he was put to death.

This same conflicted Jesus launched a movement moored in seemingly implacable contradictions. These conflicts have served as a source of theological disputes, persecutions, holy wars, and other forms of factionalism over nearly two millennia.

Throughout this narrative, we have characterized two distinct dimensions of heresy—those of substance versus style. The pioneering roles of Matthew, John, James and Thomas are primarily centered on matters of substance or belief. Those of Mark, Luke, Peter, Mary and Constantine center on questions of style or practical application. And for Paul, Luther and Jesus, prevailing orthodoxies were concurrently challenged regarding matters of both belief and practical application.

The Legacy of Heresy

What are we to make of this legacy of Christian heresy? Four thoughts come to mind:

1. **Success of the Christian movement can be directly linked to the willingness of its leaders to risk heresy—to work through the contradictions.** While Matthew failed to bring Christianity and Judaism together within the same fold, he succeeded at establishing a spiritual and theological link between the OT Hebrew Scriptures and the revelation of a new NT covenant through Jesus as the fulfillment of God's promise. Mark told us that any credit for the Christian faith rests with the source, not the followers. Luke espoused social conscience and John the opportunity for intimate connection with the divine.

Paul advocated a religion of faith strong enough to capture the imagination of the then dominant Greek and Roman world. James reminded the early church that faith alone without evidence of good deeds is dead. Peter sought the opportunity for compromise—respecting diverse views and practices of those following the way.

Thomas aimed to expose the seemingly hidden sides of truth. Mary bridged the gap between death, resurrection and emergent Christian mission.

Constantine sealed the imperial conquest of faith, making Christianity the organizing force for western civilization. And Martin Luther's reformation stirred the work ethic leading to the industrial and information revolutions of the most recent 500+ years.

In short, taking risks to interpret the Jesus experience has changed our world—both spiritually and materially.

2. **Pioneers embrace and work through conflict, over and over again.** Jesus kicked off this pattern by stating that he had come to bring division rather than peace. Parables and actions of the master often were intended to confuse and foster division, requiring Jesus' follower to seek further for meaningful truth.

Subsequent to this brief ministry, it is not surprising that only a few years were needed before James and Paul would contend for the heart and soul of the nascent church. James would state unequivocally that "faith by itself, if it has no works, is dead." And Paul would bluntly respond to those who advocated Christianity by works: "I wish those who unsettle you would castrate themselves."

The non-canonical Thomas restated Jesus' views toward money: "Give the emperor what belongs to the emperor, give God what belongs to God and give me what is mine." Mary Magdalene propelled the disciples forward at a time when they were ready to give up. In spite of this, she would be branded a whore. For their perceived heresies, the writings attributed to Thomas and Mary essentially disappeared until rediscovery of ancient manuscripts only within about the past century.

Constantine ostensibly settled a conflict between rival theological positions by imposing a religious and secular solution—known as the Nicene Creed. Luther reopened the conflict by exposing the hypocrisy of the resulting encrusted state church.

Each conflict, each heresy has its downside—when the beneficial insights brought to faith and experience are fully extrapolated without regard to Christian balance and moderation. In short, each of these dozen conflicts lives on in various forms today—as legacies to what Christendom was and may yet be about:

- Matthew's fast and loose interpretation of Biblical prophecy enables televangelists of today to interpret prophecies to fit their own whims.
- Mark's unbridled criticism of Jesus' chosen twelve apostles lives on in the countless uncivil conflicts within church bodies and between denominations.
- Luke's social service gospel foments do-goodism independent of Christ's blunt observation that the poverty will never cease.
- John's portrait of a personally accessibly Jesus introduces the idolatry of worshipping a Son (begotten of the Father) rather than the Father.
- Paul's trashing of tradition drove a wedge between Christianity and Judaism that remains unbridged 20 centuries later.
- James' rejoinder of salvation via works easily gives way to the abuses of performance-oriented Christianity—from penance to Christian work at the expense of home and family.
- Peter's call to compromise spawns the ecumenicism of good feeling without substance.
- Thomas' veil of mystery gives rise to movements emphasizing special and mystical knowledge ranging from the Moonies and Scientology to New Age occultism.
- Mary's assertion of a special relationship with the Savior may have provoked a counter-thrust relegating women to the back rows with chauvinistic Christianity only recently challenged.
- Constantine's marriage of church and state has led to authoritarianism of church leadership that continues today—from mainline denominations to evangelicals to mega-churches.
- Martin Luther's half-a-reformation rings increasingly hollow—particularly just after the completion of the last century of world wars, ethnic cleansing and holocaust.
- And Jesus' legacy of creative ambiguity and intentional conflict has degenerated over two millennia to a fractured movement often uncertain of its bearings and shared interests.

3. **Jesus advocates and embraces conflict as the vehicle to a richer earthly and spiritual experience.** If feeling good was all there was to it, Christianity could readily be relegated to the trash-heap of philosophical and religious systems that have outlived their usefulness.

But now, for the rest of the story. Jesus says, "I have not come to bring peace, but a sword." Conflict is not just the name of the game, it is the game. Get used to it, get over it and get on with it. Over and over and over again.

To his disciples, Jesus is recorded as saying: "To you it has been given to know the secrets of the kingdom of God, but to others I speak in parables, so that 'looking they may not perceive, and listening they may not understand.'"

The non-canonical Gospel of Thomas offers perhaps the most unique insight into Jesus' potential motivation, quoting Jesus as saying: "Those who seek should not stop seeking until they find. When they find they will be disturbed. When they are disturbed, they will marvel, and will rule over all."

Settle quickly, look to the Lord who hears and acts, seek and find. God is there in and through it all. But it's not a one-way street. He looks for and supports our active participation—at times even including active confrontation.

And so it is. Jesus on the one hand is offering access to the kingdom of God, but he nonetheless purposefully sets hurdles in the way of getting there. One must be motivated to search for the kingdom, then be prepared to get frustrated along the way. But persistence leads to eventual understanding and even to opportunity for skillful workmanship if not mastery.

4. **The continued vitality of Christianity depends on encouragement of diverse viewpoints and experiences.** Starting with Paul and extending through Constantine and Luther, Christianity too often has been driven by the imperative that the "winner takes all." Each sect, each denomination pushes to find and then adhere to one correct interpretation; others all too often are belittled, excluded, and condemned.

But that's not what Jesus says. Jesus claims to be "the way, the truth and the life." In practice, there are diverse ways to get there—all somehow mediated through Jesus and via this Savior to God the Father.

To a non-Jewish Canaanite woman, the key was persistence despite seemingly bigoted remarks from the Savior. To a rich man, the suggested means is selling everything and giving it to the poor. To the learned Pharisee, it is to be born again (or from above). To the Samaritan woman, the essential ingredient is something called "living water."

The keys to the kingdom are both practical and metaphorical. Continued vitality of the faith depends on mindful diversity, not mindless conformity. It is up to the listener and follower to decide which keys apply to their own situation. It is up each individual, each community to seek, then find and, just maybe, then rule.

Which Way Christianity?

And so we reach the end of a tale of these dozen Christian pioneers—viewpoints and lifestyles that bucked the system but also changed lives. It has now been half a millennium from the last great reformation from protestants of the Christian movement—those of Martin Luther and his contemporaries ranging from Zwingli to Calvin.

The last 500+ years brought western civilization and then the world to and through the industrial age to colonial power to world war—also to the ascendancy of capitalism predicated on a Protestant inspired work ethic.

The soft underbelly of Luther's reformation is now exposed. This is apparent in contemporary indifference to matters of organized Christian spirituality. In Europe, this trend was accentuated through atrocities of the First and Second World Wars punctuated by the Jewish holocaust.

More subtly but as perniciously, modern churches—most denominations and independents—remain rooted in hierarchical (and often authoritarian) organizational structures, each denomination with its own set of dogmas. Internal dissent requires risk—whether the church is of conservative or liberal bent.

Cooperation and dialogue across faiths remains difficult—for example, despite the ecumenicism focused on traditional mainline denominations.

Maybe it's time for another heresy or two to come front and center. To challenge the established order of parochial, inbred interests. To reinvigorate dialogue within churches, between denominations and faiths, and to draw renewed interest from the wider public.

If there is a need, it is to complete the reformation that Martin Luther initiated in 1517 but proved incapable of finishing. To restore the "priesthood of believers" back to the primary position of individual and communal interaction with the Godhead—each pursuing the practice of their own faith in their own way.

Will heterogeneity spawn new conflict, new heresy? Absolutely yes!

Some passages out of the mainstream will spawn beliefs and practices wholly incompatible even with a loose interpretation of Scripture. Others will lead to life reinvigorated by a scriptural understanding seeking relevance to the unique challenges of today's global community.

At the dawn of the third millennium, the world stands at the threshold of a new era, incomprehensible only a decade ago. The planet is awash in information; people can interact globally as large groups or one-on-one. And artificial intelligence (AI) is on the verge of reshaping civilization no less than what occurred in Luther's era with commercialization of the printing press.

Reinvigorating Christianity requires a return to spiritual roots. This means a willingness to critically reexamine scriptural texts together with historical and other materials—including those from outside the canon. As exemplified by the non-canonical works attributed to Thomas and Mary, drawing from extra-Biblical sources can be useful to fill in the puzzle started by New Testament writings. Similarly, improved understanding can come by fitting together seeming inconsistencies as between the Gospels or the personalities of key NT leaders as with James, Paul and Peter.

In an age dominated by rational scientific empiricism, Christian faith must stand the test of historic authenticity. Christendom can no longer gloss over or rationalize away obvious inconsistencies. Spiritual consumers and their critics are too sophisticated to readily accept the rationalizations or overly simplified explanations of the pre-modern era.

We can and should expect that the search for our Christian roots will lead to new and perhaps unexpected discoveries. Some of the discoveries will undoubtedly prove disconcerting—challenging previous beliefs. Virtually all will prove to be enlightening if we are willing to let the information inform our knowledge and practice of the Christian way.

For those willing to experience or even embrace the conflict, there is the downstream opportunity to marvel at what we find. To truly become excited, no doubt our faith will be stretched. Others who have viewed Christianity as outmoded or irrelevant may yet be attracted to a renewed burst of robust vitality.

How best to experience conflict? And yet find peace? Every day and through every phase of childhood, then adulthood, then beyond to the life after death, there is opportunity for resolution and partnership in step and at home with Jesus.

We seek a Jesus who consistently demonstrates that, just when we think we have the answers, there are new questions. When we feel we've run the race, we find we've only just begun.